# THE LURE OF PERU

# The Lure of Peru

## Maritime Intrusion into the South Sea, 1598–1701

### Peter T. Bradley

*Lecturer in Spanish and Latin American Studies*
*University of Newcastle upon Tyne*

MACMILLAN

First published 1989

Published by
THE MACMILLAN PRESS LTD
Houndmills, Basingstoke, Hampshire RG21 2XS
and London
Companies and representatives
throughout the world

Typeset by
Footnote Graphics, Warminster, Wilts.

Printed in Great Britain by

Billing & Sons Ltd, Worcester

British Library Cataloguing in Publication Data
Bradley, Peter T.
The lure of Peru: maritime intrusion into the South
Sea, 1598–1701.
1. Peru. Expeditions, 1598–1701
I. Title
918.5'043
ISBN 0–333–48086–4

For Mum and Dad
(Doris and Ernie Bradley)

'One of the greatest problems that the kingdom of Peru has is to be so far away from the whole world.'

L. de las Llamosas, *Manifiesto apologético* (Madrid, 1692)

'This Province above any other in America, is abundant in rich mines of Gold and Silver ... by which abundance, not Spaine onely, but all Europe also is more stored with pure and fine Coine, than ever formerly it was.'

G. Mercator, *Atlas* (London, 1636)

# Contents

# List of Maps

# Glossary

| | |
|---|---|
| *Alcalde* | magistrate |
| *Almiranta* | vice-admiral (the ship) |
| *Armada del Mar del Sur* | South Sea fleet or squadron |
| *Capitana* | flagship |
| *Casa de Contratación* | House of Trade (in Seville) |
| *Chinchorro* | small boat |
| *Consulado* | merchant guild |
| *Corregidor* | crown district governor |
| *Encomienda* | grant of Indians with right to exact tribute |
| *Escribano* | notary, clerk |
| *Junta de Guerra* | War Committee |
| *Maestre de campo* | batallion commander |
| *Navío de permiso* | ship with special licence to trade in a port |
| *Sargento mayor* | adjutant |
| *Real Audiencia* | high court of a region with administrative powers |
| *Real cédula* | royal decree |
| *Real Consejo de las Indias* | Royal Council of the Indies |
| *Real Sala del Crimen* | criminal court |

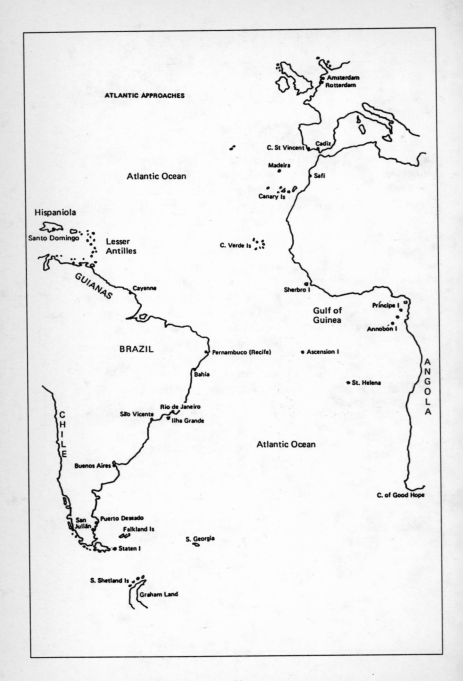

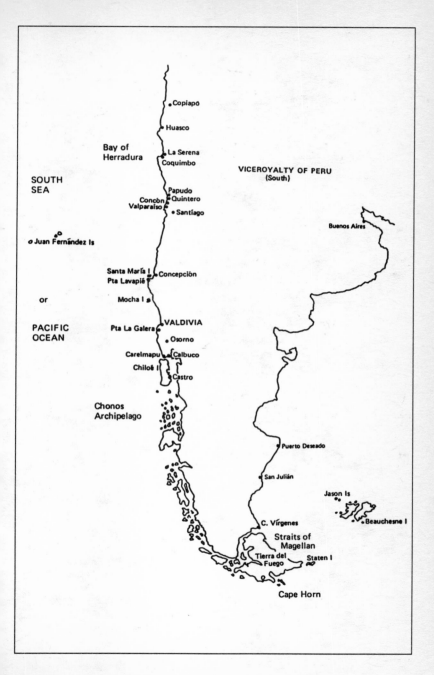

Copiapó

Huasco

Bay of
Herradura

La Serena
Coquimbo

VICEROYALTY OF PERU
(South)

SOUTH
SEA

Papudo
Concón Quintero
Valparaíso Santiago

Buenos Aires

Juan Fernández Is

Santa María I Concepción
Pta Lavapié

or

Mocha I

PACIFIC
OCEAN

Pta La Galera VALDIVIA

Osorno

Carelmapu Calbuco
Chiloé I

Castro

Chonos
Archipelago

Puerto Deseado

San Julián

Jason Is

Beauchesne I

C. Vírgenes
Straits of
Magellan
Tierra del
Fuego Staten I

Cape Horn

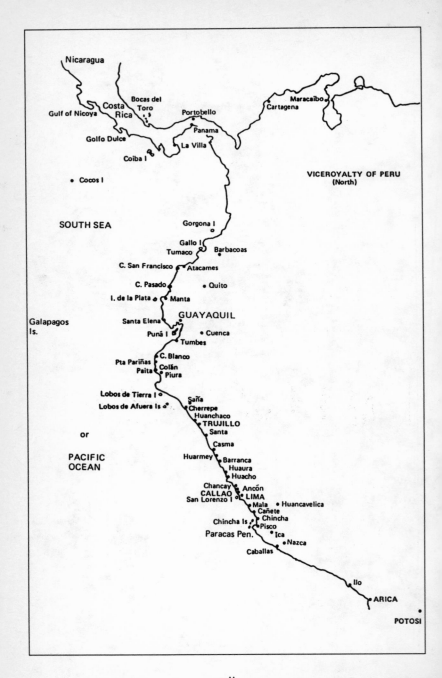

Nicaragua

Costa Rica

Gulf of Nicoya

Bocas del Toro

Portobello

Maracaibo

Cartagena

Golfo Dulce

Panama

La Villa

Coiba I

VICEROYALTY OF PERU
(North)

Cocos I

SOUTH SEA

Gorgona I

Gallo I

Tumaco

Barbacoas

C. San Francisco

Atacames

C. Pasado

Quito

I. de la Plata

Manta

Galapagos
Is.

GUAYAQUIL

Santa Elena

Puná I

Cuenca

Tumbes

C. Blanco

Pta Pariñas

Colán

Paita

Piura

Lobos de Tierra I

Saña

Lobos de Afuera Is

Cherrepe

Huanchaco

TRUJILLO

Santa

or

Casma

PACIFIC
OCEAN

Huarmey

Barranca

Huaura

Huacho

Chancay

Ancón

CALLAO

LIMA

San Lorenzo I

Mala

Huancavelica

Cañete

Chincha

Chincha Is

Pisco

Paracas Pen.

Ica

Nazca

Caballas

Ilo

ARICA

POTOSI

xii

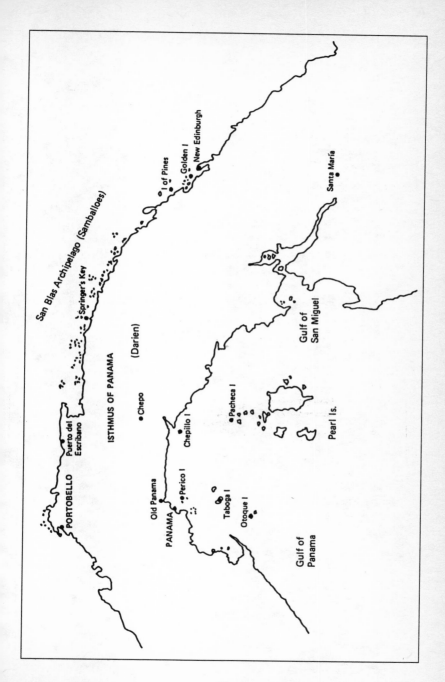

# Introduction

Today in Europe particularly, the name Peru, despite the world-wide achievements of some of the country's most notable figures in the spheres of literature or international diplomacy, often calls to mind the image of an economically poor, and socially and industrially backward, distant South American republic, forever incapable of creating internal sources of finance for development, hopelessly indebted to international creditors and unable to achieve stable political government. Only a part of this, the region's remoteness, could be considered to have much relevance to European perceptions of Peru in the seventeenth century. At that time Spain's empire in the New World was divided into a northern viceroyalty, New Spain or Mexico, and a southern counterpart from the Isthmus of Panama, generally referred to as Peru. This gave rise to the Spanish saying that 'what is not Mexico is Peru', conveniently overlooking Portuguese Brazil. In the present context we are concerned above all with the South Sea coast or Pacific coast of the southern viceroyalty, from the Isthmus of Panama to the Straits of Magellan. It is an area which never gained the same regular attention of Spain's enemies as shores of the Spanish Main or islands of the West Indies, but which, nevertheless, continued to be a beguiling attraction to Europeans long after the conclusion of the ventures described in this study.

To understand this, one has to recall the impressive impact in Europe caused first by the arrival of Aztec treasure from Mexico, recorded in awe by Albrecht Dürer among others,[1] and later that of precious items of Inca craftsmanship from Peru, shipped to Spain as gifts for the crown. Furthermore, by the 1540s, the alluring legend of El Dorado seemed to be strong confirmation of the wealth in the south. In one of its most widespread versions, it recounts how a gilded ruler bathed in the waters of a sacred lake, washing off the gold dust with which he had been covered as a form of ritual offering. Amplified with every telling, it soon came to signify a city or land of fabulous wealth, and the river which flowed through it. By this time also the looting of valuable objects had begun to give way to direct searches for the sources of mineral wealth, through mining, particularly following the discovery of the most famous silver mine in the New World, Potosí, in 1545. Here, a mining camp was to be transformed into the largest city of the Spanish empire, with a population of 160 000 by the mid-seventeenth century.

Out of the need to control effectively the extraction of silver and ensure its regular and safe shipment to Spain, Lima and its port Callao were designated by the crown as the administrative centres for imperial trade in Spanish South America. The Straits of Magellan were closed to regular Spanish shipping as a means of commercial access to the South Sea coast, and the port of Buenos Aires was restricted legally to the trade required for the mainten-ance of colonies in the area of the River Plate, although contraband flourished. Therefore, Potosí silver was taken overland to the coast at Arica and from there transported by sea to Callao, joined by the products of other mines and thence by armed convoy, the Armada del Mar del Sur, carried by sea to the Isthmus of Panama. Once there, it would be transferred to galleons waiting to carry it to Spain, or else be used to purchase at the trade fair in Portobello, incoming goods from the Peninsula, vital to the upkeep of Peru.

And so, at the beginning of the seventeenth century, Europeans were likely to recognise Peru as the principal contributor to Spain's wealth in the Americas, the home of Indian civilisations of undreamt of riches, a source of booty in the form of precious stones and metals and the site of rich mines, along whose coasts sailed ships bearing bullion exports of staggering value, American products commercially exploitable in Europe and items of local trade required by the major population centres along the South Sea coast and in Mexico.

The Spanish language still recalls the treasures that once were synonymous with the name Peru, in phrases such as *valer un Perú, valer un Potosí* and *vivir en Jauja*. Roget too in his thesaurus of English words and phrases includes both El Dorado and Potosí under the heading 'wealth'. Portuguese dictionaries invariably record Potosí as signifying a *grande fonte de riquezas*, and Littré refers to *les mines et les trésors du Potose*. Francis Drake, during his voyage of circumnavigation from 1577 to 1580, had seized bullion at least to the value of 447 000 pesos off the coast of Peru alone, returning home, it has been said, with plunder worth more than £330 000, to prove beyond doubt the existence of fabulous wealth for the taking only indifferently guarded by Spain.[2] And as a sad reminder of those past riches, in view of the present state of the republic, the arms of Peru, beneath the vicuña and the cichona tree representing the animal and vegetable wealth of the region, depict a golden cornucopia pouring forth mineral treasures.

In addition there seemed to be prospects for European trade, by supplying the demands of settlers along the South Sea coasts for manufactured goods, by a more direct route than the awkward and costly crossing of the Isthmus, at more competitive prices and with a greater range of items. All of this, trade and plunder alike, was further inspired by religious and political antagonisms against Spain in Europe, as indeed were those who sought some more permanent and effective challenge to Spanish supremacy by the implantation of rival colonial settlements, counting on alliances with the local Indian population.

And lastly, one should not neglect to suggest as components of the lure of Peru, the persuasive power of myth in interpretations of a New World where reality seemed to surpass the bounds of European imagination and the fiction of the novels of chivalry. For beyond El Dorado and stories of hidden pots of gold, chroniclers from the time of Columbus onwards had discussed the location there of legends classical, medieval and Biblical in their inspiration, such as tales of the Fountain of Eternal Youth, warrior women, Atlantis, giants and cannibals. To these were added myths American in origin, such as the Enchanted City of the Caesers, the silver river (River Plate) or the mountain of silver, the latter fortuitously realised at Potosí. In this respect, the authors of the journals or of the reports of the voyages discussed herein are at times no less bemused and puzzled in seeking to understand what they saw or heard described than those early chroniclers. To a certain degree, the exotic, strange and even the remote can be considered as sources of attraction from the time of Columbus and Peter Martyr, to the English and Dutch writers of the sixteenth and seventeenth centuries.[3] In fact the best known of Latin America's contemporary novelists, García Márquez, has written of the inspiration he derives from those who first sought to interpret the New World, and whose difficulties of interpretation he still encounters in his own writing. 'There are no writers less believable and at the same time more devoted to reality than the chroniclers of the Indies, for the problem with which they had to struggle was that of making believable a reality which went beyond the imagination.'[4]

By the seventeenth century, then, the kingdom of Peru had already gained a fame among the nations of northern Europe

which inevitably enticed to its shores their seafarers and bold
adventurers, the merely curious, the dreamers and the practical
merchants. The prospects were the discovery of new seas and
lands, treasures of gold and silver, the desire to institute, via a
westerly route, round-the-world trade links to the East Indies,
China and Japan, and perhaps even the hope of settling some
'undiscovered shore', 'secret island' or 'peaceful desert yet un-
claimed by Spain'.[5]

There can be no doubt that the latter years of the previous
century belonged to the English in this matter of foreign penetration into the South Sea. The exploits and fame of Francis Drake we
have already recalled. His worthy successor in those waters was
Thomas Cavendish, the third circumnavigator of the globe from
1586 to 1588, in pursuance of his goal to expand English trade by a
westerly route, beyond South America to China, Japan and the
Philippines. Like Drake, he proved the existence off the coasts of
Peru and Mexico of spoils for the taking, returning to his queen
with silks, pearls, satins, damasks, spices and bullion, possibly
worth as much as £125 000. She is reported to have commented:
'The King of Spain barks a good deal but he does not bite. We care
nothing for Spaniards; their ships loaded with gold and silver from
the Indies come hither after all.'[6]

In reality, although Drake and Cavendish justly deserve the
prominence which history has ascribed to them, they represent
only a part of a continuing English attraction towards the Straits of
Magellan and the South Sea, for purposes of geographical discovery, potential trade and certain plunder. Through the merchant
Robert Thorne, based in Seville, there had been English investment and participation in the Sebastian Cabot expedition of 1526,
which had set out to pass into the South Sea, but ultimately
explored the River Plate waterways. Just how powerful the lure
was to become is apparent from Cabot's comment that, in 1550, he
had been approached by the Admiral Lord Warwick concerning a
plan the latter had formulated to take Peru in a surprise attack, by
sending 4000 men up the Amazon in pinnaces.[7]

By the 1570s, eager English eyes were being drawn more
persuasively to what we now refer to as the southern cone. On 19
April 1570, the Spanish ambassador reported from London that a
Portuguese seaman, Bartolomeu Bayão, had been discussing with
interested parties a project 'to occupy and colonize one or two
ports in the kingdom of Magellanes, in order to have in their hands

the commerce of the southern sea . . . as well as getting as near as they wish to Peru'.[8] Four years later, Richard Grenville put before Elizabeth a proposal for English action which would lead to settlements in the area from the River Plate to Chile, which held out 'the likelihood of bringing in great treasure of gold, silver and pearl into this realm from those countries, as other princes have out of like regions'.[9] Though neither of these projects was translated into immediate action, clear similarities could be traced with Drake's venture of 1577, particularly when one recalls that his original objectives seem to have been limited to Peru and the South Sea, with circumnavigation becoming advisable, if not the only practical alternative, after he had experienced the rigours of the Straits of Magellan.

By the following decade, Drake and Cavendish in their turn were to entice Edward Fenton, George Clifford, Earl of Cumberland, John Chidley and Andrew Merrick to emulate their success. But sadly all of these, whilst revealing the fascination of the lure of the South Sea and beyond, demonstrated the magnitude of the obstacles that barred the way, for none passed through the Straits. Cavendish himself, on his fateful final voyage of 1591–3, when surely he hoped to become the first double-circumnavigator, perished after a reckless attempt to reach the South Sea as the turbulent and icy months of winter approached.

Two others who did cause apprehension by their presence in Peruvian waters were John Oxenham and Richard Hawkins. The former, who had been on the Isthmus of Panama with Drake in 1572–3, returned there in 1576 to steal a march on his former leader both by crossing to the South Sea and by taking there the first English prize in those waters. Though this northern, overland access was the first penetrated by the English and that regularly used by Spain, it was not for a century that such intrusions became more common, as we shall see. The fate of Oxenham and most of his crew, subsequently captured and executed by the Spanish, can hardly have endeared the area to the English. Although ultimately not so tragic, Hawkins' voyage to the South Sea in 1593–4 had decidedly mixed fortunes, for after taking prizes bearing general cargo and some gold, his own ship, the *Dainty*, was forced to surrender in a battle with a Spanish naval force. Unlike Oxenham, however, Hawkins managed to return to England in 1602, preceded by most of his crew.

Therefore, the evidence of European, especially English, attraction

to the South Sea is consistent and strong in the last decades of the
sixteenth century. However, it is equally obvious that the practical
and climatic obstacles to reaching Peru were of such magnitude
that they could dissuade or defeat even the most enthusiastic.
Moreover, although Spain had failed in its attempt to close access
via the Straits of Magellan, with the disastrous yet heroic failure of
the Sarmiento de Gamboa expedition to locate two permanent
colonial settlements there in 1584,[10] a Spanish squadron had
effectively thwarted Hawkins' plans for plunder in 1594, and a year
later the feared Drake was to succumb to the hardships of crossing
the Isthmus. Already, before the end of the century, English
interest in the South Sea had begun to wane in favour of North
America and the East Indies via the Cape of Good Hope. Here, and
not in the South Sea, the British Empire would be born. But the
interest did not die and the early voyages were not entirely in vain.

Richard Hakluyt, in 1579 and 1580, had suggested the seizure of
the Straits of Magellan by the English pirate Thomas Clarke, and its
population by *cimarrones* and convicts of both sexes from England.
This was to be merely the first stage in a direct challenge to Spanish
control of Peru. 'The Strait of Magellan is the gate of entry into the
treasure of both the East and the West Indies. And whosoever is
lord of this Strait may account himself lord also of the West Indies.
...There is no doubt but that we shall make subject to England all
the golden mines of Peru and all the coast and tract of that firm of
America upon the Sea of Sur.'[11] This most famous recorder of
English maritime enterprise was fired by the desire to destroy
Spanish supremacy in the New World, to such an extent that while
applauding the fertility of the land on either side of the Straits, and
the abundance of fish, mussels, limpets, seals and stags, he totally
fails to recall the trials and the perils. Nevertheless, he must surely
be, at least in part, responsible for handing on these fanciful and
outlandish aspirations in the South Sea to the Dutch, who were to
inherit English preoccupations with the region before the turn of
the century.

The starting point, therefore, for the new era of interlopers
which we aim to describe, is the close of the age of Elizabethan
advocates and pioneers of the southern route to Peru. Its conclusion is marked by the arrival of French traders following the
accession of the Bourbon Philip V to the Spanish throne in 1700,
and by the voyages of the last of the privateers. Between these
limits, we shall assess to what degree European aspirations in the

South Sea changed during the seventeenth century. The deeds of those lured by real or imagined gains to be gathered are of interest to historians of maritime affairs and of European overseas expansion, reflecting the changing fortunes in politics and commerce of the northern European nations concerned. Additionally, we shall be witnesses to events of geographical significance – the discovery in the south of a more open, though still perilous, route of entry via Cape Horn, and from the north the creation of an alternative overland access across the Isthmus of Panama, thanks to the audacity of buccaneers from the West Indies.

In terms of the impact on the historical progress of the Viceroyalty of Peru, our awareness of the importance of these intruders into forbidden waters has increased in recent years, as we have come to look more closely at the consequences of their actions. For these must be measured not simply in terms of the sensational and the tragic, that is booty captured, prizes taken, towns sacked and burned or individuals brutally murdered, but from the point of view of longer term effects on local and imperial trade, and above all the need to create a defensive apparatus as a form of retaliation and dissuasion. As the century progressed, viceroys of Peru were to become more concerned for the safety of the seas and security of coastal towns, attending with various degrees of alacrity, enthusiasm and conviction to requirements for defence forces, militias, warships, armaments and fortifications. At a time when we have begun to realise the full cost to the royal treasury in Lima of providing such measures, and have quantified its significance in the broader context of the financial operations of the viceroyalty as supplier of bullion to Spain, it is all the more important to have a clear and modern appraisal of whom and what the defences offered protection against.

Furthermore, in respect of repercussions in Peru itself, we may notice that on several occasions the arming of a ship or the erection of a fort or defensive wall is the culmination not of some crown instruction emanating from Madrid, nor even from a Spanish viceroy in Lima, but due to the resolve of a local population who otherwise would be defenceless. In a number of instances, inhabitants of Peru act to serve their own interests as much as those of a distant crown. They are united by a common cause in the face of adversity, and while this may not be construed as evidence of national identity, it does nevertheless offer examples of regional solidarity, it pinpoints common regional worries and directs attention to the inability, and perhaps the unwillingness, of the crown to respond effectively to local concerns. The lessons of this are not easily forgotten.

Finally, and again of long term importance, we should remember that intelligence gained by observation, conversation, or the written word led to a tremendous expansion in the store of knowledge in northern Europe about Spanish activities in Peru. Drake and Cavendish most certainly possessed the resolution and daring that were remarkable characteristics of their unrepeatable age, but those who came after in the seventeenth century, whether they be French or Dutch or English, took the first steps towards establishing the viability of the southern route discovered by Spain but neglected by it. They also amassed the practical information that would be of use to future navigators and, ultimately, to those eager to invest in and exploit new resources of the region in the nineteenth century. Moreover, even when commercial success or material gain was slight, reports carried back in the form of maps, journals, personal reminiscences or oral tales, with their stock of references to strange and exotic sights, unusual peoples and their habits, fabulous wealth and sometimes fanciful happenings, were to contribute enormously to the maintenance and, indeed, growth of interest in the area. They answered a popular demand throughout Europe for books of travel and voyages to distant lands.[12] They also strengthened rather than weakened the dream of commercial profit on the west coast of South America, as they recognised the shortcomings of Spanish imperial trade and the eagerness for foreign goods, mocked the weak defences and recorded the Spaniards' fear of Indian and negro risings. None of the expeditions studied have left a permanent base on the mainland of South America, but to choose a topical and pertinent example, today's British presence in the Falkland Isles ultimately derives from voyages of exploration, commerce and adventure such as these. In fact, at least two of them have direct connections with those islands.

# 1

# The Arrival of the Dutch: Jacob Mahu and Olivier van Noort (1598–1601)

The United Provinces of the Netherlands were born out of war, a struggle which was fought first of all, largely for nationalistic and religious motives, to wrest control of land from Spain. It was to last from the first abortive rising in 1568, to the signing of the Treaty of Münster in 1648 which recognised Dutch independence. But in 1572 the successes of the Sea-Beggars, to be followed in 1581 with the formal renunciation of allegiance to Philip II of Spain, were already an augury of the final, if long awaited, total victory. Moreover, they indicated the emergence of a powerful maritime force that would soon extend its activities throughout the globe. In the 1580s, following the unification of the crowns of Spain and Portugal, restrictions imposed on Dutch trade with the Iberian Peninsula encouraged this expansion, by prompting the search farther afield for vital commodities such as salt and spices. This expansion of the area of trade, and conflict, was especially inspired by the first of Philip's arrests of Dutch ships in Iberian ports in 1585.

Thus, the success of new commercial transactions and the birth of the challenge to Iberian domination of the seas, became the means of survival for the emergent northern provinces which began to attract from the south its wealthiest citizens, most influential merchants and its more enterprising artisans. This movement of refugees from the south was encouraged, again in 1585, by the capture of Antwerp by the Duke of Parma, who granted two years grace to those Calvinists who wished to transfer their homes and businesses northwards. But among the 20 000 who may have emigrated, there were many who chose Amsterdam and other northern ports for mainly commercial reasons, including two individuals who were to play a part in the first Dutch venture into the South Sea, Simon de Cordes and Sebald de Weert. And so,

Amsterdam was to replace Antwerp as the port of Europe, as Dutch commercial interests spread first into the Atlantic (the Canaries, Madeira and the Cape Verde Islands), and before the end of the sixteenth century to the New World (Brazil, the Guianas and the West Indies) and to the East Indies.[1]

Before 1600, there was little doubt that a new maritime nation had been born. It is not surprising that in the full tide of its expansion it should assume the legacy of English voyages to the East and West Indies. For it is certain that news of the exploits of Drake and Cavendish was avidly read and discussed, that documents were smuggled and scraps of information were gleaned from visits to Portugal and Spain, and that personal contacts, such as those of Hakluyt and Emanuel van Meteren, facilitated the spread of knowledge and enhanced the lure of distant parts. Two maps associated with Cavendish's voyages in the southern Atlantic, based on lost Spanish originals, may have found their way to Holland through this connection.[2] Nor is it to be wondered at, in a country where the printing and circulation of books were to flourish, that interest in navigation and geography had already before the end of the sixteenth century produced such landmarks as Wagenaer's *Spieghel der Zeervaert* and Linschoten's *Itinerario*.[3] The journals and the reports of the Dutch expeditions we shall discuss further stimulate these interests. Moreover, Mahu and van Noort spring from an age in which the quest for overseas expansion had seen the successful return of the first exploratory Dutch venture to the East Indies via the Cape of Good Hope in 1594, led by Cornelis Houtman. Within three years it was to spawn a considerable number of *Compagnieën van Verre* (Companies of the Far Lands), among which were those that looked towards the Straits of Magellan and the South Sea coast of Peru, petitioning the States-General for permission to trade in new waters.

These two voyages, therefore, may be considered together because of their proximity in time and the similarity of their aims and experiences. They represent the vanguard of Dutch attempts to carry their vigorous commerce to the Viceroyalty of Peru during the first half of the seventeenth century, and ultimately to establish permanent bases there. Being the first, they are modest in aim and largely exploratory in nature, for while en route to the East Indies, both parties were to test the reaction of Spanish settlers and the authorities in Chile and Peru to offers of trade. They were, nevertheless, well prepared in case open conflict with the Spanish could not be avoided, and doubtlessly the strength of Spanish defences in the region was also to be assessed.

Each of these features becomes quite clear from an examination of the informative declarations made by several members of the Mahu fleet who surrendered at Valparaíso and were later sent to Lima for interrogation. They claimed that the ships had left Holland with full capacity cargoes of Rouen and Dutch cloth, haberdashery, cutlery and articles in iron, lead and glass, to be traded for silver, but that large quantities of arquebuses, muskets, coats of mail and other trappings of war had been taken aboard also. These were intended not only for their own personal use, but to be given to the Indians in the hope that they might be induced into an armed alliance against their Spanish masters – a somewhat naive belief that seems to have been shared by the backers of several Dutch expeditions. However, the importance of commercial success is verified by the presence of supercargoes on three of the vessels, who were to supervise and duly record commercial transactions, thereby protecting the interests of the backers.[4]

In addition, the revelations of one of the Dutch captains illustrate the dual preparation for peaceful trade or a more violent course of action. First, he confessed that 'the main purpose for which they left their country was to carry many goods to the East and West Indies, to wherever they could best pursue their voyage, and to sell their merchandise or exchange it for other goods and riches'. But he acknowledged also that both he and his promoters knew that they were not allowed to trade in Peru, being driven to do so by the need to find new trades for unemployed ships and crews. Therefore, it was clear that the pressure for commercial returns could lead to the use of force, when he commented 'that if the Spanish refused to buy them willingly and they, consequently, could not make a profit, in order not to return home without any benefit, they must try to sell their goods by force or take whatever they might find, both supplies and gold and silver.'

This last informant is, in fact, a person of some renown, Dirck Gerritszoon Pomp, or Dirck 'China', who had considerable personal experience of the trade routes to the East Indies, may have been the first Dutchman to reach those parts and certainly was a valuable source of intelligence for those eager to collect and publish material on distant lands. In Chile he was to alarm the Spanish with tales of Dutch intentions to settle on the South Sea coast, disclosing plans to discover viable sites and to take back to Holland representatives of the local native population, who might learn Dutch and become useful allies in establishing closer contacts with their fellow Indians in the future. As regards the location for such activities, although no firm decisions had been reached, already Valdivia was an area of great interest, because it was 'remote from [Spanish] fleets and danger, and they wished to sell and barter their goods there since it was a town possessing much gold and trade, and if they could not do this, he said, their instructions were to take the port and add to it the island of Santa María'.[5]

Again it is in Hakluyt's collection of English voyages that we find identified the locations which the Dutch were now to frequent, references to the gold of Valdivia, to what was already being called 'the famous province of Arauco' by the time of the Chidley and Merrick expedition,[6] and to fertile lands where provisions and supplies were plentiful, such as Santa María, an island well placed to serve as a point of rendezvous for ships dispersed during the passage of the Straits.

Similarly, the ostensible purpose of van Noort's voyage was to trade with settlers in Peru, while en route for the East Indies. This is the gist of the instructions given in The Hague and reported in Peru:

> We have seen fit to send a good number of ships, well ordered and protected, to the coasts of Asia, Africa and America, and to the islands of East India to carry on their business and commerce with the subjects of these provinces.

The peaceful nature of this activity was stressed in the orders to one of the vessels concerned, which had been given 'a particular and express order and charge to seek the aforesaid islands and to resist making war, and causing all possible offence and damage to the Spaniards and Portuguese.'[7] In pursuance of these aims, van Noort also carried a commercial cargo of cloth, haberdashery, cutlery and glassware.

Once more, however, the fact that van Noort's ships also carried substantial amounts of arms suggests that recourse to force was rather more than a remote possibility. Indeed, a direct witness of the Dutchmen's mode of operation, a Franciscan named Agustín de Cavallos who became their prisoner off the coast of Central America, recalled that the letters of authority issued to van Noort, of which he carried a Spanish translation, granted permission for this when the opportunity to trade was denied. They contained the statement that in such circumstances 'they will do what they can by force of arms, provided that they do not wrong ... the King of France, nor the King of Scotland, nor the Queen of England (but at this point the documents did not say King Philip because he is our enemy)'.[8]

Therefore, these first two expeditions are closely allied in their proposal to reach the East Indies via a westerly route, investigate the potential for trade along the South Sea coast of Chile and Peru and in being well prepared for any offensive or defensive action that might become unavoidable, or merely desirable. The first venture was organised by the company of Pieter van der Haghen during the early months of 1598. In its final form it consisted of five vessels manned, armed and commanded as follows:[9]

| Ship | Tons | Guns | Men | Captain |
|------|------|------|-----|---------|
| Hoope (Hope) | 500/600 | 28 | 130 | Jacob Mahu |
| Liefde (Charity) | 300 | 26 | 110 | Simon de Cordes |
| Geloof (Faith) | 320 | 18/20 | 109 | Gerard van Beuningen |
| Trouw (Fidelity) | 220 | 18 | 96 | Jurien van Bockholt |
| Blijde Boodschap (Glad Tidings) | 150 | 16 | 56 | Sebald de Weert |

All major sources agree on the participation of Englishmen, several of whom sailed as the principal pilots of the fleet. One of them at least, Timothy Shotten, had been around the world with Cavendish, and another may have accomplished the same feat with Drake. The link between their pioneering voyages and the arrival of the Dutch in the South Sea is, therefore, again clearly established. In his confessions to his Spanish captors, Dirck Gerritsz was later to affirm that 'English pilots are, for all regions, more trustworthy and experienced than the Dutch'.[10] The balance of experience was soon to shift in favour of the latter, in part as a result of the expeditions we shall examine.

Leaving Goeree in the last week of June 1598, the ships headed for the African coast to pick up vital supplies of fresh food before attempting the Atlantic crossing. The hazards of this at once became apparent in the Cape Verde Islands (1–10 September), where they were obliged to resort to force since all efforts to persuade the Portuguese to sell them provisions had failed. Soon afterwards their foraging was to be rewarded when two captured turtles yielded some 200 eggs, with which a giant omelette was made.

While sailing from these islands towards the mainland on 23 September, the expedition leader Jacob Mahu died and was succeeded by Simon de Cordes. As a result other promotions occurred in the fleet. Gerard van Beuningen became vice-admiral in the *Charity*, Sebald de Weert was appointed captain of the *Faith* and Dirck Gerritsz assumed command of the *Glad Tidings*. During the next two months the principal concern remained the need to acquire supplies of fresh meat and fruit, now even more urgent as scurvy began to ravage the crews. Unfortunately the Portuguese remained uncooperative, as did the local natives who fled inland, doubtlessly fearing that the Dutch were slave traders. Such delays ashore in search of provisions eventually created a further danger, an outbreak of fever brought on by the climate, culminating in 16 deaths. Their final port of call before striking out for the Straits of Magellan was the island of Annobón where, from 16 December to 2 January, they gathered and loaded fruit and cattle to help restore their health for the coming voyage.

Only at this late stage, when its further concealment was no longer possible, was it revealed to the officers and men that their true course to the East Indies lay through the Straits. Hitherto they had been encouraged to believe that they would sail via the traditional route, the Cape of Good Hope. Such deception was to be a feature of early Dutch voyages, suggesting that the backers in .Holland had succumbed somewhat more readily to the lure of Peru than many of those they employed to pursue its wealth. The reason must surely have been the fear that men would be reluctant to serve on what was generally considered a dangerous enterprise, with virtually no hope of a return home except by circumnavigating the globe, and with the unpleasant possibility of falling into the hands of the Spanish, or of savages.

Following the disclosure of what to many must have been bitter news, Cordes crossed the Atlantic and headed southwards along the coast of Brazil towards the River Plate. The spectacle of a sea coloured red by vast numbers of shrimps (or more precisely krill), now being commercially exploited by vessels using the Falkland Islands as their base, led to fanciful accounts of the phenomenon, including the theory that they were small creatures expelled from the bodies of whales. On 6 April 1599 the five ships finally came to anchor at the mouth of the Straits. Although the hardships of the voyage had been considerable and sickness was daily becoming more prevalent, the real test of endurance was yet to come in the long sojourn within the Straits themselves.

On 18 April the fleet entered Great Bay, subsequently renamed Cordes Bay, where they were to remain throughout the winter season, until 23 August. It has already been pointed out that the suffering undergone during these months was due in large part to the negligence of Cordes, who ought to have taken advantage of the north-east winds to pass into the South Sea as quickly as possible. The English pilot William Adams records the favourability of such winds in his first letter. 'We had the wind at North-East, some five or six days, in which time we might have passed through the Straits.'[11] Instead, during the rigours of winter 120 men died, including van Bockholt who was succeeded in his command by Baltasar de Cordes, brother of the admiral. For four months they suffered frequent storms of wind, rain, hail and snow, and an intense cold which only increased their craving for food. Already one man had been hanged as an example to the rest, for his nocturnal visits to the food locker to steal provisions. Another had suddenly collapsed and died, foaming at the mouth and with a vacant look in his eyes. The rest devoured roots and shellfish, eaten completely raw in their haste to satisfy their appetites. To the more needy were distributed lengths of cloth from the cargoes of trading goods, in order to give them some protection from the cold.

During an excursion on shore to collect seals for food, the Dutchmen made their first contact with the local natives. These are generally described as being of reddish skin, with long hair, and between 10 and 11 ft tall. Such stories of giants, capable of running as fast as a horse and so tall that ordinary men reached only to their waists, were first recorded by Pigafetta in his chronicle of Magellan's circumnavigation.[12] They were repeated by Hakluyt in his publication of the discourse of the Portuguese, Lopes Vaz, and in an account of the Cavendish voyage around the world. The author of the latter suspected that some were 'men-eaters' and claimed to have measured one of their feet, found to be 18 inches long.[13] They were, of course, nicknamed *patagones* – big feet, by Magellan. Despite the fact that one Dutchman, Dirck Gerritsz, appears to have seen them more clearly and reported more honestly, describing them as 'people small in body and dressed in skins', the belief in Patagonian giants continued to satisfy European appetites for the exotic in the New World for many years to come.[14] In later encounters small parties from the ships were attacked and killed by these Indians. Although buried by their companions, the bodies were subsequently discovered to have been dug up, mutilated, disfigured and shot through with arrows. With rumours and facts such as these to be recounted and overheard by seamen, it is hardly surprising that the Dutch promoters chose to keep the route through the Straits a secret as long as possible.

Soon after leaving Cordes Bay on 23 August, in memory of the experiences undergone, the admiral created the Order of the Unchained Lion, into which were enrolled the six principal officers whose names were inscribed on a plaque. They swore an oath to do nothing against their honour, whatever danger this might bring them, and to uphold the cause of Holland wherever the King of Spain held sway. Such ceremonies completed on 3 September 1599, the five vessels made to enter the South Sea for the first time, but high seas, mists and an accident to the *Glad Tidings* caused the company to divide. Therefore, from this point onwards we must consider the fate of each ship independently. They can, however, be grouped into two sections: first the *Hope* and the *Charity* which reached Santa María and eventually headed out to the East Indies, and secondly those which with varying fortunes struggled to free themselves from the furies of the Straits. By this time, the number of survivors is judged to have been 233 or 235 men, or less than half those who had departed from Holland over 14 months ago. Nine others were to die soon after leaving the Straits and all were unwell.[15]

While the other ships remained behind at the western entrance to the Straits to aid repairs to the *Glad Tidings*, Simon de Cordes sailed onwards in the *Hope* unaware of their predicament. Fortunately, before entering the South Sea, it had been agreed that in case of separation they should all meet at the island of Santa María. However, before reaching the island, Cordes spent 28 days in the Chonos archipelago where he was well received by the Indians. Sailing from here he landed on the mainland at Punta de Lavapié on 7 November, and assuming that the Indians would be equally friendly and willing to trade, he disembarked with 23 of his men. Disastrously, the Indians, unaccustomed to seeing strangers other than the Spaniards whom they had cause to fear, attacked them ferociously and killed them all, including Thomas Adams brother of the pilot. Those who had remained on board ship decided to proceed to the planned rendezvous at Santa María, and on their arrival found that the *Charity* had anchored there four days previously on 4 November. The experiences of her crew in their contact with the Indians had been no less tragic, for after parting company with the *Faith*, *Fidelity* and *Glad Tidings*, she had called at the island of Mocha to trade. Van Beuningen and 27 men went ashore but were massacred.[16]

This second group of three ships had kept company until 8 September, when the *Faith* and *Fidelity* lost sight of their companion the *Glad Tidings*. The former were driven southwards by strong winds and for 24 days strove to make headway northwards past the mouth of the Straits. Finally, on 26 September, finding themselves in danger of being driven ashore and still only three leagues north of the entrance to the Straits, they decided to take refuge in one of its bays. They were obliged to remain there until 2 December, amid the growing discontent of the crews who began to plead for an early return home. In particular, the crew of the *Faith*, under the command of Sebald de Weert, were in a near mutinous state as a result of hunger, cold and sickness. When finally the two ships were able to weigh anchor, it became clear that the *Faith* was in no condition to sustain a long voyage. By 11 December she found herself alone, separated by wind, storms and the superior sailing ability of the *Fidelity*.

Alone and with a disaffected crew, de Weert realised that he must renounce his plan to join the others at Santa María, and thus he set out eastwards intending to return home. However, he must have felt that his luck had begun to change when on 16 December he made contact with a party from the van Noort expedition which had left Holland a few weeks after his own. But with the gradual recognition that van Noort was unable, or unwilling, to share his provisions, and that the *Faith* was in no state to return to the South Sea, reluctantly de Weert left the Straits on 21 January 1600 bound for Europe. Yet the memory of Sebald de Weert was to live on in those regions, for he was soon to sight islands to which mapmakers gave his name – the Sibbel de Wards or Sebaldine Isles, at one time thought to have been the Falklands but now felt more likely to have been the Jason Islands.[17] When she reached Goeree on 13 July, only 36 of the crew of the *Faith* were still alive. Even so, she was the only vessel of the entire expedition to return home safely.

The *Glad Tidings*, meanwhile, commanded by Gerritsz, on emerging from the Straits for a second time was driven far to the south to about 64°, beyond the point reached by Drake, where the crew sighted a mountainous land covered in snow, possibly the South Shetlands or Graham Land. When the storms abated Gerritsz turned once more for Chile, and on 17 November 1599 the 23 survivors gave themselves up to the local authorities in Valparaíso, pleading for supplies and treatment for their ills.

As part of the measures for the defence of the Chilean coast, the *corregidor* of Santiago, Jerónimo de Molina, had been sent to the port of Valparaíso with all the men he could muster. It was Molina who prepared an ambush for Gerritsz and six men who came ashore bearing a flag of truce, and who finally convinced them that any resistance would be in vain.[18] After their surrender, the *Glad Tidings* was sailed to Callao with a Spanish crew and six of its original Dutch complement. Their statements and those of Gerritsz and company before the *audiencia* of Santiago, are the main sources for this story of misfortune. As regards the fate of those taken prisoner, we learn from Spanish sources that three were put aboard the 1602 squadron leaving Callao, their destination being Seville. However, although some 22 had surrendered with Gerritsz, the viceroy makes specific reference only to a further six or seven, whom he had decided not to return to Europe at the same time, because they were 'informants and too knowledgeable', especially the captain and the pilot.[19] Some were obviously held in the viceroyalty and one of these, a carpenter from Leiden known in Peru as Adrián Rodríguez, was to play a part in a later expedition to the area, that of Jacques l'Hermite.

By this time the Spanish were, of course, aware of the presence of the *Hope* and the *Charity* at Santa María, and consequently Captain Antonio Recio de Soto was dispatched thither in order to assess the strength of the opposition. Although impressed by their military preparedness, he saw enough to convince himself that the two Dutch ships had food supplies for only two months, and not two years as they boasted. Their petitions to be allowed to barter for, or purchase, fresh supplies since they came in peace as Dutch vassals of the Spanish king, expecting a warm welcome, were denied.[20] Unwilling to challenge the defences of the alerted mainland coast, they judged it best to depart for the East Indies on 27 November 1599. The *Charity* was lost on the voyage and the *Hope* reached Japan where her English pilot, William Adams, lived under partial detention for about 20 years until his death.

In terms of its operations in the South Sea, perhaps the most successful vessel was the *Fidelity* under the command of Baltasar Cordes, which after parting company with the *Faith* at the mouth of the Straits managed to make headway towards the north. She reached Carelmapu overlooking the island of Chiloé in March 1600, but unlike those of their countrymen who found hostile receptions elsewhere in Chile, the crew of the *Fidelity* were received with enthusiasm by the Indians. It was only with their support, for their own numbers were now reduced to about 50 men, that the Dutch were able to devise a bold plan to attack the settlement of Castro on Chiloé island, in April 1600. This was achieved, apparently, by convincing the commander of the fort, Baltasar Ruiz del Pliego, that he was in danger of attack from a horde of Indians, and offering to reinforce his defences in exchange for fresh food. Having gained admittance to the settlement by this simple trickery, and with the aid of Indian allies, the Dutch killed or put to flight the majority of the Spanish.[21]

But the invaders themselves were driven out of Castro a few months later, when it was reoccupied by about 100 men brought across from Osorno on the mainland at the initiative of one Francisco del Campo. His report sums up a bloody encounter in which 300 Indians died along with 26 Dutchmen. The Dutch version of events admits to only 23 survivors leaving the area on 4 June in the *Fidelity*. They finally reached Tidore on 3 January 1601 where they were imprisoned by the Portuguese authorities. While accounts in Spanish of the Castro episode tend to dramatise murder, rape and the plunder and destruction of the local church, del Campo himself shows the ferocity of Spanish retaliation, since for their part in aiding the Dutch almost 50 Indians were executed as a warning to the rest. 'All Chiloé is calm, as if they had never rebelled', he concludes.[22]

The second of these first two Dutch intrusions into the South Sea, that of van Noort, was financed by a trading company formed in 1598 by three merchants, Pieter van Beveren, Huyg Gerritsz van der Buys and Jan Benning. Two ships, the *Maurice* and the *Concord* left Rotterdam on 2 July 1598 heading for Goeree, that is only a few days after Mahu's departure. On 1 August they pressed on towards the English coast where they intended to await the arrival of two further ships from Amsterdam. When the latter had not arrived by the end of the month, van Noort returned to Rotterdam. Therefore, the complete fleet only left Goeree on 13 September, by which time Mahu was in the vicinity of the Cape Verde Isles.

The four ships, carrying in all 248 men, were commanded as follows:[23]

|                        | Tons | Guns  |                          |
| ---------------------- | ---- | ----- | ------------------------ |
| Mauritius (*Maurice*)  | 250  | 24    | Olivier van Noort        |
| Hendrick Frederick     | 300  | 25/28 | Jacob Claesz van Ilpendam |
| Hoop (*Hope*)          | 50   |       | Jacob Jansz Huydecoper   |
| Eendracht (*Concord*)  | 50   |       | Pieter Esaisz de Lint    |

Following Mahu's example, they took aboard an English pilot, Melis, at Plymouth, and then the four ships struck out for the African coast on 21 September, passing the Canary Isles in the first week of October. Portuguese opposition became evident at this early stage, as it had done in the case of the Mahu fleet, for when a strong force landed at Príncipe Island in the Gulf of Guinea on 10 December, it was engaged before it was able to gather supplies of food and fresh water. The pilot Melis was killed in this encounter. But the most serious confrontation was to come across the Atlantic soon after the expedition sailed into the bay of Rio de Janeiro on 9 February 1599. Van Noort had hoped to collect large amounts of fruit here to compensate for the failure to obtain adequate supplies on the African coast, but the Portuguese again refused all trade, except for 50 or 60 oranges. When a Dutch party secretly slipped ashore, it was ambushed, seven were killed, several captured and the rest put to flight. The situation was further complicated at this time by the need to remove and redistribute the cargo of the *Concord*, now in danger of sinking after weathering Atlantic storms. She was later burnt.[24]

Beset by these problems and the fast approaching winter season, van Noort concluded at a council meeting on 20 March that the wisest solution would be to await the summer for the passage of the Straits, rather than to winter there as Cordes had done. Thus, amid storms, growing starvation, sickness and the unrest of his men, whom he reports at one stage to be dying at the rate of three or four a day, he sought the shelter of St Helena or Ascension Isle. Until the end of May the search continued without success, and when land was finally sighted it proved to be merely the coast of Brazil a little further to the south. Therefore, they were forced to spend the winter in the vicinity of Puerto Deseado and Cape Vírgenes close to the eastern entrance to the Straits, surviving on a diet of penguins in vast numbers (Purchas says they captured 50 000), their eggs, and fish.

Attempts to enter the Straits of Magellan began on 13 November, but were unsuccessful until the 24th of the month due to storms and winds. The three ships eventually emerged into the South Sea on the last day of February 1600, having experienced to a rather lesser degree the hardships endured by Cordes. However, accounts of van Noort's expedition seem to indicate some unrest among the crews. This is evident from a meeting of the Council of War on board the *Maurice* on 28 December 1599. At that session the vice-admiral Jacob Claesz was found guilty of causing mutiny throughout the fleet and sentenced to be set on land and abandoned. His position was assumed by Pieter Esaisz de Lint, former captain of the *Concord*. It was during the resolution of this problem that contact was made with that section of the Mahu expedition under the command of Sebald de Weert.

Inevitably in the midst of storms, the small expedition departed from the Straits and headed towards the island of Mocha. Of the 248 men who had set out, only 147 were now left alive, and many of these were suffering from disease and the lack of fresh food. During the confusion of the exit from the Straits, the *Hendrick Frederick* became separated from the other two ships and was not seen again by them. The story of her solitary course must therefore be considered apart. Van Noort, meanwhile, landed at Mocha on 21 March 1600, taking ashore some trinkets and other small items to win the favour of the Indians. He clearly found them in a much more friendly disposition than had van Beuningen and the crew of the *Charity* a few months previously, for on the second day a more useful trade took place, and they were able to exchange knives and hatchets for hens, maize, sheep and various fruits. As a token of their friendship, the Indians invited them into their huts to share a cup of their traditional fermented maize beer, chicha.

While sailing between Mocha and Santa María on 25 March, van Noort sighted a Spanish ship ahead trying to make her escape. The vessel, the *Buen Jesús*, commanded by Francisco de Ibarra, was taken on the following day. She had formed part of a small squadron dispatched from Callao in January 1600 to investigate rumours of Dutch attempts to infiltrate the South Sea. As a prize she yielded little more than 30 sacks of flour, some up-to-date information about the state of Spanish defences, and a pilot, Juan Sandoval, who must have imparted useful knowledge of sailing conditions in the area. Dutch sources, however, indicate that during her stay in Chile, the ship had collected a cargo of gold for shipment to Callao, and that this had been cast overboard before van Noort's crews had reached her. It was from the *Buen Jesús* that he was to learn of the fate of his countrymen under Cordes.[25]

Still seeking the rewards which would make this venture financially rewarding, van Noort sailed on with his new prize to Valparaíso. On 28 March he burnt two vessels and captured a third, the *Los Picos*, with a cargo of wine, leather, apples and olives, destined for sale in Lima. This action perhaps compensated to some extent for a second piece of bad news, letters from Dirck Gerritsz telling how his own activities in the South Sea had ended in that port a few months previously. At Huasco on 1 April welcome fresh provisions were loaded – melons, figs, raisins and chickens, the *Los Picos* was burnt and the *Buen Jesús* and her crew were released, with the exception of two negroes who had told the story of the jettisoned gold and the pilot Sandoval, said to have corroborated their tale under interrogation. The latter met a sad end, when on 30 June he was cast overboard for some misdemeanour. 'A prosperous wind happily succeeded.'[26]

Nevertheless, the lack of opportunity for trade on the coasts of Peru and Chile, and the growing reports of Spanish efforts to drive them from the area, persuaded van Noort to set out across the Pacific to the Ladrones, Philippines and Borneo on what was to become the fourth circumnavigation of the globe, and the first by a Dutchman. The *Maurice* finally returned to Rotterdam on 26 August 1601 with 65 men, having gained her greatest victory against the Spanish in a close engagement off Manila, but the *Concord* fell into enemy hands in the same encounter.

The *Hendrick Frederick*, separated from the rest of the expedition on entering the South Sea, followed a course initially to the agreed rendezvous at Santa María, where a bark of little consequence was captured and fresh meat supplies obtained. Similar engagements and sorties ashore followed at Concepción (2 May) and Arica (18 June). Callao was given a wide berth, a delinquent crew member, Christian Haese, and four Spanish soldiers who had deserted in Chile were put ashore near Guayaquil, then course was set for the Gulf of Panama, where a becalmed vessel with a useful cargo of maize was taken on 11 August. On board her was the priest Agustín de Cavallos, who has left an account of his experiences with the *Hendrick Frederick* for 16 days on the coasts of Costa Rica and Nicaragua. He revealed, on being set free, that it was the intention of her crew to abandon their unhappy stay on the coasts of Peru and New Spain and sail for the East Indies. The ship was finally stranded on the island of Ternate and her crew entered the service of the Dutch East India Company.[27]

As we come to assess the results of these first two Dutch expeditions lured to the coasts of Peru, it is patently obvious that whether the South Sea was a destination in itself, or merely a link in a round-the-world trade to the East Indies, reaching it exacted a terrible toll in terms of hardships, illness and death. Both expeditions verified that European penetration, for purposes of trade or settlement, would be far more hazardous than it had been hitherto in the Caribbean. It necessitated a continual search for fresh supplies and provisions in hostile lands – among the Portuguese or local native population on the African coast in preparation for the crossing of the Atlantic and, again among the unfriendly Portuguese along the coast of Brazil, then the scavenging of whatever a barren and inhospitable land offered as they entered and passed the Straits of Magellan. Finally, it necessitated dependence in the South Sea on the willingness of generally hostile Spanish settlers or wary Indians to provide daily sustenance and a store of food to carry them across the Pacific.

Actual trade seems not to have advanced much beyond the exchange with friendly Indians of novelties of European origin for small amounts of food. Reactions of the Indian population ranged from outright hostility and violence, in the case of the landings of Simon de Cordes and van Beuningen at Punta de Lavapié and Mocha Isle, where 50 men were lost, to cooperation as in the joint Dutch-Indian action at Castro, and the more hospitable treatment accorded van Noort at Mocha. The Dutch correctly perceived that the Indians were hostile towards the Spanish in Chile. But it was difficult, on the basis of these early contacts with them, to reach a conclusion as to whether this could be translated into a Dutch-Indian alliance, for they had arrived at a time when Indian resistance to Spanish domination had reached a climax with the destruction of Valdivia and the massacre of its inhabitants on 24 November 1599. Those Dutch who perished at Indian hands most certainly did so because they were mistaken for Spaniards. Later expeditions, therefore, continued to embrace the hope of enlisting the aid of Indians, and perhaps negroes, for anti-Spanish action.

Clearly, each expedition disposed of sufficient military strength for its own defence, and indeed to enable it to move to the offensive against Indians, Spanish shipping or, in the case of

Baltasar de Cordes, against the isolated colony at Castro. But the acquiring of fresh provisions or plunder by these means can hardly be considered the basis for establishing a regular and profitable commerce in the future. In each case the remoteness of the destination, its isolation from any supporting Dutch base and the perils of the long, unbroken voyage were to become a test of endurance and discipline in often appalling climatic conditions. The Mahu group reached the South Sea in a little more than 14 months, whereas van Noort required almost 18 months, the former with about 48 per cent of those who had set out and the latter with 59 per cent, perhaps an indication of the advisability of wintering before entering the Straits rather than within them. Above all, there was ample confirmation of sailors' fears that the dangers and the rigours of a voyage to the Straits of Magellan were a powerful challenge to the strongest and most determined of men. For although by choosing the calmer season and allowing the furies of winter to pass, van Noort entered the South Sea with greater ease, his stay there was still a desperate struggle for survival. Stormy seas, tempestuous winds, hail, rain, snow and biting cold feature prominently in the written accounts, and likewise must have figured in the tales told in the taverns of Amsterdam and Rotterdam. Natural perils such as these, hunger, illness and the ungodly end met by those who fell into the hands of barbarian 'giants', must have placed an almost unbearable strain on those whose task it was to maintain discipline and still pursue the objectives of the voyages to a successful, or at least safe, conclusion. [28]

This was all the more so in view of the practice of revealing the course via the Straits of Magellan only several months into the voyage. It certainly created an element of mistrust and contributed to the unrest of the crews as the conditions worsened. If they had had any loyalty to the enterprise at the outset, this would the more easily be shaken in times of trial. In more practical terms, it meant that sailors were not prepared for the intense cold of the Straits and did not possess the heavy clothing with which to withstand the biting winds and driving rain and snow. Dirck Gerritsz claims to have protested when he received the news, and Agustín de Cavallos appears to support this cause of agitation, adding that the rather different implications of entry into the South Sea were a further motive for discontent. 'They complain that the captain of this vessel had led them by deceit, saying that they came to trade, but that once they had emerged from the Straits he told them that they came only to steal and do all the damage they could.'[29] It is also significant, with regard to unrest and problems of discipline, that the insubordination of van Noort's vice-admiral, Claesz, appears to have occurred during the passage of the Straits.

Charles Boxer seems to support the general notion of tightly run Dutch ships, with crews on minimum wages and low rations, creating an undercurrent of dissent, but one must confess also that previous non-Dutch approaches to the Straits had been marked by alleged mutinies.[30] Both Magellan and Drake (the famous case of Thomas Doughty) felt obliged to resort to execution. There were seditious plans afoot during Cavendish's last voyage, and Richard Hawkins firmly believed in the need to exercise an iron discipline. Obviously, the remoteness of the voyage and the delays caused by wintering taxed any crew to its limits, but more so when their presence in those regions was unexpected and unplanned for.

And yet, van Noort's exploits, enhanced by his role as the first Dutch circumnavigator, further stimulated European interest in the southern lands of the Viceroyalty of Peru, as is proved by the number of translations of his journal. For despite the dangers and the afflictions, he still records the lure of precious metals and fertile soils. For example, with reference to the region from Santiago to Valdivia in southern central Chile, he reports in the words of Purchas that it 'is the most fertile in the world, and of the most wholesome ayre, insomuch that few are there sicke; yea, a sword put up into the scabbard all wet with dewe, doth not therewith rust. Fruits, Mays, Hogges, Horses, Kine, Sheepe, Goats, are plentiful and wander in great herds, besides Gold-mines.'[31] As we have seen already in the comments of Dirck Gerritsz to his captors in Valparaíso, the Dutch like the English before them were developing the image of distant lands, far from the centres of Spanish government and population, and only barely within the orbit of Spanish colonial jurisdiction, which might contain new sources of wealth and ultimately become the home for settlers.

Even the *Faith* which made no significant headway into the South Sea contributed to those who were to pursue her course later, for her mate, Jan Outghersz, was to publish a crude but practical pictorial guide to the Straits of Magellan following his return home. This was a marked improvement on the English sources of information available previously, and signals the first shift in the balance of knowledge in favour of the Dutch.[32]

Finally, we must consider the repercussions in the Viceroyalty of
Peru to this unwelcome irruption into the South Sea by a nation
already proved to be a redoubtable foe in Europe. In a sense the
response from Lima had been adequate to the threat perceived,
since the disclosure to the intruders of preparations being made to
obstruct and challenge their operations had persuaded captains
from both ventures to sail for the East Indies, and delay no longer
in Peru. In practice, hitherto the viceroy's principal lines of defence
had been reliance on ignorance and isolation, and the utilisation of
a flotilla of four or five crown vessels to scour the seas for signs of
intruders, before accompanying the annual silver shipment to
Panama. In response to warnings of fresh English arrivals in 1597,
viceroy Luis de Velasco had expressed scepticism based on the
inclemency of the winter season, but adding that 'the entire
defence of the Indies in general consists more of the ignorance
which enemies have of specific aspects of it, and the obstacles
posed by land and weather, than the forces which there are to
resist them'.[33]

On 22 June 1599, when the Mahu/Cordes expedition was
wintering in the Straits, and van Noort still in the Atlantic close to
Puerto Deseado, the Peruvian viceroy was informed, by way of
New Spain and Guatemala, that a Dutch fleet had left Holland. The
initial reaction was again one of scepticism, reinforced by disbelief
that anyone should equip a fleet for the Chilean coast, where 'there
are only Indians with whom to trade and the land is the poorest in
the world',[34] a viewpoint which is markedly different from that
expressed by van Noort. However, the doubts were shattered on 2
December, when a ship from Chile brought news of a positive
sighting of intruders at Santa María, on 4 November. Four days
later, Velasco was in receipt of communications from the governor
of the River Plate, which chronicled the progress and action of van
Noort off that river in August, and also at Rio de Janeiro the
previous February. On 8 December, the viceroy was able to make
his own observations and inquiries of the nature of the intervention when the *Glad Tidings* sailed into Callao ironically with the bad
news, and incontrovertible evidence of the Dutch presence,
following Gerritsz's surrender at Valparaíso. Only at this point did
he judge it necessary to take action beyond the usual alerting of
local militias and the distribution of warnings along the coast.

Since it was considered at that time that the most effective
defensive measures could be adopted at sea, viceroy Velasco

prepared eight armed vessels. These included the *Dainty* captured from Richard Hawkins and now known as the *Visitación* or *Inglesa*. Together with a launch, they embarked in all 1119 men. On 1 January 1600, two galleons and a patax carrying some 300 men were dispatched to Chilean waters with instructions to search the coast and islands and to engage, or merely observe, the enemy depending on the strength of his forces. If no contact were made by 20 March, this squadron was to return northwards to Arica to collect the year's silver shipment and convey it to Callao. Already, therefore, the viceroy was confronted by the dilemma posed by the twin duties of the Peruvian fleet – its coastal defence role and its convoy protection function. Furthermore, the possibility that the Dutch might evade detection in the south led to the decision to send out the remainder of his ships, under the command of his nephew Juan de Velasco, to act as a second line of defence off Pisco.[35]

After waiting anxiously for a month with no news from either squadron, it seems that the viceroy's certainty and scepticism were under stress, for he altered his original plan. First, a vessel was detached from the Pisco group to collect the silver from Arica and transport it to Callao. This was done by the end of February. Secondly, in March, Juan de Velasco was instructed to convoy the silver to Panama with all speed, and then to commence a search for intruders in the north. Tragically, during the latter operation, the viceroy's nephew and the crew of the *capitana* lost their lives in a wreck off the coast of California.[36] Meanwhile, in the far south, the smaller squadron had supposedly scoured the coasts and islands expected to be frequented by any interlopers, but failed to make contact with the participants of the two Dutch expeditions at that time active in the vicinity of Carelmapu, Castro, Mocha and Santa María. Therefore, it departed on 21 March, in accordance with the instructions, leaving behind the patax under the command of Francisco de Ibarra. It was this ship which eventually fell into the hands of van Noort and company. During the next two or three months, reported sightings of strange ships provoked the despatch of crown vessels down to the area of Pisco, at times with elaborate orders as to how to induce the enemy to surrender peacefully, or by using as little force as necessary.[37]

Therefore, although the Mahu and van Noort expeditions can never in any sense be considered a serious threat to the coastal zones of the Viceroyalty of Peru, nevertheless, their presence did seem to rebuff the reliance on isolation and ignorance, and did reveal the practical problems confronting a viceroy who must, as a priority, maintain regular silver shipments to Spain while at the same time protecting his kingdom from attack, both with the same squadron of ships. In a somewhat resigned frame of mind, viceroy Velasco commented in 1600 'that it is not possible to guard this port [Callao] and at the same time scour the coast without forsaking the one to attend to the other, and even when this were done what resistance can four ships offer to the many which it is known are being fitted out in Holland?'[38] He might also have appended comments on the impracticality of trying to find intruders once in the South Sea.

His answer, therefore, was the suggestion that a fleet be sent from Spain to patrol the Straits of Magellan and prevent intrusions, a proposal rejected at this stage but taken up by some of his successors later in the century. Velasco was supported by Pedro Ozores de Ulloa, who had formed part of the Pisco squadron, and who urged a larger South Sea fleet, part of which should be permanently stationed off the Chilean coast, to engage the enemy before he had the opportunity of refreshing on any of the handy islands. Without undertaking to strengthen its commitment to sea defence, the crown counselled the annual dispatch of two of its ships from Callao to the Chilean coast, from November to May, since it was not to be expected that intruders would pass the Straits in winter.[39]

As had occurred at the time of the incursions of Drake and Cavendish, the mere presence of enemy ships was sufficient to raise voices proclaiming impending doom. Ozores again commented that 'if one of these pirates carried orders to sack this port [Callao] and the city of Lima, which is guarded only by its reputation, it would be easier to achieve it than it had been in Santo Domingo, Cartagena, Cadiz or in other areas'.[40] He found an ally in Juan Vázquez de Loaysa, who had seen service at Lepanto and Tunis, and who suggested that the security of Peru dangled by a mere thread when entrusted to its geographical position. A force of 1500 men would soon overrun the unenthusiastic and unskilled resistance offered by the citizens' militias of Callao and Lima.[41] Both Vázquez and Ozores called for the erection of two forts at Callao, whose crossfire might protect ships at anchor and deter landings. Both plans were put off in 1601 and again in 1603 due to cost, the uncertainty about whether the Dutch would follow up their first interventions, and doubtlessly by the fact that viceroy Velasco was reaching the end of his term of office.[42]

But although he and the crown were probably right, on this occasion, to hold firm against the more active supporters of costly defensive strategies, it is equally true that in areas remote from Lima, the sightings, both real and imagined, of enemy vessels were the source of some fear and alarm. Particularly in Chile, whose inhabitants were already beleaguered as a result of effective and ferocious Indian resistance, the prospect, however remote, of a European ally for the Indians and the destruction of shipping, endangering the lifeline to Peru and income from coastal trading, were cruel blows of fate.

# 2

# The Defeat of the Peruvian Fleet by Joris van Speilbergen (1614–17)

Already at the time of the Mahu and van Noort expeditions, the States-General had begun to urge that similar commercial enterprises should merge, or coordinate their efforts, with a view to attaining a greater Dutch share of trade. This was achieved in 1602 with the creation of the East India Company, which had been granted a monopoly charter over Dutch trade eastwards via the Cape of Good Hope and westwards from the Straits of Magellan, initially for a period of 21 years. However, although the Dutch were to continue to advance in both directions, to the west this was limited to the Caribbean, the Guiana coast and Brazil for more than a decade. In fact, in the years immediately following the foundation of the company, there had developed a struggle for supremacy between Willem Usselincx, another refugee from the south, proposer of schemes for Dutch expansion in the West Indies and leader of a group generally referred to as the 'war party', and Johan van Oldenbarnevelt who directed the 'peace party' towards the conclusion of some form of understanding with Spain.

Usselincx had advocated the theory that Dutch colonies be established in the New World to exploit the rich and fertile soils, rather than simply to plunder the mineral wealth for which parts of the region had become so famous. With the benefit of European techniques, valuable commercial crops could be produced for a European market, and new outlets be found for manufactured goods from the home country. Being a fervent Calvinist, he would offer the native population conversion in the hope of creating a bond of belief with the Dutch, which might serve as the firm basis for an armed alliance against the Spanish. As is apparent from the two ventures we have already described, the plan was not to seize colonies in Spanish or Portuguese hands, but to identify those areas still open to settlement, for example south of the River Plate and southern Chile.

Increasingly, however, Usselincx and his supporters were confronted by the powerful proponents of peace with Spain, led by the lands advocate van Oldenbarnevelt, who sought to rid the treasury of the costs of the conflict and who pointed out that American products could be acquired more cheaply in Spanish and Portuguese ports. The result of an intense dispute was the conclusion of a twelve-year truce with Spain in 1609. Though carefully worded so as not to constitute an affront to Spain, the treaty, none the less implied a tacit acceptance of Dutch expansion in the East Indies in an effort to safeguard Spanish holdings in the New World. Therefore, it did amount to a check on the most ambitious proposals by Usselincx. But it did not totally eliminate Dutch activity in areas such as the Guiana coast and Brazil, and it most certainly did not deter Usselincx from continuing to advance proposals for Dutch action in the New World, particularly from about 1613 onwards. Moreover, after a short period of neglect, the States-General also began to renew its interest in the west, and as evidence of this the expedition of van Speilbergen sailed for the South Sea.[1]

Perhaps reflecting the greater unity of recent Dutch maritime undertakings, this fresh act of trespass into Spanish territory in the New World had an official commission from 'Their High Mightinesses the States-General and His Princely Excellency',[2] and the financial support of the coordinating agency, the East India Company, apparently now desirous of exercising, somewhat tardily, its monopoly of trade through the Straits of Magellan. Under this sponsorship a fleet was gathered during the early months of 1614. In addition to the principal Dutch journal, we are fortunate to have an unofficial insight into its aims and experiences through the declarations to Spanish officials in Peru of four men: two Germans who deserted the fleet in the Chilean port of Papudo, namely Andreas Heinrich, a soldier from Emden and Philip Hansen from Königsberg, a third, Nicolas de la Porte, who declared himself a pastrycook from Paris and who slipped ashore at the Peruvian port of Huarmey, and the last, Francisco de Lima from Madrid, who had been a prisoner of the Dutch since his capture near São Vicente on the coast of Brazil.[3]

From the information passed on by the latter in Peru, with regard to cargoes and armaments, it is clear that this is another instance of a Dutch fleet fitted out for trade but capable of using force, perhaps simply to obtain booty through privateering activities.

Lima specifically states that everything taken as plunder was for the benefit of the backers of the venture, and that each ship carried a merchant whose job it was to keep an account of such items. But more specifically on this occasion, and as a reflection of the interests of the East India Company, the voyage was seen as a challenge from the west to Spanish and Portuguese investments in the East Indies, which might be achieved by an attack on the Manila galleon, or merely by diverting Spanish attention from Dutch pretensions in those parts as a result of action along the Peruvian coast. Presumably those charged with the provision of supplies had taken note of the plight of Cordes and van Noort in this respect, for van Speilbergen was stocked with large amounts of fish, meat and biscuit, calculated by Lima to be sufficient for three years.

However, this did not totally eliminate problems due to dietary deficiencies, nor did it diminish outbreaks of unrest in the fleet, for as Heinrich explained to his Spanish interrogators, 'the principal officers eat well and the common sailors badly, and for this reason, as he has said, this declarant deserted'. Furthermore, there are indications that the practice of not revealing the true course of the expedition at the outset was again adhered to, thereby contributing to the poor discipline. Heinrich again declared that 'he came as a soldier in this fleet, which he was told was to sail for India, and en route they changed course and came to steal'. His statement was supported by his companion Hansen and by La Porte, who refers to the opening of secret orders. Such comments deserve to be heard with a degree of suspicion, because obviously their effect, if not their design, was such as to shift the blame for involvement in hostile acts off the Peruvian coast from the individual participants to the promoters of the venture. However, Francisco de Lima too, on the basis of his observation of the Dutch crews, confessed that 'he learnt that everyone there came unwillingly, some saying that they had been deceived'.[4]

Therefore, in these circumstances, a fleet of six ships left Texel on 8 August 1614 commanded by an experienced seaman and leader, Joris van Speilbergen, who had previously sailed to the East Indies via the Cape of Good Hope between 1601 and 1604. There were to be a number of occasions on which his firm and capable leadership greatly contributed to the overcoming of the dangers and disorders that were to arise. The ships were armed and commanded as follows:

| Ship | Tons | Guns | Captain |
|---|---|---|---|
| *Groote Sonne (Great Sun)* | 600 | 28 | Joris van Speilbergen |
| *Groote Manne (Great Moon)* | 600 | 28 | Claensz Marten Thoveling |
| *Morgensterre (Morning Star)* | 350 | 24 | Maerten Pieterssen Cruyck |
| *Aeolus* | 350 | 24 | Job Cornelissen |
| *Meeuwe (Gull)* | 60 | 8 | |
| *Jager (Huntsman)* | 60 | 8 | |

They carried somewhat more than 700 men, of whom 350 were soldiers. The majority were Dutch, though as we have already seen Germans and Frenchmen participated also. According to Lima, in each of the four major vessels there were four pilots, but he makes no comment on their nationality, and clearly following Mahu and van Noort the Dutch were now able to draw on the experience of their own navigators in the South Sea.

The crossing of the Atlantic by way of the Canary and Cape Verde Islands was without incident, and the mainland of Brazil was sighted on 13 December, but no landing attempted until a week later when they reached Ilha Grande beyond Rio de Janeiro. At this point on the coast of Brazil the remoteness of their enterprise became apparent to expeditions such as this, particularly with the revelation that their course lay through the Straits of Magellan. For the commander, van Speilbergen, it was the moment at which to demonstrate a firm hand both in dealing with Portuguese settlers and authorities from whom he needed to obtain fresh supplies, and in ending outbreaks of unrest among his crews. At São Vicente, from 18 January 1615, they negotiated for supplies of fruit, fowls, pigs and sugar, but before the handover was completed the authorities dissuaded the local population, causing van Speilbergen to employ force, burning a church and a sugar mill after an attempt to ambush his men. It was here that they took a prize bound for Angola, and from her seized the prisoner Francisco de Lima to whose testimony we have referred above. From her cargo, which also included books on law and theology, and 'relics, crosses, grants of absolution, and such-like foolery', they were able to extract fresh oranges and lemons before putting to sea once more.[5]

It was no coincidence that at this same stage of the venture there were outbreaks of mutinous activity aboard the *Gull*, most probably reflecting a division in the fleet between those who favoured wintering in Puerto Deseado and those who preferred to sail directly for the East Indies via the Cape of Good Hope. At a trial on 5 January two men, Hieronimus and Jan Hendricksen, were found guilty of treason, hung up at the yardarm and their bodies shot through by musketeers. When they finally left São Vicente on 4 February it was clearly van Speilbergen's intention to proceed without delay to the Straits, anxious to offer no further opportunity for dissent. But despite the firmness of his first response and despite the partial redistribution throughout the fleet of the *Gull*'s crew, further incidents occurred while they were dispersed by stormy weather early in March, and when entry to the Straits of Magellan was finally gained on 2 April, it was without the company of their troublesome companions in the *Gull*.

Although the five remaining vessels were separated during the passage of the first channels of the Straits, they rejoined one another with great rejoicing in Cordes Bay on 16 April, where they remained until the 24th of the month, collecting water, wood, seafood and berries to restock their depleted supplies. Sightings of the local natives produced the predictable judgement that they were 'of very big stature'. To celebrate their happy reunion, van Speilbergen organised a feast for the principal officers on board the *Sun*, best described in the official narrative of the venture.

> For joy at our re-union, the Admiral invited all the principal officers to dinner on board his ship, and they were well regaled there with many fresh dishes of meat, pork, poultry, oranges, lemons, candied peel and marmalades, most of which we had procured at Saint Vicente; also with olives, capers, good Spanish and French wine, Dutch beer, and many other things which it would take too long to mention here; and, moreover, we enjoyed there a fine concert of various instruments, and music of many voices.[6]

The rest of the crews were also able to celebrate and recuperate here, but on a more prosaic diet of mussels, cress, parsley and berries.

Clearly then, in spite of the disputes of the past, it was a more good-humoured and fitter fleet which passed into the South Sea about nine months after leaving Holland, and after a dramatically improved 34-day passage of the Straits of Magellan. They were certainly more able to withstand the toils ahead on the coasts of the Viceroyalty of Peru than either of their Dutch predecessors, but this was doubtlessly due to the general knowledge and practical navigational information and expertise gained during those two experiences. Francisco de Lima confirms the assurance they demonstrated later on the Chilean coast, stating that:

> they came with as much confidence as if they had sailed and travelled through these regions all their lives, so that when in the port of Concón [north of Valparaíso] . . . they said that they were not worried by failing to take on water there for three leagues ahead they would do so, and they went on to collect water . . . at Papudo with as much certainty as if they were natives of this land.[7]

Before chancing a landing on the mainland, however, it was already established as desirable to obtain rest and refreshment on one of the islands off the Chilean shore, where Spaniards might be few in number or totally absent. The latter was the case at Mocha, where a party went ashore on 26 May in boats laden with trading goods, but well guarded by soldiers because of uncertainty concerning the Indian response. In the event armed men were unnecessary for, as in the instance of van Noort, the Indians were keen to barter sheep, poultry and fruits for items such as axes, knives and beads. The Indian chief and his son were invited aboard the flagship and gun salutes fired in their honour. The journal records that they were 'well-mannered, very polite and friendly, very orderly in their eating and drinking, of good morals, and almost equal to Christians'.[8]

On dropping anchor at Santa María on 29 May the omens were clearly not so auspicious, as two dozen or more Spanish cavalrymen appeared riding to and fro, and a bark at anchor nearby was able to escape and warn the mainland of intruders. Nevertheless a Spanish negotiator, Juan Cornejo, delivered an invitation to the principal Dutch officers to dine ashore on the evening of 30 May, but no sooner had they landed when they were recalled by the *Huntsman* whose crew had seen armed men making directly for the spot where the dinner was to take place, and concluded that some mischief was afoot. On the following day van Speilbergen landed a force to punish the Spanish for their deception, but since they fled before it the town was looted of wheat, barley, beans, 500 sheep and some poultry before being set on fire.

From Juan Cornejo, now held as a prisoner in view of the

embittered relations with the Spaniards, it was learnt that the viceroy, the Marquis of Montesclaros, had dispatched his nephew, Rodrigo de Mendoza, as commander of a squadron of two galleons and a patax to search for intruders in the area of Mocha, Santa María and Valdivia, following receipt of warnings about a possible invasion. They had left Callao at the end of December 1614, carrying over 500 men and 42 guns, at a time when van Speilbergen's force was still off the coast of Brazil. In his secret instructions to Mendoza, the viceroy personally expressed his confidence of victory in any coming encounter with the enemy, to the extent that 'with a few hours of battle you may bring him to the point of surrender without any irreparable damage to your-selves'.[9] Yet it is clear that his judgement was not without criticism from those who favoured a different response to foreign inter-vention.

Some counselled that in view of the uncertainties concerning the route any interlopers might take, it would be better not to risk losing them at sea but to concentrate land and sea forces at Callao to protect the port and its shipping. At the same time more trustworthy news of the enemy's progress along the coast could be gathered from sightings, or as a result of his excursions ashore.[10] Such a point of view reflects the interests above all of the merchant community at Callao and the citizens of the capital, displaying a readiness to subject the minor ports of southern Peru and Chile to whatever hostilities the Dutch might embark upon, granted the minimal level of defence in those ports.

However, at this juncture, given the rate of progress of the van Speilbergen fleet, such issues were hypothetical for Mendoza returned to Callao on 13 May, that is before the Dutch had reached Mocha, reporting no sightings. Viceroy Montesclaros, neverthe-less, had recognised the potential threat to the year's shipment of silver, finding himself in a situation similar to that which had confronted Luis de Velasco, and responding in like manner. For while his nephew was still in Chilean waters, the remainder of the crown fleet under Antonio Beaumont had collected the silver from Arica and sailed onwards to Panama from Callao on 12 May. The already small Peruvian naval force was thus, once again, divided in its operations.

Van Speilbergen's confidence was such that, unlike his Dutch predecessors, he was not intimidated by news of the viceroy' offensive and defensive measures. On the contrary, he drew up detailed strategy for an encounter at sea, assigning to each Dutch ship its role in the coming battle and to each man the precise function he was to perform. The search for the Peruvian squadron began on 1 June as the Dutch headed for the bay of Concepción, anchoring without attempting to land on the 3rd of the month. Some Spanish-American writers attribute this to the fact that the port was defended by Alonso de Ribera, governor of Chile, and a man well respected in Flanders. Certainly, in writing his own report of the events for the crown, Ribera claims to have gathered a considerable defence force of 900 Spaniards and 300 Indians, strategically placing them in trenches or behind earthen breast-works.[11]

The next port of call for van Speilbergen was Valparaíso on 12 June, where the crew of the *San Agustín* at anchor were forced to abandon her, but not before setting her ablaze to prevent her cargo of wheat and biscuit from falling into enemy hands. Similarly when 200 Dutchmen landed, driving off a force over three times larger augmented by reinforcements from Santiago, it was the Spanish themselves who burnt their dwellings as they retreated. At Papudo on 13 June the scene was more peaceful, as they were led to fresh water by wild horses coming down to drink from streams.[12] Before departing on 16 June, van Speilbergen released two prisoners taken at São Vicente (one of them being Francisco de Lima) and the Spaniard Cornejo taken at Santa María. At the same time Andreas Heinrich and Philip Hansen seized the opportunity to desert.

A brief visit to Arica on 2 July seems to have been due in part to disappointment at not finding any silver galleons at anchor, as well as to hasty defence measures. The local townspeople had rallied round to dig trenches and erect adobe parapets and wooden palisades, but even so were fearful of the outcome of any attack because of the shortage of basic equipment – arms, artillery and powder. A fresh supply of firearms had been promised from Lima but never sent. Consequently, at most, about 200 muskets and arquebuses were collected from private sources. Moreover, the three best guns in the port had been appropriated by the viceroy for use in the silver fleet under Antonio Beaumont, leaving only seven pieces, some of them very old and of short range. Neverthe-less, the general clamour and beating of militia drums, together with the absence of any attractive prize persuaded to the Dutch to press on.[13]

The defence situation at Arica is a good indication of what must have been the case in other similar ports. Although, as the Dutch themselves well understood, it was a vital link in the silver chain from Potosí to Seville, it depended largely at this time on the efforts of its own townspeople for its security. This was attained despite the disinterest of a viceroy who had expressed the unsympathetic opinion that if Arica suffered a serious attack, its buildings of wood and adobe could more easily be repaired or replaced than the stone built dwellings of Lima and Callao.[14] Furthermore, following van Speilbergen's visit to the port, when the *ariqueños* had spent 1000 pesos from their own resources to construct a half-moon shaped redoubt and a small fort to house artillery, overcoming the earthquake of 16 September in the process, they were dismayed by a further order from Montesclaros to hand over their cannon, in pursuit of his policy of withdrawing artillery from smaller ports. Therefore, by December 1615, they were left with only two demi-cannons and a single gunner whose wages were paid by the town.[15]

Off Pisco on 16 July, the Dutch captured a trading vessel captained by Juan Bautista González, bound for Callao with a typical cargo of olives, but unexpectedly also surrendering a booty of 7000 pesos in silver.[16] Then, at last, on the following day towards evening, a more formidable sight appeared as the sails of the Peruvian fleet hovered on the horizon near Cañete. After the long search since they had departed from Santa María, the conflict which the Dutch had sought was now upon them.

By this time, Spanish officials both in the Peninsula and Peru had been in receipt of warnings about a new Dutch intervention into the South Sea for some sixteen months. As early as 28 February 1614, that is over five months before van Speilbergen sailed, the crown had dispatched preliminary warnings to the viceroy about Dutch commercial projects, and the Council of the Indies was regularly receiving detailed accounts of preparations in Holland from the Duke of Lerma, between May and September of the same year. These eventually carried such alarming news as Dutch plans to blockade Callao and Panama, plunder Acapulco and await the Manila galleon, capture a treasure fleet, perhaps at Arica, and encourage the Indians of Chile to join an alliance against the Spanish.[17] However, the crown was apparently satisfied, on the basis of reports from the viceroy in Peru, that any expedition which entered the South Sea would be so shattered as a result of its experiences, that the Peruvian squadron of four galleons would have little difficulty in destroying it. These ships are described as being 'of excellent build and well suited for sailing those coasts'.[18] It was the viceroyalty's reliance on its isolation and the fleet for its defence that was now to be put to the test off Cañete.

The Marquis of Montesclaros took the decision to concentrate his defence on the fleet following news of contacts between the Portuguese and Dutch near Rio de Janeiro, and after receiving details in November 1614 of what was in reality a false sighting of enemy ships off Valdivia.[19] It was the latter which had led to the fruitless search by the squadron under Rodrigo de Mendoza along the Chilean coast. The same commander was now in charge of a fleet of seven ships, hurriedly gathered, armed and crewed after receipt in Lima on 22 June of news of a positive sighting off Santa María at the end of the previous month. Perhaps somewhat rashly, they were preparing for their first engagement in the gathering gloom of the evening of 17 July. The composition of the Peruvian armada, according to most Spanish sources, was as follows:

| *Crown galleons* | *Tons* | *Captain* | *Armed men* | *Guns* |
|---|---|---|---|---|
| *Jesús María* | 400 | Rodrigo de Mendoza | 150 | 22 |
| *Santa Ana* | 250 | Pedro Alvarez Pulgar | 130 | 14 |
| *Merchant ships* | | | | |
| *Nuestra Señora del Carmen* | | Diego de Saravia | 100 | 8 |
| *San Diego* | | Jerónimo de Peraza | 100 | 8 |
| *Rosario* | | Iñigo de Ayala | 60 | 4 |
| *San Andrés* | | Juan de Nájera | 40 | 0 |
| *San Francisco* | | Juan Arce de Albendrín | 40 | 0 |
| *Total* | | | 620 | 56 |

Whereas the Spanish were twice as numerous in respect of armed men, the Dutch were twice as powerful with regard to the firepower of their ships, since the majority of the Peruvian armada were only merchantmen hastily rushed into service. Moreover, although perhaps too keen to criticise the viceroy with the benefit of hindsight, for once more dispatching a maritime force to seek out intruders, some commentators alleged that in the heat of the moment care had not been taken to ensure that the shot fitted the artillery and muskets, nor that there were adequate supplies of powder, flasks and medicines. The Peruvian force may have been larger in numbers of men but many of them are described as being 'inexperienced in the use and practice of firearms, mestizo and lacking fighting spirit'. The entire plan to confront the Dutch at sea is therefore considered to be a 'foolish decision'.[20]

Already on the first evening there were signs that this was so, for the tide of battle had begun to turn against the Peruvian fleet as the unarmed *San Francisco* was sunk in an early encounter with the *Great Sun* and the *Huntsman*. Some 90 men were lost, but her captain was saved by floating to safety, it is said, on a Dutch drum.[21] Such a swift loss was merely a portent of the desperate situation to befall the Peruvian fleet on the next day, 18 July. For in spite of having kept a light out all night, Mendoza awoke to find that his fleet was widely scattered, and for eight hours only the crown galleons *Jesús María* and *Santa Ana* took part in the combat. After several hours of bitter struggle, the Peruvian flagship was reduced to the point of surrender and a white flag hoisted, though apparently against the wishes of Mendoza. But as her crew took to wondering about their fate in Dutch hands, it was decided to run for the nearest safe port, Pisco. Thus abandoned, the *Santa Ana* was soon to feel the effects of the full weight of Dutch firepower and rapidly became unseaworthy. Her captain, Alvarez de Pulgar, was invited to leave his ship and surrender, but this he declined to do and consequently went down with her.[22] Such an end had already been foreseen by him, for despite having recently cost 100 000 pesos to construct and despite the crown's confidence in its ships, Pulgar was reported to have said of the *Santa Ana* that 'he was sure to die in her since she was very heavy and a poor sailer'.[23] By this time, the armed merchantmen which had taken no part in the battle on the second day had left the scene and effected their own escape. The *Carmen* and the *Rosario* made a landfall at Pisco, and the *San Andrés* and the *San Diego* eventually reached Callao.[24]

As one might expect, estimates of Dutch losses in the journal are low. No ship was seriously damaged. The gravest casualties occurred on the *Morning Star*, where 16 men were killed and between 30 and 40 wounded. As for the remainder of the Dutch fleet, the journal records 24 killed and between 16 and 18 wounded. The margin of the Dutch victory can be gauged from Spanish calculations of their losses as between 400 and 500 killed or drowned, plus the loss of one of the largest and newest crown ships in the South Sea and a merchantman. Realising the importance of the military aspect of his victory, and the psychological reaction this must provoke in the minds of defenders elsewhere in

Peru, van Speilbergen set out to press home his advantage at Callao and Lima, unlike his predecessors who had avoided any contact with the capital and its port. But delayed due to calm weather, his five ships did not begin to approach the bay until 20 July, during which time viceroy Montesclaros had made some attempt to atone for previous misjudgements and over-optimism by creating at least the semblance of an effective, planned defence policy.

For their part, the Dutch naturally hoped that their rout of the Peruvian fleet had left the heart of the viceroyalty open to assault and, therefore, were astonished to find flags flying, trumpets blowing, guns firing, men shouting as if giving orders, and rather perplexed when a cannon shot came close to sinking the *Huntsman*. Such apparent readiness and zeal for defence cautioned them to anchor at the entrance to the bay of Callao. What van Speilbergen did not realise is that he was the witness of a well-planned deceit by the Marquis of Montesclaros to cover up the weaknesses of his defence. Since learning of the defeat of his fleet off Cañete, the viceroy himself had felt the need to become involved personally in the digging of trenches and building of earthworks to defend Callao, as well as calling upon every sector of the community, including some 300 clergymen and a number of university students to take the place of those who had sailed with the silver fleet to Panama and Mendoza's armada to do battle at Cañete. If one is to believe the journal, the Dutch estimated that they were opposed by eight companies of horse and 4000 infantry.

A view of Callao's defences rather different from the impression gained by van Speilbergen, is that of eyewitnesses on shore who were sceptical of their chance of success if attacked, although they may well have had good reason to exaggerate the weaknesses of the defenders. Typical of these is the comment that:

> everyone came down to Callao to protect it against the approach of the enemy, who on the feast of Mary Magdalen suddenly appeared in the port with his five ships, opposite Callao. And we were all stationed along the shore with our weapons in our hands and under penalty of death that none should leave his post, waiting until the obliging adversary should begin to fire his artillery and dispatch us to the next world.[25]

The Provincial of the Jesuits also reveals details which would certainly have given heart to the Dutch if they had caught wind of them.

Two or three thousand gathered on the shore for the defence. But what men! Merchants, dapper young gallants straight from the town square, lacking skill or experience in firing an arquebus, the ammunition so unsuitable that the balls did not fit into the mouths of the barrels with the result that they split them into pieces with daggers.[26]

In fact the single cannon shot which had damaged the *Huntsman*, fired by one of only three pieces of artillery left in Callao after equipping the maritime forces, had been fired by a Franciscan, Father Gallardo, for lack of anyone else with sufficient skill. The cannon disintegrated soon afterwards, presumably not having been embarked on any of the ships because it was virtually unserviceable.[27]

Unable to gain any advantage by prolonging his stay near Callao, van Speilbergen set sail on 26 July, capturing a small coastal trading ship off Huaura laden with salt and 80 jars of honey. She was kept as a prize and a crew put aboard her under Jan de Wit. Huarmey was found deserted on 28 July, the inhabitants having fled inland because of a warning of impending attack by the Dutch. The latter, therefore, were able to collect fresh supplies of oranges, poultry, pigs and water at their leisure. For the benefit of those who might follow in similar circumstances, the journal reports a constant pool of fresh water here. Before departing northwards on 3 August, 16 prisoners were released and the Frenchman Nicolas de la Porte handed himself over to the local authorities. The last port of call on the Peruvian coast was that of Paita, where they dropped anchor on the evening of 8 August to debate tactics for the following day. Boats were then sent ashore bearing 300 well-armed soldiers, but finding the defenders well entrenched they were obliged to retreat. The *corregidor*, Juan Colmenero de Andrade, had positioned his smaller force of about 120 men skilfully, so that in this first encounter they were able to withstand the assault. However, on the second day when the Dutch brought up their ships to bombard the town, Colmenero found himself deserted by a good proportion of his force with result that the Dutch occupied and burnt the port.

Paita, with only a few dozen regular Spanish inhabitants but of importance as a port of call on the voyage to and from Panama, is another example of a minor port obliged to rely on its own resources against the superior military strength and ability of its attackers. On several occasions during the century its townspeople were to be confronted by this choice of standing their ground and risking their lives, or else retreating inland leaving their property to be plundered. Van Speilbergen and his crews were obviously attracted to the location and stayed for almost two weeks, marvelling at the bird life, observing and conversing with Indians fishing from balsas, and collecting supplies of fish from Lobos Island, the latter in such quantities that some soon began to complain of the unvarying diet.[28] But a major source of diversion appears to have been an exchange of communications with Doña Paula, the wife of the *corregidor*, who accompanied her entreaties for the release of prisoners in Dutch hands with a supply of fresh foodstuffs. Moved by her 'beauty, good grace and discretion',[29] van Speilbergen regretted having burnt the town and did release a number of sick and infirm captives, retaining about thirty more including a chief pilot and others likely to provide useful intelligence.

Probably the principal reason for delay at this point was the fact that van Speilbergen had decided that their last action on the coast of Peru should be a dramatic one, the seizure of the fleet returning from Panama to Callao. His informants had revealed that it was expected to number among its passengers the new viceroy, the Prince of Esquilache, and he had sufficient intelligence about maritime operations on the coast to know that it was likely that the fleet would put into Paita. And so the recently taken prize, under the command of Jan de Wit, was sent out daily to watch for signs of its approach. In fact, the new viceroy set sail from Panama on 9 August, seemingly unaware of the danger, at a time when the Dutch were still struggling for control of Paita. En route he was met by another squadron sent out by viceroy Montesclaros, again under the command of his nephew, and as a result decided to land at Manta, north of the Gulf of Guayaquil, on 9 September, proceeding to Lima overland.

However, impatient at the non-appearance of this fleet, the Dutch had already abandoned Paita on 21 August, heading towards Cape Santa Elena. Thus they failed to effect the capture of one who would have been a most valuable hostage, but almost simultaneously they narrowly missed another rich prize. For on 27 August, as they passed Cape Santa Elena they caught sight of a vessel ahead but soon lost her in the growing darkness. She was the *Nuestra Señora del Rosario* sailing from Acapulco to Guayaquil, carrying the baggage, family and person of Antonio de Morga, on his way to take up his new appointment as president of the *Real Audiencia* of Quito. What would have been equally attractive to the Dutch was the fact that part of her cargo consisted of Chinese silks worth one million pesos, part of which Morga had listed in the ship's register as his personal library.[30] Not realising the magnitude of this loss, van Speilbergen set course for Acapulco in the hope of intercepting the Manila galleon, but the most he achieved was an amicable exchange of prisoners for fresh supplies of food and water. After cruising along the coast of New Spain until the end of November, the expedition headed for the East Indies, returning home on 1 July 1617, via Manila and Ternate, completing the fifth circumnavigation of the globe.

The expedition of Joris van Speilbergen was remarkable in several respects. From a financial point of view the time spent on the coasts of Chile and Peru was not profitable. Trading took place only with Indian communities, although these now showed themselves to be more favourably disposed to the Dutch, and sorties on land or attacks against ships at sea generally yielded little more than was vital for overcoming deficiencies in the store of provisions. Nevertheless, van Speilbergen was more successful than his two Dutch predecessors. There are fewer indications that his men were engaged upon a constant energy sapping struggle with the elements, as in the previous cases, and the feast celebrated in Cordes Bay is in complete contrast to the interval spent there by those who had given it that name. Although troubled by unrest, even mutiny, especially on the *Gull*, and suffering a few desertions, the fleet was expertly and firmly managed and controlled, particularly after its entry into the South Sea. On each occasion that trouble occurred, van Speilbergen acted swiftly and decisively, taking care to ascertain the facts and keep a true record of the events. The meticulous preparation for battle and the keeping of rendezvous are further evidence of this effective control.

Moreover, the victory over the Peruvian fleet off Cañete is clear proof of the rise of Dutch sea power in the early years of the seventeenth century. This feat seemed to render more viable the dispatch of expeditions from Europe to prey on Spanish wealth in the South Sea, while ultimately pursuing the East India Company's objectives across the Pacific. Cordes and van Noort had served to reveal the immense obstacles of such a proposition. Van

Speilbergen had shown that they were not completely insuperable, and that the Spanish were certainly not prepared to repulse strong attacks directed against the best of their shipping or lesser, but not insignificant, ports. Even so the major prizes had eluded him, for example the capture of Arica or Callao, the seizure of a ship from the Peruvian treasure fleet, or the interception of the Manila galleon. The lure of these was to remain a temptation for the future.

The memory of the attractions was to be kept alive by the publication of the journal and its translations, with their references to opportunity for profit and to the pleasant and fertile nature of many of the places visited. Characteristic of these is Arica, pictured as a 'pleasant green spot, planted with all kinds of trees, amongst others oranges and citrons', and to which all the silver of Potosí is brought. Or Papudo, which because of its fresh water, 'being very clear and sweet of taste', abundance of fish and timber, 'must be regarded as the fittest of any for revictualling or getting the necessary supplies'. Santa María now 'has no gold or silver mines', but 'abundance of wheat, barley, beans, sheep, fowls, and the like'.[31]

Knowledge of the South Sea coast and its ports, the understanding of local maritime operations and of defensive capabilities were additionally intensified by the interpolation within the journal of two descriptions of areas visited. The first, longest and most detailed is of Peru, by a captured *limeño* whose name is given as Pedro de Madriga. His account refers to the system of government and its seat in Lima, listing churches, hospitals and colleges and describing its population, both Spanish and Indian, their trades and occupations. It further includes descriptions of mining activities at Potosí and in other zones, and lists ports from Arica to Huanchaco with details of their commerce. The second, only two pages long, portrays the ports of Chile, among which figures Valdivia, 'very rich in gold', with the information that the wives of its former Spanish inhabitants who were massacred in 1599 'can be re-purchased for a pair of spurs, a bridle, a rapier or a pair of stirrups'.[32] Such were the comments guaranteed to keep Dutch interests in Peru alive! Optimists in the East India Company may well have been gratified by such comments, as well as by the manner in which van Speilbergen's expedition had completed its passage of the Straits of Magellan and crossing of the Pacific, but none was persuaded to invest immediately in another similar venture.

From the perspective both of crown officials and ordinary citizens going about their day-to-day business in the coastal areas of the viceroyalty, the intrusion of van Speilbergen grew to be a source of severe consternation and concern. This reached its climax following the sea battle off Cañete and the arrival of a hostile force in the bay of Callao. Initially, viceroy Montesclaros seems to have reacted in much the same way as his predecessor Luis de Velasco, resisting the temptation to act precipitately on receipt of vague rumours, and then balancing the need to ensure the safe and prompt shipment of the year's bullion with the requirements for ensuring security, above all close to the capital. Only when first the customary reliance on isolation and the perils of the Straits had been proved to be unsound, and secondly the principal military force of crown galleons had been shown to be insufficient in number and in firepower, did Montesclaros show some signs of urgency. However, since he was later able to claim that he had saved Peru on the brink of disaster by his well-designed, if last minute, defensive ploy on the shore at Callao, in the official account of his administration he felt justified in asserting his belief that his original strategy had been correct. This was founded on the infrequency of invasion, the insignificance of most South Sea ports, and the long and open coastline which made any land-based fortification easily circumvented. [33]

And yet losses of some magnitude had been suffered and costs incurred both by private individuals and the crown. Indeed, as we have noted, several hundred lives were lost, many more put in peril, property burnt or sacked and vessels plundered, entire coastal communities left to fend for themselves. Some criticism of policy and strategy is to be expected in such circumstances, but this was intensified by the impending arrival of a new viceroy in Lima. Our so-called 'dispassionate' or impartial commentator hinted that losses and damage could be valued at as much as two million pesos as a consequence of this intervention. [34] More emotionally, father Alvarez de Paz, an ally of the new viceroy, questioned from where one could expect protection against attacks on haciendas, the murder and dishonouring of women, assaults on convents, the destruction of churches and the desecration of their images and relics. [35] Eventually representatives of various branches of the church in Lima, including the archbishop, were to join the criticism of the negligence of Montesclaros, and support the need for a more permanent and sure response based on the (mistaken) assumption that van Speilbergen would swiftly be followed by others.[36]

The only concession which Montesclaros was disposed to make in the last months of his administration, in face of the criticism directed at him, was to recommend the construction of a battery or small fort on the shore at Callao, and a platform to carry seven or eight pieces of artillery in the country, to deter any approach to the town from the landward side.[37] The former certainly appears to have been executed with little conviction or enthusiasm, sited on unstable ground with shallow foundations, and offering little or no protection to men and guns inside it. But the arrival in Lima, on 22 December 1615, of the Prince of Esquilache, a man of literary talents as was the outgoing viceroy,[38] signalled a new phase in the defence of Peru against those lured to its shores, a new phase which is attributable directly to the deficiencies revealed by this second period of Dutch intrusion into the South Sea, and by the fears aroused by it.

As a result of an enquiry carried out by a group of military advisers appointed by him, Esquilache embarked on three courses of action which were to be of long-term significance for the viceroyalty and its ability to counter attacks at its heart. These were the construction of a line of three forts on the shoreline at Callao, sited in such a way that their crossfire would protect ships at anchor and dissuade a hostile force from landing, the creation of a permanent and paid body of soldiers, five companies each of 100 men, who would be divided between service in Callao and in the squadron transporting silver to Panama, and lastly the rebuilding and expansion of the fleet with the result that by the time of his recall in 1621 it consisted of 4 galleons, 2 pataxes and 2 launches. A pattern of maritime operations had by then been established, which to some extent overcame the dilemma faced by Velasco and Montesclaros, for half the fleet (2 galleons and 1 patax) sailed to Panama with the silver, while a second similar group of vessels operated between Callao and Arica, remaining at the heart of the viceroyalty as a defence force. The launches were used to transmit messages and warnings, and to search the coasts for intruders before the Armada del Mar del Sur sailed.[39] The need for a stronger fleet seems to have been the only point of agreement between the defence plans of the old and new viceroy.

However, whereas the action of the Prince of Esquilache won the firm backing of those fearful of a repetition of the van Speilbergen venture, he was firmly censured by the crown and members of the Council of the Indies because of the costs involved, particularly when there appeared to be a lull in Dutch preoccupations with Peru. Dispatches to the viceroy, *Real Audiencia* and other crown officials warned that the downward trend in returns of silver had been noted and attributed to the new defence measures. But although the reaction in Spain was highly unfavourable to what had many supporters in Peru, it is now clear that the van Speilbergen expedition had sparked off the commencement of a regular commitment by the exchequer to the support of defensive measures there. This was to peak at times of subsequent incursions, and fall back only during the lapse in activity between the last of the Dutch and the first of the English interlopers in the middle of the century. The crown was alarmed at the financial implications of its new viceroy's response to van Speilbergen, but can hardly have foreseen the requirement in the future to devote an increasing proportion of the product of Peruvian mines to this branch of administration.

# 3

# Jacques l'Hermite, the Nassau Fleet and the Blockade of Callao (1623–6)

Following the entry of van Speilbergen into the South Sea and until the expiry of the twelve years' truce in 1621, Dutch maritime enterprises were directed towards successful advances against Spain and Portugal in the East Indies, the English in the Malay archipelago, and the maintenance of commercial links with the Wild Coast, especially the Guianas and the vicinity of the Amazon. However, already by 1619 a new climate of national feeling had begun to coalesce, marked by the execution of van Oldenbarnevelt on a charge of high treason and the rise of Prince Maurice of Nassau and the 'war party' of militant Calvinists. Hardly was the treaty period complete, when on 3 June 1621 the States-General granted a charter to a new West India Company. Though there were obvious parallels with the earlier sister organisation, it has been clearly shown that the new company was envisaged from the outset as being predominantly warlike in its purpose and, therefore, markedly distinct from Usselincx's concept of a corporation that would seek trade and settlement as its objectives in the New World. The West India Company, following the expiry of the peace agreement, would move to the offensive against Spain in a bid to deprive it of the resources of its overseas possessions. In a way, then, the new organisation offered private individuals, under licence and control, the opportunity to express their anti-Spanish attitudes through profit-making raids against Spanish settlements and shipping. Privateering would now become an expression of Dutch hostility towards Spain. But the West India Company was more than this, for it did also envisage the creation of colonies, and then commerce, but through the process of military conquest.

Generally speaking, the new company was granted a 24-year monopoly of territories not specifically mentioned in the charter of the East India Company. Relevant to the present context is the fact that these included the east and west coasts of America, north and south. The company was to endeavour to make alliances with the local native populations, construct fortresses, appoint officials and promote the settlement of unoccupied lands. In practice potential subscribers hesitated to back the new organisation, early ventures were purely trading enterprises, and there were doubts with regard to the choice of the most profitable locations for its activities. As far as the New World was concerned, with the Dutch attack on Bahia in May 1624 and its occupation until Easter of the following year, it emerged that Brazil had been selected as the most favoured site for the challenge to Iberian possessions. In fact, in 1621, the West India Company had turned down an invitation from the States-General to participate in an attack on Peru and the South Sea coast by what we now know as Jacques l'Hermite's Nassau Fleet, a project in which the East India Company had already invested considerable amounts. The refusal was partially due to the shortage of funds at its incorporation, but also induced by fears of an unprofitable outcome. Nevertheless, although denied West India Company financial support, the Nassau Fleet displayed certain characteristics of Dutch maritime enterprises sponsored by that corporation after 1621.[1]

Several years before l'Hermite sailed, the rivalry between those who favoured the East India Company's predominantly commercial outlook, and those who demanded a more aggressive quest for expansion at the expense of the Iberian powers, was to produce a search for a new route to the South Sea which did not transgress that company's monopoly over the Cape of Good Hope and the Straits of Magellan. The instigator was Isaac Lemaire, whose eldest son was to sail as supercargo on the voyage of exploration, and die in the East Indies. His ally and supporter was the experienced Willem Corneliszoon Schouten, master and chief pilot.[2]

By 25 January 1616, after passing the entrance to the Straits of Magellan, they traversed a second strait (which they called Lemaire), between Tierra del Fuego and a coast they named Staten Landt. Four days later they glimpsed a hilly land covered in snow to which they gave the name Hoorn, Schouten's home town in North Holland, and sailed on into the South Sea. Europe, and more specifically that part most antagonistic to the Iberian powers, had acquired a new route by which to pursue its defiance of their partition of the globe.

This momentous advance in geographical knowledge with its

implications for access to Spanish colonies on the South Sea coasts of America, coming so soon after the alarm aroused by van Speilbergen, at once demanded a response from Spain. The decision had already been reached in 1616 to fit out a small expedition designed to gather information to acquaint Spanish pilots and sailors with the navigation of the Straits of Magellan. Following disclosure of the work of Lemaire and Schouten, the latter incidentally having returned to Holland with van Speilbergen, the voyage of Bartolomé and Gonzalo García de Nodal, in 1618 and 1619, took them through the Lemaire Straits, around Cape Horn and back into the Atlantic via the Straits of Magellan, thus completing the first circumnavigation of Tierra del Fuego.[3] They returned with accurate observations of land, natives, flora, fauna and tides, and with practical sailing directions, but it is ironic to consider that the results of their efforts, published in Madrid in 1621, were destined to be of greater benefit to other European nations than Spain.

Accordingly, the l'Hermite voyage has to be set into the context of the discovery of an open sea passage which might facilitate its entry into the South Sea, and a mood of greater readiness to resort to warlike methods in pursuit ultimately of commercial supremacy and new colonial outposts. As one version expresses it, 'he would come to this kingdom of Peru and set fire to all the ships in the South Sea, sack Lima and Callao and burn Panama and would do as much damage as possible and this would be legitimate since it was action taken against people opposed to his religion.'[4] In general terms, therefore, the Nassau Fleet was drawn to Peru by the prospects of undermining Spain's hold of territory and control of sources of wealth, for this would inevitably weaken it at home and diminish its ability to compete in commercial enterprises where it was a rival of the Dutch. In furtherance of these general aims, a blockade of Callao was finally mounted when other more precise objectives proved impossible to achieve.

For at the outset the Dutch journal, later accounts by two Greek deserters and the declarations of a German, Carsten Carstens, who became a prisoner at Callao, all concur in pointing to Arica as the principal destination.[5] Visited already by vessels from the two previous incursions into the South Sea, it was favourably described by the most recent. The journal states that:

the fleet was intended to attempt the conquest of Peru . . . and it was concluded that we should go and refresh at the Juan

Fernández Islands, and then proceed to Arica to do battle with the Spanish galleons, and try to make ourselves masters of the place, in order to press our plans further with the help of the Indians.[6]

The plan, therefore, was not merely a privateering raid on the silver fleet, but a more ambitious, some might say chimerical, attempt to cut off the supply of silver to Spain through one of its principal outlets in America. The rather forlorn hope of an alliance with the Indians, and perhaps too with negro slaves, which is a consistent feature of so many of these Dutch proposals, was obviously a necessary prerequisite to the fulfilment of the wilder dreams of conquest. The plan to regroup at the Juan Fernández Islands, rather than at Mocha or Santa María as in the case of l'Hermite's predecessors, must derive from the favourable reports of Lemaire and Schouten on the larger of the two islands. They provided practical advice on the best approach, and their landing party returned with news of a 'fine, verdant valley', fresh water, sightings of goats and pigs, and two tons of fish.[7]

Although the West India Company had declined to participate, the general objectives of the Nassau Fleet can be seen to agree with the more aggressive nature of that organisation. By the spring of 1623, in the name and authority of Prince Maurice of Nassau, final preparations for the sailing had been put into the hands of three commissioners appointed by the East India Company, Hugo Muys, Albert Joachim and Adrian Bruyning. Finally, an impressive force of 11 ships bearing 1637 men and 294 guns was assembled, clearly the most powerful hostile force yet to enter the South Sea. It came well supplied with firearms, explosive grenades and devices with sharp prongs to obstruct the manoeuvres of cavalry, as befitted its largely military role, and reflecting the shift to a more openly belligerent attitude after the expiry of the truce. The precise composition of the fleet was as shown.

Leaving Goeree on 29 April 1623, the fleet did not round Cape Horn until early February of the following year, taking some seven weeks longer than Lemaire and Schouten. In part this may be due to the fact that during the crossing of the Atlantic, there occurred a series of incidents which ought to lead us to harbour some doubts about its ability to carry out its objectives, in spite of its apparent strength. Whether one judges them to be cases of misfortune or weak and ineffective command, they can hardly have induced a

| Ships | Tons | Men | Guns |
|---|---|---|---|
| *From the city of Amsterdam* | | | |
| Amsterdam | 800 | 237 | 42 |
| Admiral Jacques l'Hermite and Captain Leendert Jacobsz Stolck | | | |
| *Delft* | 800 | 242 | 40 |
| Vice-admiral Hugo Schapenham and Captain Cornelis de Witte | | | |
| *Arent (Eagle)* | 400 | 144 | 28 |
| Captain Meyndert Egbertsz | | | |
| *Haeswint (Greyhound)* | 60 | 20 | 4 |
| Captain Solomon Willemsz | | | |
| *From Zeeland* | | | |
| *Orangien (Orange)* | 700 | 216 | 22 |
| Rear-admiral Johan Willemsz Verschoor and Captain Johansz Quirguen | | | |
| *From Rotterdam* | | | |
| *Hollandia (Holland)* | 600 | 182 | 34 |
| Cornelis Jacobsz, counsellor to the admiral and Captain Adrian Tol | | | |
| *Mauritius (Maurice)* | 560 | 169 | 32 |
| Captain Jacob Ariaensz | | | |
| *Hoop (Hope)* | 260 | 80 | 14 |
| Captain Pieter Harmensz Slobb | | | |
| *From North Holland* | | | |
| *Eendracht (Concord)* | 600 | 170 | 32 |
| Captain Jan Ysbrantsz | | | |
| *Koningh David (King David)* | 360 | 79 | 16 |
| Captain Jan Thomasz | | | |
| *Griffoen (Griffin)* | 320 | 78 | 14 |
| Captain Pieter Cornelisz Hardloop | | | |

sense of confidence and security in the crews as a whole. Even before leaving the English Channel, the *Eagle* sprang a leak necessitating a halt at the Isle of Wight for repairs, the *Orange* and the *Hope* were in collision, and on the night of 13 May a signal gun exploded in the flagship, tearing up decks, demolishing cabins but causing only one fatality.

The coast of Spain seemed to forbode better fortune ahead, for at the beginning of June four of a fleet of ten sails were captured and their cargo of sugar from Pernambuco taken aboard. Since the Dutch fleet was already overloaded it was decided to proceed to Safi on the coast of North Africa, there to unload the precious cargo on to a Dutch ship known to be in port. The sugar was eventually transferred to the *Overijssel* and sent to Holland together with the *Greyhound* which had become unseaworthy. The crew of the latter continued their voyage in one of the prizes. However, after leaving Safi on 24 June, as they progressed along the African coast towards the island of Annobón, which they reached on 30 October, the shadow of misfortune again settled on the venture. Through carelessness the *Maurice* was almost lost, 'for having careened, they forgot to shut the Scupper-holes; and by this means, she had Eight Foot water in her Hold before it was perceived'.[8]

Illness had also begun to take its toll, for between 11 August and 5 September 40 men had died mainly from scurvy, a figure which was to rise to over 200 before they even attempted to cross the Atlantic. Carstens' reference to the disease as 'mal de Olanda' (Dutch sickness) would seem to be entirely appropriate on this occasion, although usually in Spanish today it is 'mal de Loanda' (Luanda). Crews had already at several points been sent ashore for supplies of lemons and oranges to combat the illness.[9] The admiral too was noted to be suffering from a sickness which caused the swelling of his legs, doubtlessly gout, which led to an increasing share of the burden of command being transferred to the less experienced Schapenham.

But in addition to these predictable illnesses, there were other cases of death which caused some alarm. Following investigations, it was verified that a surgeon had been administering poison rather than medicine. Remarkably he withstood the torture of being 'drawn up to a great Height by a Rope, and then suddenly let fall, having great Weights at his Hands and Feet'.[10] But this only induced the other sailors to believe that black magic was involved, especially after the discovery that the surgeon wore around his neck a bag containing the skin and tongue of a serpent. Finally, he willingly confessed to having poisoned seven men whom he disliked, and to his desire to make a pact with the devil, for all of which he was beheaded.

Amid such distasteful circumstances, the fleet prepared to head for the South American coast, first taking on supplies of pigs and poultry at Annobón, under a flag of truce. Departing on 4 November, they plotted a course which would bring no landfall north of the River Plate, with the intention of depriving the Peruvian viceroy of advance warning of their arrival, for example from Rio de Janeiro, as had happened in the case of the previous expeditions. Consequently, they entered the Strait of Lemaire on

2 February 1624 and a few days later, on 6 February, caught sight of Cape Horn. After several weeks of storms and strong winds, the Chilean coast was a welcome sight on 28 March. By the beginning of April, the fleet which had scattered during the bad weather began to reunite and refresh at the planned rendezvous in the Juan Fernández Islands. One further advantage of this location was that it kept them out of sight of the Chilean coast near to populated areas, and again made it more likely that they might come upon their chosen targets in the South Sea with a greater degree of surprise and unexpectedness. It was here that the tactics for an assault on the Peruvian treasure fleet at Arica were worked out. Although at this stage l'Hermite was probably still able to issue orders on this matter, it is clear that his condition had worsened and as a result he was now confined to his bunk, leaving the management of the fleet to Schapenham and the other officers.

On 13 April they set sail for Arica in three divisions, each of which was equal to the crown squadron then operating in the South Sea, but a combination of ill luck and the cunning of a Spanish captain was to deprive them of great booty. To deal first with the question of ill luck, a number of interrelated factors combined in 1624 to encourage the viceroy, the Marquis of Guadalcázar, to ensure that the annual shipment of silver to Panama sailed as promptly as possible. These were delays and resulting hardship in Spain in the previous two years, repeated warnings of an impending Dutch invasion since November 1622, despite their precautions, and finally sightings (later proved to have been false) of ships off the Chilean coast as early as April 1623.[11] Yet, although the reports were premature, all of this was sufficient to persuade Guadalcázar to dispatch crown silver on 3 May, unwilling even to wait a further week as he had been requested by owners of private silver and merchandise. Even so the lack of hesitation on the viceroy's part did not deliver crown silver safely from the clutches of the Nassau Fleet, already rapidly approaching the heart of the viceroyalty by early May. This was due to the cunning of a Spanish captain.

Having received definite proof of the sighting of enemy ships off Mala on 7 May,[12] the viceroy dispatched two *chinchorros* from Callao to ascertain whether it would be safe to allow the departure of the second shipment of private silver and goods. Unfortunately, before he realised his error, the captain of one of these vessels, Martín de Larrea, had sailed into the midst of the Dutch fleet and was unable to escape. The details of his interrogation and that of his negro crew members vary slightly according to the source consulted, but the substance of the ploy used by Larrea remains the same, namely to draw the attention of the Dutchmen away from the recently departed silver fleet by convincing them that it had sailed some two weeks before, rather than a few days ago. One version explains that the negroes insisted that the fleet had left only three days ago, whereas Larrea stated that it had departed thirteen days before. When brought face to face with the negroes, he explained the error as one of pronunciation, in that for *trece* (thirteen) the negroes said *tres* (three). [13]

It was at this point, therefore, that the Dutch captains were faced with the dilemma of either pursuing the silver fleet, one of their original objectives, or turning their attention to the coast of Peru. From the journal one is led to deduce that there was some division of opinion. What prevailed was the view that they should now opt for a blockade of Callao, since the silver fleet had eluded them and would be able to unload under the shore batteries at Panama, and in any case they lacked pilots familiar with those northern waters. This decision was further strengthened by evidence from the negro crew of the captured *chinchorro*, which confirmed their own suspicions, based on a source of information that we shall discuss presently, that Callao and Lima were relatively weakly defended. The Dutch, then, were all too ready to believe that any assault on their part would swiftly gain the backing of 4000 negroes, while discounting the warnings of Larrea who once more tried to dissuade them with stories of effective precautions and a force of 6000 defenders. Moreover, the Dutch were correctly aware that the flagship of the Peruvian armada, the *Nuestra Señora de Loreto*, was still in port awaiting the chance to sail for Panama with the second shipment of private silver. Therefore the Nassau Fleet sailed for Callao with three possible objectives in mind: a landing and assault on the port and capital, an attack on the flagship and a general plundering of merchant shipping.

As the site for their first attempt to land on 10 May, the Dutch chose Bocanegra about two miles north of the port, from which point a direct assault might have been made on Lima. Some 17 launches set out for the shore bearing 800–900 men from a total force now reduced by over 20 per cent to about 1300, but they were compelled to renounce their plan due to strong undercurrents. Later on the same day a second approach was made, but by this time the Spanish had been able to bring up artillery to the threatened sector and repulsed the attack, inflicting losses of about twenty dead.

On 11 May, late at night, the Dutch began diversionary action again in the vicinity of Bocanegra, while now directing their main thrust at the fifty or so vessels anchored in the bay. Though the majority of these were smallish craft engaged in carrying and distributing the agricultural produce of the coastal valleys, the flagship of the Peruvian armada lay among them. This new attack was not particularly damaging nor rewarding, having been beaten off by the fire from the new coastal forts. Some nine merchantmen were set on fire, but immediately began to drift towards the Dutch fleet and force it to take evasive action. The Dutch account of the attack tends to exaggerate the damage inflicted on the vessels at anchor, stating that between thirty and forty were burnt, though adding wrily that if they had acted with foresight, it would have been sufficient merely to have cut their cables and allowed them to drift into their clutches. It was in this attack that the German Carstens was captured.

These fresh setbacks can hardly have been encouraging to crews that had suffered so much disappointment already. Above all, they had arrived convinced that Callao and Lima would be weakly defended, and now in their first sorties they found themselves repulsed. And, in fact, there was as yet not a great deal in the defensive preparations of the viceroy to deter them. It is true that he had had early warning of an impending Dutch intrusion into the South Sea, but when the initial sightings proved to be false, he disbanded the supplementary forces he had collected. Moreover, the silver fleet which had recently sailed for Panama carried, for its own protection, the best armed and trained personnel. When l'Hermite's force sailed into Callao, the port's main land based defences were two of the forts built by the Prince of Esquilache in 1616 and 1617, one in the centre of the shoreline with seven guns, and the other in the north with nine. To these the Marquis of Guadalcázar had added another fort in the south, where Esquilache's third projected fort had never progressed beyond the levels of the foundations, equipping it with eight guns. In the bay, the flagship with 42 guns and two pataxes bearing 12 guns each were available to protect merchant ships at anchor. According to his own estimate, the viceroy expected to be able to count on 2000 men to defend the port and its immediate vicinity.[14]

At this stage of the proceedings, the Spanish in Callao and Lima still believed themselves to be besieged by a strong and determined enemy. Eyewitness accounts reveal both a recognition of their own weak position and the degree of alarm which the presence of the Dutch provoked. Friar Andrés de Lisón, for example, pointed out that neither the viceroy nor his advisers had any training in military affairs and clearly did not inspire confidence with their faces 'as white as snow' out of fear and concern.[15] The population of Lima flocked to the churches to pray for deliverance, until the glow in the sky of ships burning in the bay sparked off the rumour that Callao had fallen, and caused men and women to gather their belongings and head inland.

The best opportunity for the Dutch was during this first day or two of the blockade, when panic and confusion reigned, above all in Lima. In the coming weeks, the chance of salvaging some minor success from their once grand plan was gradually to slip away. However, not all the expedition was to maintain the blockade during the coming weeks. On 14 May Cornelisz Jacobsz sailed southwards with the *Concord, David, Griffin* and *Greyhound* with the intention of making a landing at Arica in accordance with the original plan. Again, they had been given to believe that the port was not well defended, but on arrival found sufficient activity to be dissuaded from attacking. This may be some indication of the depression and sense of failure which was by now sapping the vigour of the expedition as a whole. For General Juan de Salas, the *corregidor* of Arica, had only recently reported that there was a woeful lack of arms in the port and nothing but a rapidly decaying adobe fort in which to place his four pieces of artillery.[16] Similarly, at Pisco during the return voyage to Callao, this squadron was driven off when it tried to land several launches. The Dutch journal speaks of a 15-ft defensive wall, whereas Spanish sources merely describe the digging of trenches, building of parapets and mounting of artillery on a platform. This was achieved due to the efforts of the *sargento mayor* Francisco Chirinos de Cabrera and the *maestre de campo* Diego de Rojas y Borja, the latter hurriedly dispatched from Callao with four guns and 300 armed men whose upkeep fell on the local townspeople.[17] This squadron returned to Callao to rejoin the blockade on 15 June.

Meanwhile, a second party of 200 men, commanded by Verschoor had set out northwards on 23 May in the *Maurice* and the *Hope* for the island of Puná and the important trading and shipbuilding centre of Guayaquil, which was destined to attract a variety of intruders in the seventeenth century. As a result of a dispute between the *corregidor* and other influential citizens, there had been few efforts to heed the warnings of an early attack, and so the Dutch were able to take the island without resistance, looting its buildings, capturing at least four vessels at anchor and plundering cargoes of cacao, wine, cheese and biscuit. A few days later, on 6 June, they were briefly masters of Guayaquil where only 80 of the 200 defenders possessed firearms, and were free to burn and pillage at will, the churches especially being objects of their rage, until uncontrollable fires drove them out closely pursued and suffering some casualties.

The journal records 35 killed, although the most conservative of Spanish estimates is 55 killed with several suggesting twice that number. The Dutch were quick to take their revenge, 17 Spanish prisoners being thrown into the sea off Puná, according to the journal. Spanish accounts, on the other hand, record that two prisoners were murdered, one, a friar, by hanging and the second by the knife, and the remainder thrown into the sea tied back to back. Another version, keen to make its point about the cruelty of the heretics, describes the poor friar's death more vividly. 'There the privateers took him by surprise, split his head with a cutlass and opened up his stomach, removing his entrails whilst he was still alive.'[18] The point is also made that the lives and property of Indians were deliberately excluded from these depredations and cruel acts. This Dutch party, with a somewhat unedifying victory to its credit, returned to Callao and the blockade on 5 August.

The remaining five vessels and crews which maintained the blockade during this period, had now made their base on the island of San Lorenzo, facing Callao. Their principal activity seems to have been to prevent ships entering and leaving the port, which they achieved because captains were not forewarned of their presence, and later through the foolhardiness of those who risked running the blockade in search of a profit. When it was only a few days old, they took an unsuspecting vessel from Trujillo with a cargo of soap, sugar and leather, and soon afterwards three others from Pisco with typical cargoes of wine, dates, figs and fruits. On 19 May, when the viceroy's warning had had time to travel to neighbouring ports, they seized two ships from Huaura with loads of wheat, salt and timber, to be followed by the *San Ambrosio* from Guayaquil with wood, cacao and rigging (20 May) and a further

prize from Barranca with wheat, maize and honey (3 June). Several
of these were later burnt.

Apart from these events, the occasional exchange of fire with the
defenders of Callao, and an unsuccessful attempt to sail a fireship
into the midst of merchant ships at anchor on 6 June, the scene had
become one of stalemate by June, and was to continue so. The
death of the admiral, l'Hermite, was reported on 2 June, although
it is clear that he had played a passive role for some time, and had
taken little part in the blockade. The cause was more certainly his
gout, rather than 'sorrow because the silver had eluded him', as
one report claims.[19] He was succeeded by Hugo Schapenham,
who seems to have enjoyed little popularity among the men as a
whole and who had already shown himself to be wanting in
experience. One of his first actions as leader of the expedition was
to try to arrange the exchange of prisoners held by each side. On 13
June a launch was sent ashore under a flag of truce, offering to give
up some 30 Spaniards. When the viceroy refused to negotiate, 21 of
these were hanged. The Spanish for their part, at the end of June,
put to death one of their early informants, the German Carstens.
'They burnt him for being a pirate, and he died a good Catholic
because the fathers of the Company [of Jesus] had taught him
well.'[20]

The execution of their prisoners may reliably be construed as a
sign of despair in the Nassau Fleet, and of the fact that the balance
of advantage was beginning to tip in favour of the defenders. Their
arrival had struck panic and fear into the citizens of Callao and
Lima, but the failure of their attempted landings and the limited
success of their action against shipping, generated a growing sense
of confidence among their opponents on shore. The Dutch, it was
true, controlled the outer approaches to the port, but had not been
able to penetrate as far as the anchorage of the *Loreto*. The
townspeople dominated the land and were able to offer adequate
protection to the majority of merchantmen at anchor close to the
shore.

Signs of despair and dissatisfaction can also be recognised in the
desertions which occurred. The first of these had happened before
any significant action in the South Sea, at the Juan Fernández Isles,
where five gunners and a carpenter chose to leave their fate to the
Spanish or the Indians, rather than stay with the fleet. When the
blockade of Callao was still not two weeks old, on 21 May, two
Greeks referred to in Spanish documents as Juan and Antonio

Nicolás slipped ashore to seek refuge. When the Dutch departed the Spanish were to find the bodies of two men, perhaps would-be deserters, hanging from a gallows. The Pisco venture, which produced only a handful of Dutch casualties, was followed by the desertion of 14 or 15 men. And as the Nassau Fleet was making plans to depart in mid-August, a Frenchman called Jean de Bulas in the Spanish documents went ashore at Ancón, asking to be taken to the viceroy.[21]

Apart from the fact that they might be indicative of a more widespread unrest, these desertions are significant because of the information they disclosed to the Spanish authorities: accurate details of the ships, crews and armaments, of the specific aims of the expedition, and above all of the problems that had begun to undermine its effectiveness. They refer to discontented crewmen, many of whom had been deceived into believing that they were engaged for a voyage of only six months duration, to a general shortage of fresh water and the suggestion that supplies of meat and fish were adequate but unfairly allocated. Given the opportunity, Bulas stated, because of this unrest, poor command and illness, six or seven hundred would desert. It was noted that 'he has heard the sailors say that they would rather make two voyages to India than the one they are engaged upon at present. And he knows for sure that if they returned to Flanders, they would not come back even if each were given 2000 florins.'[22] While there may be exaggeration in such statements which contain a number of the traditional grievances of sailors anywhere at the time, and while those who deserted may have a clear motive for wanting to distance themselves from their former commanders and shift the blame for their actions elsewhere, they were the basis for growing confidence among the defenders of Callao, especially since they were supported by the lack of any positive and resolute action by the Dutch and their own gradually improving state of defence.

Since the arrival of the enemy, the viceroy had been busy during the remainder of May and June, hastily organising defensive preparations to compensate for his originally weak situation.[23] Because there was so much of value in the bay itself, by way of merchant shipping and the flagship of the Peruvian fleet, the front line of defence had been carried out into the very waters of the bay. Two hundred armed men were placed on the flagship and around it on a floating platform for its protection, and a further hundred on board the two pataxes which were to guard the merchant vessels. Particularly successful were some thirteen small oared craft built during May and June, which could traverse the bay quickly bearing armed men, forestalling attempts to land and forming a barricade around any Spanish ship threatened with attack. A final element in the defence of the bay was a flat bottomed boat or barge equipped with three or four large pieces of artillery, with the intention of demasting any Dutch ship that might venture close to it.

On land between fifty and sixty pieces of artillery were ranged along the shore in strategic positions, and a score of cannon made ready in the forts. The viceroy was also particularly successful in recruiting defenders, once the initial panic had subsided. He called upon most sections of the community in Lima and Callao to come to his aid, including students, the clergy, free negroes and mulattoes. Individuals raised companies of men and brought them from as far afield as Cuzco. In this way, by using every available source, he was able to gather a body of men which totalled some 4600, outnumbering the Dutch by four to one. However, one must remember that these were not professionals nor skilled in warfare, but men drawn from every trade and walk of life, whose effectiveness might have been seriously tested by a determined assault. Furthermore, because of the Spanish custom of riding mules, the viceroy had found it difficult to gather cavalry forces, so important in preventing landings. He subsequently ordered that in future Spaniards should ride not mules but horses.

The new confidence among the defenders can further be gauged from suggestions to the viceroy, during the absence of the Guayaquil and Pisco squadrons, that now was the time not merely to consolidate defences but to move on to the attack. Encouraged particularly by the statements of the Greek deserters and the prisoner Carstens, it was proposed to launch a pre-dawn attack with the largest ships in the port, lest the Dutch might be able to build their own defences on the island and await the arrival of reinforcements.[24] This represents one view put forward by those attending a meeting of defence advisers on 12 June. But the opinion to prevail, less reckless and more prudent, was that which recommended no action, other than the prevention of landings. The viceroy, therefore, had chosen to preserve the stalemate, to allow the Dutch to consume their provisions and their strength, and to await their next move.

This did not come until 14 August when the fleet finally abandoned San Lorenzo island and gave up the blockade, leaving

70 of their number buried there, including the admiral l'Hermite whose body was later disinterred and burnt on a bonfire by the local population. There is further evidence, in the form of newly dug wells, that the Dutch were short of water, but finding insufficient quantities on the island they transferred to the mainland a few leagues north of Callao, landing at Ancón. Here, under cover of rapidly constructed earthworks and trenches, and with the protection of artillery, they searched with some success and planned future action. Remembering that their only victory had been the brief seizure of Guayaquil by 200 of their number, a second assault was planned with the backing of the full expedition. Between 500 and 600 men landed on 27 August, but in a fierce conflict were driven off. Since the assault in June, modest reinforcements of 50 arquebusiers had arrived from Quito, plus 100 men from Chimbo and Cuenca. This reversal of fortunes persuaded them to abandon an earlier resolution to sail to Chile to form an alliance with the Indians, one feature of their instructions they had not as yet attempted to carry out, and instead they departed for New Spain. At Acapulco on 28 October a council meeting resolved to follow a course for the East Indies, where the expedition can be said to have ended since the ships sought their own individual fate at this point. The *Concord* bearing the writer of the journal arrived in Holland on 9 June 1626.[25]

Evidently the outcome of the Nassau Fleet was far from satisfactory. By fitting out a formidable force in terms of ships, men and armaments, thus anticipating the sort of warlike enterprise in which the West India Company would participate, the Dutch backers had hoped to realise their expectations of gain from the South Sea. The success of other ventures throughout the world, the maritime victory of van Speilbergen and the discoveries of Schouten and Lemaire all seemed to support their vision of a round-the-world commercial empire, dependent upon permanent bases in South America and the East Indies. L'Hermite's expedition can be viewed as a further step in these grandiose schemes, which ultimately involved transferring European military conflicts and religious rivalry across the oceans of the world.

Significantly, l'Hermite sought no opportunities for trade or barter in the South Sea, not even with Indian coastal communities. After refreshment at the Juan Fernández Islands, the plan was to pursue a direct confrontation with the Spanish at Arica, on land or sea, for the purpose of intercepting the silver trade. Following the discovery that the silver armada had eluded them, or so they believed, the alternative actions chosen were similarly of a warlike nature, assaults on Callao, Arica, Pisco and Guayaquil. Neither these nor the seizure or destruction of coastal trading craft yielded much more than welcome, fresh additions to the diet, and an outlet for frustrated energies. When one compares the dream of the conquest of Peru with the results of the venture, it is not surprising to learn that in a vain effort to compensate for their failure, some participants concocted the story of a furious battle fought against overwhelming odds off the coast near Lima. In vivid details it recounts how an inferior Dutch fleet encountered 30 Spanish galleons and 10 000 men, but after several hours had sunk 22 Spanish vessels for the loss of two of their own.[26]

Turning from these fantasies to the realities, the only true benefits must have been experience gained and information acquired: experience especially of the new route via Cape Horn leading to recuperation in the Juan Fernández Islands, and information about the defensive capacity of the Viceroyalty of Peru. They now knew that it was not entirely true, as some believed, that defences around Lima and Callao were very weak. Although hastily patched together, condemned by some who had close knowledge of them, and of an effectiveness more apparent than real, they had all the same proved adequate to hinder any landing of long duration. Similarly, although Puná and Guayaquil had suffered great losses in the first Dutch assaults in that region, a subsequent setback there and in ports such as Pisco and Arica further showed that the local population of such towns was not completely unprepared nor totally disinclined to offer some resistance. Perhaps it is significant, therefore, that the next Dutch attempt to establish a foothold in the area, that of Hendrik Brouwer in 1643, aimed not at Callao nor Arica, but the then unpopulated site of Valdivia in southern Chile.

If one is seeking to apportion blame for the failures of the Nassau Fleet, there is ample evidence in the incidents we have quoted, in the comments of those who strayed into Spanish hands and in the journal, to suggest weaknesses of leadership. The belief that prizes were still temptingly to be had was confirmed, for example by the narrowly missed silver fleet, but emphasised once more were the obstacles. The sheer remoteness of the region and the perils of the voyage still delivered Peru from effective Dutch attack. To overcome this those in command needed to be men of great courage and exceptional ability, able to convey enthusiasm and impose their authority without question. But the accidents during the early stages of the venture, indecision over action to be taken when the silver fleet seemed beyond their grasp, the humiliating defeat at Guayaquil and the fact that a fruitless blockade was allowed to continue so long, merely increasing the unrest and misery of the crews, all seem to point to a shortage of the required qualities. Since he was already incapacitated before leaving the African coast, and must be supposed to have enjoyed little effective authority after entry into the South Sea, blame would seem to rest not with l'Hermite but with Schapenham and his subordinate officers. Very evidently a dearth of talented and decisive command only served to exacerbate what one has come to accept as the normal grievances associated with the passage into the South Sea: the unpopularity of the route, inadequate provisions and the ravages of illness which had reduced their numbers from over 1600 to about 1000 (or by nearly 40 per cent) before they left Peru.

Some of these problems might be minimised if the Indians could be relied upon to cooperate, even if it were only in the matter of provisions and shelter. The neglect of the Nassau Fleet to attend to this aspect of its instructions meant that only the Brouwer voyage would put this possibility to the test. For the present, in the words of the English version of the journal, 'all the fine projects of Indian conquests formed in Holland, appeared to them so many romantic dreams',[27] and 'thus cheaply were the Spaniards freed from the most formidable armament that ever at any time before or since threatened their possessions in the South Sea'.[28]

Seen through the eyes of the ordinary townspeople and local authorities alike, in the central and northern coastal zones of the viceroyalty, both the sightings and the reports of the Nassau Fleet can have been nothing less than awesome and frightening. At once it must have been recognised, with some panic in view of what had happened at Cañete, that the maritime force at the disposal of the Dutch admiral was far superior to anything available to their viceroy. Happily for them, the consequences were by no means as disastrous as might have been initially expected, although the damage inflicted, deaths caused and commercial losses suffered were the most serious yet experienced.

During the period of the blockade at the heart of the viceroyalty, specific, itemised losses totalling 527 000 pesos were incurred as a result of prizes taken and vessels burnt.[29] Unquantified losses of this nature must have raised that figure to at least 700 000 pesos. Nine small craft were taken by the squadron which sailed northwards and there were losses of ships and valuable cargoes, such as timber, textiles and cacao, at Puná and Guayaquil, with one report mentioning the burning of a crown galleon in process of construction and on which 30 000 pesos had already been spent. Indeed, Guayaquil suffered more than any other area as a result of the l'Hermite invasion, its homes, public buildings, churches, monasteries and hospital reduced to ashes. Such was the despair of several of the principal families, fighting to overcome setbacks to traditional commerce in textiles and wool by expanding the cacao trade and manufactures associated with the shipbuilding industry, that they abandoned the town to re-establish themselves elsewhere. The squadron which had chosen the coast south of Callao for its operations captured some 17 craft.[30]

As far as the viceroy and the crown were concerned, the most pressing worries aroused by the Nassau Fleet were the devising of an immediate, effective response, and the degree to which long-term planning should seek to match similar potential threats in the future. As ever, the crown balanced such necessities against the effects they would have on silver shipments to Spain. It was for this reason that the Marquis of Guadalcázar did not inherit in 1622 a defence system that embraced in full the improvements planned by his predecessor, for pending his arrival the *audiencia* had introduced a number of restrictions, paying heed to the crown's censure of viceroy Esquilache.[31] In the first instance, therefore, his task was to complete and return to their full strength the innovations introduced by the former viceroy, expanding and modifying where necessary once the Dutch fleet was anchored before Callao. The groundwork had been done by the Prince of Esquilache, following the van Speilbergen intrusion, but it was only when the Marquis of Guadalcázar was confronted by a similarly desperate situation that it became clear that the emphasis was shifting towards the formulation of a defence policy on land. On the occasion of the entry of the Nassau Fleet, a Peruvian viceroy for the first time in the seventeenth century turned down proposals to seek out the enemy and carry the conflict to him with a maritime force, and the strategy of land-based defences prevailed. In the less disturbed and more tranquil years of what was left of the 1620s, this trend became even more marked.

The crown and its advisers had evidently been distressed by the ease with which an intruder could now reach the heart of the viceroyalty and delay or, as in 1625 prevent the departure of silver shipments from Peru by creating alarm and uncertainty. The merchant community was understandably reluctant to entrust its wealth to the armada when such powerful foes were at hand, or presumed to be so, and discussions with royal officials keen to avoid delays were at times lengthy.[32] Guadalcázar himself summed up the greater vulnerability now felt in Peru by the phrase 'there is no longer any strait for these enemies, they pass through that of San Vicente, which they call Lemaire, in 24 hours'.[33] The degree to which the crown was troubled by l'Hermite can be measured by the fact that it now urgently requested a detailed plan of Peruvian defences in 1626. It is the viceroy's response a year later which reveals his recent course of action.[34]

By 1627, Callao enjoyed the protection of five main forts in close proximity to the town. The two new sites now chosen by Guadalcázar, in addition to the three which his predecessor had planned to fortify, seem to have been selected on the basis of experience gained from the latest Dutch blockade. The first was in the north, but further inland, to forestall attempts to enter the port from the rear through the countryside. It was precisely at Bocanegra, about two miles north of Callao that the l'Hermite expedition had first sent men ashore with this aim. The second was located at La Punta with the aim of preventing a landing from the open sea, and also to protect the passage between the mainland and the island of San Lorenzo. Dutch control of this island had afforded them a useful base from which to mount raids on shipping heading to and from Callao bay. Furthermore, all but the last fort were linked by an embankment of adobe running the whole length of the bay, which in turn had incorporated into its structure three batteries, placed roughly equidistant between the central forts on the shore. Thus, on the sea side at least, we have a slender line of defences that mark the first stage towards the total encirclement of Callao. Moreover, although Guadalcázar was instructed to be stringent in his application of crown funds for these measures, he was none the less authorised to appropriate them in this way.

With both crown and viceroy now agreeing to pursue land-based defences as a reaction to l'Hermite and as a preparation for any possible repetition, one might rightly expect the Peruvian maritime force to decline. In practice, Guadalcázar struggled to maintain the larger galleons in seaworthy condition, ordering one replacement to be built in Guayaquil. This had still not been delivered by 1630, due to the interruption to its construction and the havoc done to the shipbuilding industry in general by the first Dutch attack. The major concern of the viceroy in terms of seagoing craft was the rather effective collection of small vessels built to roam the Bay of Callao and protect shipping at anchor there.[35] He may be forgiven any lack of resolve in constructing more prestigious vessels since the crown had taken the initiative over the matter.

First, in the clamour for action following the earliest indication of a new Dutch interest in Peru in 1623, it had ordered the arming of all private merchant ships sailing in the South Sea since they had proved to be such an easy prey to intruders. Guadalcázar pointed out the impossibility of this due to the burden of cost to ship-owners, and the shortage of the necessary arms and guns, but the instruction was repeated in 1626.[36] Secondly, and on a much grander scale, in December 1624 the crown had undertaken to solve the problems caused by the multiple roles assigned to its Peruvian armada by undertaking to build in Spain a South Sea fleet of 10 galleons, to carry a force of 3000 men. There was little that was new in the proposition, since it followed the advice given by a number of individuals in Peru who had felt the need to express their views on defence requirements after the van Speilbergen expedition. Crown support for the scheme now did generate fierce discussion over many months, with those in Peru generally welcoming the commitment to the protection of their, and the crown's, interests. But, of course, the fleet never materialised, becoming a victim of increasing financial burdens falling on the crown in other parts of its empire, and the realisation by 1626 that the outcome of the Nassau Fleet was hardly likely to encourage a swift reprise from the Dutch.[37]

Nevertheless, whereas it is difficult to conceive what might have been the material gains to the backers of the l'Hermite expedition, its impact on viceregal administration, turning questions of de-fence into regular and prominent areas for discussion among officials, experts and laymen who had a point to make, cannot be in doubt. Above all, the practical efforts were still concentrated in the vicinity of the capital, and more especially its port, but the exchange of views revealed a growing awareness of the need to consider the requirements of lesser ports, for the fate of these could not be considered totally separate from that of the capital.[38] Arica relied on 240 muskets and arquebuses, and six pieces of artillery following a direct crown order to the viceroy to deliver four, but it still lacked a stone fort in 1627. Paita required four pieces of artillery. Pisco, with a population of some 150 Spaniards and Cañete with about a hundred, each important for the survival of Lima through their regular supply of foodstuffs and wines, demanded a small garrison and artillery. The former had four pieces of artillery hastily hoisted on to a platform when a party from the Nassau Fleet visited it, and by 1627 possessed 200 firearms. Guayaquil, with a population of over 400 Spanish, was the only one of the above to have paid dearly for its lack of protection, still possessing only 120 firearms in the post-van Speilbergen period, but subsequently gaining the attention of the crown with a request for information on the desirability of erecting a platform to hold artillery in 1627.

The Count of Chinchón who replaced Guadalcázar in 1629, dispatched an inspector who reported that Guayaquil could muster a force of 300 men for its defence, including negroes and mulattoes, and that a further 200 reinforcements might be expected within a space of 12–15 days. But although there were no military fortifications of any sort, Chinchón rejected their construction since an enemy could easily take, hold and fortify the island of Puná.[39]

The islands and coastal settlements of Chile, due to their proximity to the Straits of Magellan, had naturally attracted the attention of Dutch intruders, but it was felt that towns such as Concepción, Valparaíso, Coquimbo and the island of Chiloé were relatively safe since in an emergency they could draw on the support of soldiers stationed in those regions to hold the frontier against the Araucanians. Valparaíso, as the gateway to Santiago and producer of hemp for the shipping industry, needed some strengthening, but Concepción had an adobe fort, artillery and a garrison of 100 men, Santa María island the protection of a palisade and a garrison of 12 soldiers and Chiloé 50 Spaniards in a single castle.

Indubitably, the Nassau Fleet had provoked a fresh response in Peru to hostile acts directed against Spain by its European enemy, and an unprecedented inquest into the most appropriate counter-measures in expectation of future attacks, but in some ways more sinister was the light shed on the matter of potential dangers lurking within the viceroyalty. This is apparent on two fronts. On the one hand, it is clear that the Dutch were convinced that they could spark off revolts of Indians and negro slaves, and on the other that they were receiving information about the area from residents in the viceregal capital, from persons acting as spies. The Greek deserters, the prisoner Carstens and the writer of the journal all refer on occasions to the help expected, particularly from negroes in Lima. In his report of the incursion, the viceroy states his belief that the Dutch carried boxes of letters granting freedom to negroes, duly drawn up with a space left for the names to be entered.[40] That the possibility of a negro and Indian rising was taken seriously, is borne out by the viceroy's decision to keep them under guard during the blockade, and by the town council's request later that he give due attention to the consideration of this threat.[41]

However, despite one councillor's fears over supposed drinking bouts involving Indians, negroes and Dutch sympathisers, it was unrealistic to expect any long-standing alliance with these groups close to Lima, and certainly unwise of Schapenham to allow the blockade to drag on for so long in the hope that a rising, or some expression of support, might occur. In contrast to Dutch expectations and Spanish fears of negro slave behaviour, free negroes and mulattoes served so willingly and with such distinction during the defence of Callao that they were later relieved of an annual tribute of 400 pesos as a recompense.[42]

The Dutch entertained these hopes as a result of news from within Peru, from sources which also tended to be unduly optimistic about the ease with which defences in the Lima–Callao region could be overcome. But in most respects, information from these sources was reliable. This is especially true of that relating to the features of specific ports and to the timing of the operations of the silver fleet. After a long voyage, l'Hermite missed it merely by a few days, in a year in which the departure was unusually prompt.

An important figure in passing on this information was Adrián Rodríguez, who had first come to Peru in 1600 in the Mahu fleet as we have seen. After being held for a time he was subsequently repatriated, found his way back to the New World and travelled widely before returning to Peru by 1620.[43] His activities were disclosed to the viceroy by the Greek deserters, and later in his possession were found letters from Prince Maurice of Nassau in reply to his own. When put to the torture on 28 June 1624 he revealed nothing about accomplices, although already a glove maker and a merchant were in prison, suspected of being agents for a foreign state, and investigations still continued. The Dutch had also made use of these informers at the time of the van Speilbergen expedition, and the fact that this had been undetected for so long was a further cause of anxiety both in Peru and Spain. Their presence was a blunt reminder of a continuing Dutch fascination with the South Sea and seems to have convinced the Spanish crown that at least one European rival still looked upon the area as a target for attacks on its monopoly there, hence the considerable concern for the defence situation in the post-l'Hermite period.[44]

# 4

# The Expedition of Hendrik Brouwer: a Project for Colonial Settlement (1642–4)

For almost two decades the lure of Peru faded, and the Dutch temporarily suspended their dreams of incorporating the South Sea coast into their vision of a world wide trading empire. The disappointments and the poor returns associated with the l'Hermite venture, must have readily convinced many that their best hopes lay in undertakings of already proven viability and profit. Therefore, although it had long been the desire of Willem Usselincx to win for Holland a share of the varied riches of Peru, the West India Company continued for some time to concentrate its efforts on the more accessible Atlantic shores of South America.

After a number of early setbacks in the mid 1620s to the concept of unifying Dutch operations in the west, including the swift demise of the colonial enterprise at Bahia in Brazil, the company's exploits began to be crowned with remarkable success, particularly in the privateering type of action, and never more so than in the hands of Piet Heyn who, after inflicting heavy losses on shipping off the Brazilian coast, attained a legendary victory with his capture of the Spanish treasure fleet off Havana in 1628. Imbued with a new confidence, the company turned once more to Brazil as the most promising area of the New World in which to mount financially rewarding colonial ventures, based on a flourishing sugar industry which it was hoped would provide sufficient income to pay for the conquest and occupation. The conquest of Pernambuco began in 1630, but following the appointment of the energetic and enthusiastic Johan Maurits to the post of governor-general in 1636, spread to embrace seven of the fourteen Portuguese captaincies by the end of 1641.

However, the West India Company was never able totally to

shed the financial weakness with which it had been born, and whereas the promotion of warlike activities had accumulated unequalled benefits, the project for a Brazilian colony proved to be a terrible drain on resources, even in such capable hands. By late 1643, when the question of the renewal of both India companies' charters was soon due for discussion, a proposal was advanced for the merging of the two organisations. The West India Company was firmly in support but its counterpart unsympathetic to the idea. [1]

The Brouwer venture, therefore, is surprising in the context of the considerable indebtedness of the West India Company, but intended as proof of its continuing vitality and vision. It is further evidence, should any be necessary, of Dutch attachment to the lure of some quick gain to be won on the coasts of Peru, and to the incorporation of that region into western enterprises including Africa, Brazil and the Caribbean. In fact, ever since the first Dutch assault on Bahia in 1624, the Spanish had feared that a Dutch foothold in Brazil could ultimately threaten the mines of Peru, and Johan Maurits, who was now to become involved in the Brouwer expedition, only did so after renouncing, in 1642, a plan of his own to take Buenos Aires and march on Peru and its fabled mines from that direction. [2] The consolidation of Dutch authority in northeastern Brazil in theory ought to have been of great assistance to Brouwer, lessening the degree of isolation felt by his predecessors, since his fleet could refresh and re-equip at Recife before setting forth anew for the Chilean coast. In short it eliminated the dependence on supplies in the past fiercely won against Portuguese opposition along the African and Brazilian coasts.

As the location for its first venture in the South Sea, the West India Company chose the port of Valdivia in Chile. Although known to the Dutch by report since the latter years of the sixteenth century, the selection of such an isolated region at this time probably reflects the lessons learnt by the Nassau Fleet with regard to Spanish defence capabilities at the heart of the viceroyalty. But other reasons surely influenced the decision. For Valdivia was the site of one of Spain's worst defeats in its conquest of the New World. What better choice could there be for a nation seeking to use the animosity of the local population to form an alliance against the Spanish? Founded in 1552, it had struggled to exist to the close of the century until, on 24 November 1599, a horde of Indians massacred most of the Spanish population and gave warning of the long war for dominance which lay before Spain in Chile. By founding the fort of Santísima Trinidad on the ruins of Valdivia in March 1602, the Spanish hoped to resettle the area, but Indian raids, the remoteness of the site and illness brought this to an end in February of the following year, when the 36 survivors of an original garrison of 220 men were relieved.[3] Thus, when the Dutch began to envisage the Brouwer expedition, the port was uninhabited by Spaniards, for all subsequent plans for its repopulation had encountered obstacles.

In the upswell of comment and discussion concerning matters of defence following the entry of van Speilbergen and l'Hermite, both viceroys and interested commentators had expressed the dangers of leaving such a tempting and safe base for an intruder without Spanish population nor protection.[4] Following a plea from the governor of Chile, Francisco Laso de la Vega, the crown issued a decree on 18 May 1635 ordering its viceroy, the Count of Chinchón, to proceed with the port's repopulation and fortification at the expense of the Peruvian treasury. The count remained unconvinced, adding to his immediate predecessor's reservations over cost, his own doubts about remoteness, the Indian threat and the availability of other ports in Chile for Dutch settlement. Further insistence from the governor of Chile led to a reissue of the decree in April 1637, but on this occasion the resourceful viceroy found a way of postponing any effective action by appointing a survey expedition which included the cosmographer Francisco de Quirós. His job was to make an assessment of the possibilities for fortification and resettlement. It is said that he was so afraid of the Indians that he executed his survey and made his measurements from on board ship.[5]

A new viceroy, the Marquis of Mancera, who came to Peru in 1639 was at once instructed by the crown to complete the work in Valdivia over which Chinchón had procrastinated so long. However, his own enquiry and the findings of Quirós enabled him to report in May 1640 that the scheme was impractical and costly, at least 200 000 pesos per year.[6] Such was the nature of colonial administration, with the effect that Valdivia was open to Dutch settlement in 1643.

In terms of suitability for Dutch designs, the choice of Valdivia is again not difficult to justify, for as we have seen, ever since their first incursion into the South Sea there was reference to the area's fertile soil and the proximity of important sources of gold. These notions were perpetuated by geographers such as Hondius, Laet, and Mercator who wrote enthusiastically of the 'inestimable value of its wealth from mines, metals, stones, water and sand, where there is scarcely a river which does not conceal grains and nuggets of gold, rating this kingdom as the richest in the Indies'.[7] The lure of gold and the possibility of using the port as a base for further Dutch expansion were both motives disclosed by a Dutch prisoner taken by the Spanish on the island of Chiloé. 'He said that he had heard tell of a great deal of gold, and that they settled there in order to go on to win other lands, and that certainly after populating Valdivia they will not be content merely with that.'[8] One should not forget either the logistical value of Valdivia to any nation wishing to challenge Spain's dominance of Peru from the south.

The same informant was also able to reveal details of the preparations made in pursuance of the objective of establishing a settlement in Valdivia. Unlike previous expeditions, on this occasion the cargoes did not consist largely of commercial goods, apart from the trifles traditionally used to ensure friendly relations with the Indians. Instead, the ships carried barrows, spades, hoes, picks, axes and two forges, together with arms and equipment of war sufficient to gain and hold a site. But in common with previous voyages, and seeking a long held objective, the Dutch once more hoped to win the backing of Indian allies, perhaps even arming a number of them, and for this purpose Brouwer was to deliver a letter from the Prince of Orange to the leader of the Indian community offering protection and the terms of an alliance. Again, as before, the precise aims of the venture were withheld and the founding of a permanent settlement at Valdivia was only publicly announced when the coast of Chile was in sight. The Dutch prisoner was in no doubt as to the reason for such deception on the part of the expedition's organisers.

He said that unless they are brought by deceit, no one will come to these parts because of the great risk that the voyage entails, and because once settled here they will not return home. Furthermore, the rumour will spread that if prisoners are taken in the mishaps of war that must occur, they will not be ransomed nor will they be treated as in the various parts of Europe.

The passage into the South Sea, whatever the route, maintained its fearsome reputation among the sailors despite the attractions which were believed to lie ahead.

Apparently it was Brouwer himself, a director of the West India Company and a former governor-general of the East Indies, who urged this enterprise in 1642 and found himself nominated to lead it, in spite of his age.[9] He sailed from Texel on 6 November, heading for Recife, where he was to enlist the aid of Johan Maurits in the final fitting out of his fleet. After a delay of a little over three weeks, a group of five vessels left port on 15 January 1643, as follows:[10]

| Ship | Guns | Captain |
| --- | --- | --- |
| *Amsterdam* | 30 | Hendrik Brouwer |
| *Vlissingen* | 30 | Elias Herckmans |
| *Eendracht (Concord)* | 24 | Elbert Crispijnsen |
| *Dolphijn (Dolphin)* (yacht) | 6 | |
| *Orangie-boom (Orange Tree)* | | |

They carried about 600 men, of whom 350 were soldiers chosen from Dutch garrisons in Brazil.

For three months the expedition pressed on southwards through heavy storms and without sight of land. It was to be characterised by Brouwer's strict control and enforcement of discipline, neither of which has won him many friends then or now. His purpose was to preserve the military effectiveness of his soldiers and combat boredom by regulations governing regular weapon inspection and training. He also displayed some concern for the welfare of his men by distributing extra clothing to any unprepared for the biting cold, and sought to preclude disputes over rations by firmly establishing and enforcing the allowances due to each man. These were:

a good cheese for the whole voyage; three pounds of biscuit, half a pound of butter, and a quartern of vinegar per week; about a pint of fresh water *per diem*; every Sunday three quarters of a pound of flesh; six ounces of salted cod every Monday and Wednesday; a quarter of pound of stock-fish for every Tuesday and Saturday; grey pease, and three quarters of a pound of bacon, for Thursday and Friday: Besides this, as much oatmeal boiled in water as they could eat.[11]

By 5 March, only four months after leaving Holland, all five ships had reached the entrance to the Strait of Lemaire but because of continuing storms were unable to pass through. In fact, by subsequently sailing to the east of Staten Landt, Brouwer proved its insularity and was the first to follow the open route around Cape Horn into the South Sea. The first important mishap to be suffered by the fleet occurred as a result of the failure to find a suitable harbour in which to shelter from the winter winds: this was the disappearance of the *Orange Tree*.[12] Her loss was serious since she carried the bulk of the essential food supplies. Nevertheless, the four remaining ships sailed on without her, sighting the coast of Chile on the last day of April.

Until late August the expedition remained in the vicinity of the island of Chiloé and nearby ports on the mainland. From their ships at times they glimpsed groups of men both on horse and foot but whenever they landed on the island, as at Puerto Inglés on 9 May,[13] or Castro a month later, all they discovered were signs of human habitation such as smouldering fires and footprints, and indications that the Spanish themselves had deliberately set fire to their houses and the few public buildings. Frustrated by such tactics, Brouwer determined to provoke a confrontation by sending a Major Bleauwbeck to Carelmapu on the mainland. Some 70 men landed on 20 May, overran the defenders who this time had sheltered behind a palisade under the command of the *corregidor*, Andrés Muñoz Herrera, and on the following day were joined by the rest of their companions in plundering a store of honey, wine, wheat and flour. Before departing on 25 May they found a letter written in Concepción on 28 February 1642, which reported the expectation of a fleet of 12 Dutch ships to come to Chile in the following year.[14] This belief could account for the policy of deliberately destroying property and goods on Chiloé, which might be of benefit to foreign intruders, a policy which in fact was to be widely applied in respect of several of the offshore islands of the viceroyalty during the buccaneer intrusion of the 1680s.

The following relatively unproductive but tranquil weeks were soon to be disturbed by unrest when the true objectives of the venture were publicly revealed at Puerto Inglés on 17 June. Once more it is the prisoner Antonio Juan, rather than the official journal, who conveys the resentment that this announcement caused.

All the soldiers became very bitter because when they embarked they were told that the voyage was for four or five months there and back. And they regretted very much having to remain in these parts, and the fact that they had been deceived because the agreement which had been concluded in Brazil was for seven months.[15]

The restiveness of the crews and soldiers was most certainly further heightened by the growing shortage of provisions, which had prompted the decreeing of the death penalty for anyone found guilty of stealing meat, bread or tobacco. Remarkably, however, according to Antonio Juan, no one had yet died on this voyage.

Better fortunes seemed to be heralded on their return to Carelmapu on 11 July, site of the only incident with positive outcome during this phase. The hiding place of a small amount of silver (325 pesos and 25¾ lbs of silver plate) was uncovered, but more importantly for the long-term future of their enterprise, an agreement was struck with 470 Indians, which involved their transport to Valdivia along with considerable supplies of peas, barley, potatoes and sheep, food badly needed after the loss of the *Orange Tree*. Unfortunately before they could depart, a sad note was also recorded with the death of Brouwer on 7 August, a victim of old age and the climate. In his dying moments he had asked to be buried in Valdivia, and to this effect, to preserve it from decomposition, his body was cut open and the entrails removed. His command was replaced by Elias Herckmans.[16]

Somewhat overloaded with its new passengers, the expedition sailed for Valdivia in better spirits on 21 August, arriving at the mouth of the river three days later. Friendly contact was made with a small party of Indians willing to trade, and so on the 28th the *Dolphin* and the *Concord*, the two vessels able to clear the sandbanks, anchored before the site of the town, saluting it with six guns each. The amicable relations continued, though eventually were to cause mild alarm as the Indians were discovered to be purloining everything movable, particularly the compasses and metal objects. Eager to take advantage of this happy mood, Herckmans disembarked with two companies of soldiers on 29 August to present his credentials to the *cacique* Manquipillan, and to offer peace and protection in an alliance against the Spanish. On 3 September, they began to land their equipment and the rest of their men and offered a further elaborate explanation of the hostility between Spain and Holland, expressing the hope that their recent conquests in Brazil might soon extend to Chile. In return for military assistance, the Dutch obviously expected Indian cooperation with regard to provisions and the erection of a fort or stockade.

Indian support seemed to be willingly granted during these first days ashore, but perhaps already fearing a change of mood, a council meeting on 7 September resolved to dispatch Crispijnsen to Brazil in the *Amsterdam*, to give an account of the achievements to date and to arrange for fresh food and reinforcements to guarantee the future of the settlement. An air of unreal, and in fact unjustified, optimism still reigned in Valdivia at the time of Crispijnsen's departure on the 25th of the month, for he carried the news that a fleet of 10 sail and 800 men would suffice not only to conquer Chile, but to turn the whole of Peru against the Spanish. Those who stayed behind, 180 sailors and 290 soldiers, now began to lay the foundations of this dream, clearing the ground on the site of the first of three forts planned to defend the entrance to Dutch Valdivia.

The sad reality was that the work was not destined to progress very far, for within three weeks, at a second council meeting on 13 October, it was decided to prepare for the return of the whole expedition to Brazil, before the shortage of provisions became critical. During those weeks the condition of those remaining in Valdivia must have deteriorated rapidly, or some other motive for the abandonment of the port arisen.[17] The goodwill between the Indians and the Dutch certainly had begun to fade gradually as the former recognised the signs of preparation for a permanent presence. The Indians in response stopped bringing fresh provisions, withdrew their labour and therefore quickly failed to honour any bargain which Herckmans believed he had reached. Moreover, lack of tact in persistent enquiry about the proximity of gold mines must have evoked memories of similar experiences with the Spanish. Although fresh quantities of sheep, pigs and cows were presented by a second *cacique*, Manqueante, early in October, the journal stresses that no more could have been expected for some five months. The degree to which these shortages caused unrest is apparent in the report that four deserters fell into Indian hands, amid rumours that some 50 men wanted to surrender to the Spanish. Of those caught or proved to have been implicated in the plot at least six were shot following a court martial.

In a last desperate effort both to obtain supplies for his men and halt their desertion, Herckmans wrote to Manqueante.

> Sir: gladly and willingly we have received the message you sent us with three men. In answer we now reply that we are hard-pressed for provisions which those ashore here promise every day, but nothing is done, and taking into consideration the fact that we might die of hunger we have resolved it best in our council to depart with our ships, to see if we can achieve anything against our enemy the Spaniard at Santa María or Concepción. The shortage of food supplies has already caused some of our soldiers to desert, although until now they have not suffered hunger, and if by chance any of them enter your hands, do not give them passage but in your desire to do us a favour kill those you may find in the countryside.[18]

Thus, the situation was beyond remedy, and the only solution was to pursue the planned evacuation of this first and shortlived Dutch settlement in Chile.

Some of the Indian inhabitants were obviously worried by the departure, fearing reprisals by the Spaniards for having allowed the Dutch to settle, albeit briefly. For his part, the Dutch commander promised a swift return with arms, men and supplies in sufficient quantities to assure the success of repopulation. Significantly, also, the plan contained measures to relieve the Indians of the burden of labour. It promised that 'quickly he would send four ships with sufficient men and food to take that port, populate it and fortify it, and afterwards the General would come with twelve or fourteen ships, 2,000 soldiers and 1,000 negroes as slave labour to enable the Indians to be excused work, and it would be as quickly as possible'.[19] They took their leave on 28 October, only two months after their arrival, reaching Recife on 28 December after the first recorded west to east passage of Cape Horn. Their return was viewed in Brazil with dismay, particularly by Johan Maurits, who only three weeks previously had welcomed the news brought by Crispijnsen and commenced the fitting out of a relief vessel. This was on the point of putting to sea when Herckmans returned.

The failure of the intended settlement at Valdivia was to mark the end of Dutch attempts at expansion in the South Sea. That Brouwer's expedition achieved so little when the odds at the outset seemed so much more favourable than on prevous occasions, was in no small part due to the loss of provisions carried by the *Orange Tree*. This created dependence upon the Indian community and aggravated the usual dissatisfaction caused by the lack of honesty at the outset with regard to the nature and duration of the voyage. More than this, for the first time the Brouwer expedition put to the test the theory of an alliance with Indians advocated ever since the Mahu venture, its purpose being both to swell their numbers and to offset the penalties of operating far from a friendly base. Along with the right to build fortresses, appoint administrators and maintain garrisons and fleets, this is one of the main authorisations granted to the West India Company at its foundation. But the unrealistic nature of the proposal is demonstrated once and for all by this last enterprise. For there is every sign that once the Indians of Valdivia realised that the Dutch were there not merely to trade but to stay, they were far less eager to be of assistance. There is the suggestion also that the Indians were prepared, or obliged, to play a double game, for in Spanish documents Manqueante is described as being 'well-disposed towards the Spanish' and subsequently reported to be inviting them to repopulate and fortify Valdivia.[20] One can only express sympathy at their bewilderment and at their plight, when faced with the conflicting entreaties of two hostile European nations, both of whose ultimate aims they had just cause to doubt.

Even so, if the vital provisions had been preserved until a relief ship could arrive from Recife, it is still doubtful whether in the end the Indian response to them would have differed greatly from their reaction to Spanish settlers. During their very brief stay ashore, the Dutchmen's enquiries about sources of gold, as regularly reported in their accounts of Valdivia, were already an indication of the burdens that a Dutch settlement would bring to bear. In these circumstances, to consider, as some obviously did, that from a Chilean base Spanish power could be overthrown, was to lose all sense of reality and succumb totally to the lure of Peru. The Spanish, with their resources relatively near at hand, had not yet been able to guarantee total security for their settlers in Chile.

Returning to Recife just as the relief vessel was due to depart, the immediate blame for the failure fell on Herckmans, who died shortly afterwards. More recently, some have sought to soften this criticism and instead blame the original leader, Brouwer, partly for his undoubtedly stern handling of the venture. Robert Southey distinguishes between the two men. Of Herckmans he writes that he was 'one of the best Dutch, an excellent seaman, and athirst for knowledge of every kind', whereas Brouwer 'was a man of distinguished courage, conduct, and integrity, but odious to those under his command, because his discipline was strict, even to severity'.[21]

Charles Boxer is more overwhelmingly critical, for he comments, 'the greed and brutality of Hendrik Brouwer ... aroused the mistrust of the Araucanians and spoilt a promising start in May 1643'.[22] But surely, it is not in May at Chiloé, but in August and September at Valdivia, after Brouwer's death, that the vital stage of negotiations with the Indians took place. And in any case, on this occasion rather than the personality or conduct of a single leader, it is the objectives and their manner of attainment which contributed to the dismal outcome.

Dutch rewards, therefore, were insignificant. They gained further first-hand knowledge of the Chilean coast, especially of Chiloé and Valdivia, gathered information on Spanish military strength, and registered two firsts in the records of the history of navigation. Their arrival off the Chilean coast less than six months after leaving Holland was also the swiftest passage yet achieved.

The anxiety caused by Brouwer, who seemed to fulfil the fear of those who had counselled the repopulation of Valdivia for over 30 years, lingered on until May 1644, when the first of two reconnaissance squadrons sent out by the governor of Chile, the Marquis of Baides, reported that the Dutch had departed. Brouwer suffered the same fate as l'Hermite at the hands of the second of these squadrons, his body being dug up and burnt for being a heretic. On the last day of December 1644, a fleet left Callao to begin the fortification and garrisoning of the approaches to the site of Valdivia. Overall command of the maritime expedition was placed in the hands of Antonio Sebastián de Toledo, son of the viceroy the Marquis of Mancera, but the task of fortification was entrusted to the *maestre de campo* Alonso Villanueva de Soberal. Instructions had also been sent to the governor of Chile to march overland with 2000 men to link up with the fleet.[23]

The fitting out of a fleet to perform the task of resettlement and also fight off a second Dutch force should they return from Brazil as promised, proved to be one of the major maritime ventures undertaken in Peru. The force of 22 ships included the five principal crown galleons in the South Sea, two of them newly built at Guayaquil during the administration of viceroy Mancera, and the largest yet seen in those parts, being of about 1000 tons each. They carried 166 guns. The remainder were armed merchantmen and crown pataxes, whose armaments raised the final total to 318 guns, and a variety of craft transporting war materials and supplies, some of them departing from Chilean ports rather than Callao.[24]

The fleet reached the vicinity of its destination on 6 February 1645 and was soon to discover that governor Baides had excused himself the hazardous undertaking allocated to him, rather wisely since it would have exposed his army of Chile to the dangers of crossing Indian held terrain, and also left Spanish frontier forts virtually defenceless against Indian raids. A second minor inconvenience which also came to light at this point was the recognition that the plans of the cosmographer Quirós, on which they had hoped to base their choice of sites for fortification, were not entirely correct. Apart from these initial hitches, work proceeded at a steady rate for what remained of the summer and reasonably amicable contacts seem to have been made with Indians in the neighbourhood, particularly those under the leadership of Manqueante. Illness, and later winter conditions, seem to have been more of a challenge than Indian raids. When Toledo was forced to depart on 1 April to involve himself in the transport of silver from Arica to Panama, a force of 700 men and 35 guns was distributed among the newly erected fortifications on three sites down river, at Niebla, Corral and Constantino Island, protecting approaches to the interior.[25] The old town of Valdivia up river was finally formally refounded by Francisco Gil Negrete, former *maestre de campo* of the Callao garrison, on 6 January 1647, and gradually given the protection of its own fortifications. Though it was no longer open for the taking after 1645, Valdivia continued to gain the attention of those approaching Peru by the southern route in the second half of the century.

Therefore, as viceroy Mancera himself was to point out, the implications of his action for the Peruvian treasury were not simply the cost of mounting this considerable undertaking, some 348 000 pesos, but the new and regular commitment to the maintenance of Valdivia as a fortified outpost, requiring an annual shipment of supplies, clothing and other items, and at least 20 000 pesos in aid.[26] Even when informed of the conclusion of the peace treaty between Spain and Holland in 1648, he felt that the support of

Valdivia was vital, in part because of the remaining Indian challenge in Chile, but also because 'when there are no longer
Dutchmen in the world nor other nations who can enter this sea in
force as they have done on other occasions, there is enough to
justify its maintenance in having in Brazil such fearsome enemies
as the Portuguese'.[27]

These words might lead one correctly to suspect that Mancera
displayed a profound concern for the security of the viceroyalty,
and that his administration reacted decisively not only to fresh
fears aroused by the revolt of the Portuguese in 1640, but also those
occasioned by rumblings of new Dutch intrusions. The first
response was to embark on a series of precautionary measures that
were now standard practice as a result of previous intervention –
the dispatch of warnings to ports northwards from Callao to Paita
with instructions that exercises of local militias be arranged, the
appointment of lookouts at suitable headlands along the coasts,
the transmission of news to Panama and in case bullion operations
were affected, the transport of food aid to Guayaquil, which was
itself to request forces from inland to protect the shipyards and the
Isle of Puná, the distribution of warnings southwards from Callao
to ports such as Cañete, Pisco and especially Arica, and finally the
instruction of the governor of Chile to carry out a search of coastal
waters and neighbouring islands to verify or disprove the rumours.[28]
Such was the worry provoked by the mere hint of hostile intrusion,
that the entire length of the viceroyalty's coastline was involved in
safety procedures.

As soon as the rumour hardened into clearer evidence of Dutch
intent, Mancera committed himself to longer term action. A survey
of local militias in ports as far south as Nazca resulted in the raising
of new cavalry forces of 400 men, and the distribution of 500
firearms.[29] The decision was finally taken to provide two forts for
the defence of Guayaquil, and at last Arica, by a happy stroke of
fortune, was also to enjoy a stone-built fortification thanks to the
offer of a Portuguese to finance its construction in exchange for
Spanish nationality.[30]

But the viceroy's crowning triumph in matters of defence,
following the Count of Chinchón's somewhat insubstantial efforts
in the 1630s to provide the first inland enclosure of batteries and
linking parapets around Callao, was the total encirclement of the
port by a stone wall attaining a height of between 4 and 6.9 metres.
Construction was begun in November 1640 and completed in July

1647, with the appropriate celebrations and an air of festivity and rejoicing.[31] In response to Dutch threats to the security of the viceroyalty, Callao had now become a regularly fortified town encircled by a defensive perimeter. This was the logical and rational conclusion to the shoreline forts built by viceroys Esquilache and Guadalcázar, as their response to van Speilbergen and l'Hermite, and it incorporated in more durable form the inland parapets constructed by Chinchón at a time when a feared Dutch intrusion never materialised.

And so, first the report and then the reality of rekindled Dutch hopes in the Viceroyalty of Peru had embarked its viceroy on the most extensive, and costly, set of precautions from the northern to southern extremes of the viceroyalty, and spanning the entire length of his administration. The main items were the maritime expedition to refound and fortify Valdivia and the future commitment to that port's defence and maintenance, the wall of Callao which cost 876 000 pesos to build and whose future finance and repair was a legacy which several successors were less keen to bear, the construction of new galleons for an expenditure of 322 369 pesos, and the levying of forces of armed men, the purchase of equipment and the manufacture of artillery which raised this latter figure to some 560 400 pesos. One informant reports that in 1644 the viceroy expected to be shipping to Spain only 1½ million pesos, which but for the unexpected burden of defence costs might have been twice that amount.[32]

# 5

# Narborough and the Mysterious Don Carlos (1669–71)

From a reading of the preceding chapters, it is evident that the Dutch held the monopoly of intervention into the South Sea in the first half of the seventeenth century. However, in the remaining years, they were to be conspicuous only by their absence as they toiled, ultimately in vain, to hold on to conquests in Brazil, consolidated footholds in Guiana and the West Indies, and expanded their enterprises in the East Indies. Their place was now assumed largely by Englishmen and Frenchmen in the double guise of exploratory trade and buccaneering.[1]

From the mid-seventeenth century, English sailors departed from their island home to recommence a process of exploration and expansion which would span centuries, and achieve maritime supremacy at the expense of old rivals like the Spanish and Portuguese, as well as being to the detriment of northern European neighbours like the Dutch. In this undertaking, it is understandable that some should be drawn to the South Sea at a time when that region still entertained the imagination with accounts of its boundless wealth, to say nothing of the riches of the ocean beyond and the lure of the legendary Terra Australis Incognita. The voyage of John Narborough to Valdivia is evidence of the rekindling of English attraction towards those parts, stifled since the defeat and capture there of Richard Hawkins in 1594.

The motives which had brought Drake to the South Sea had gradually coalesced into a general antagonism towards Spain, expressed through the privateering war from 1585 to 1603. But the English presence in those waters which coincided with that period, was only a small part of a series of widespread, though somewhat uncoordinated, probing ventures by Elizabethan seamen, ranging from a preoccupation with a northern passage, to Newfoundland, North America, the Caribbean, and to the Straits of Magellan and beyond. With the death of Elizabeth, the accession of James I and his successful quest for a peace with Spain in 1604, this pattern changed. Though the peace did not guarantee the exclusion of the English from the Spanish New World, James' keenness in pursuing a policy of conciliation tended to encourage the main sphere of activity to shift to the edges of Spanish power, to territories she did not as yet unquestionably possess, in North America, Guiana and the East Indies. The peace also created a lull in English operations in the West Indies, certainly until 1618 and the start of the Thirty Years' War, but they were to return in greater numbers with the difference that increasingly they did so not as seaborne raiders but as colonising planters in the Lesser Antilles, in the 1620s and 1630s. Therefore, the reign of James I (1603–25) saw Englishmen embark on ventures that were to lay the foundations of a new empire, but Peru did not figure among them.

For the next twenty years or so, it was the overseas enterprise as a whole, rather than any one part of it, which suffered a restraint.

This was brought about by internal political disorders, marked above all by the estrangement of crown and parliament which had already become embittered in the reign of James I. Under Charles I (1625–49) the situation gradually became more grave during the lengthy period of direct royal rule without a parliament, the rift deepened by quarrels over the crown's desire for extra finances and the disquiet of the Puritans over the crown's Catholic sympathies, in the end dissolving into the Civil Wars of the 1640s. Therefore, we shall see no revival of English interest in the South Sea until the time of Oliver Cromwell, and no clearly documented result of this until the Narborough voyage, the outcome of proposals from commercial lobbyists for a re-establishment of contact with the area first presented to Charles II soon after the Restoration of 1660. By these dates, jealousy of Dutch commercial successes undoubtedly prompted this reconsideration of the search for new trading markets in America, but the rivalry had erupted into fall-scale war between 1652 and 1654, and again from 1655 to 1657, thus delaying once more any plans for future ventures in South America.

In a way the English had not been totally neglectful of Peru during all those years, nor totally absent from the concerns of its administrators. Indeed, although admittedly often unreliable, one source does record the presence of an English vessel off the coasts of Chile and Peru in 1616.[2] Not long after this, in 1625, a novel scheme was proposed by John Oventrout, which like the Dutch at this time identified Arica as being of major interest. The novelty was that he suggested 'that the best way to sett the Spaniards in a mutinie in Peru was to send preachers thither and with them some thousands of Catechismes, which in a short time would make dissension concerning religion amongst them'.[3] But it is not until the periods 1656–60 and 1662–63 that the occasional rumour in Peru about new English intentions appears not to be entirely groundless, but rather a reflection of the discussions in London at that time over the commercial prospects of an entry into the South Sea.[4] As we shall see, these projects then under consideration were the forerunners of the Narborough voyage.

When first envisaged, the objective clearly was to mount a reconnaissance of the southern tip of South America, both in the Atlantic and the South Sea, another examination, therefore, of an area on the fringes of Spanish power which it was felt might not be securely in its grasp. Narborough would also test reactions to offers of trade and assess the viability of what might become, perhaps in the long term, a new trade route to China and the East Indies. His orders state precisely:

> The design of this voyage on which you are employed being to make a discovery both of the seas and coasts of that part of the world, and if possible to lay the foundation of a trade there. You are not to meddle with the coast of America nor send on shore, unless in case of great necessity, till you get to the southward of Río de la Plata, and you are not to do any injury to such Spaniard as you shall meet with, or meddle with any places where they are planted.[5]

Similarly, in his dealings with the Indians, Narborough was to adopt a friendly posture, propose the establishment of trade and 'make them sensible of the great power and wealth of the prince and nation' to whom he belonged.

The peaceful intentions of the enterprise seem to be borne out by the fact that only two ships were involved, lightly armed and with small crews, in contrast to the powerful fleets of van Speilbergen and l'Hermite. They were the *Sweepstakes* of 300 tons, carrying 36 guns and 80 men, and the *Bachelor* of only 80 tons, bearing 4 guns and 20 crew. Unlike Brouwer, they carried no instructions, tools or supplies for an immediate settlement. Moreover, as we shall see,

Narborough's conduct was peaceful and in any contact with the Spanish he took pains to express such motives. For example, at Valdivia, he notes in his journal that he informed them, 'I was bound for China, and that I only touched in at this place, knowing here were settlements of the King of Spain's subjects, hoping here to have wood and fresh water, and refreshing for my men.'[6]

Nevertheless, it is evident that this attitude was only adopted since it was the most appropriate at the time, for it enabled Narborough to make his assessments of opportunities for trade and settlement. He had been instructed to explore all bays, harbours and inlets, observe vegetation and species of animals, and note weather conditions. Thus, subsequent reports in the journal reflect an almost scientific interest in noting the characteristics of each place visited. Such is the case of San Julián, now a port on the Argentine coast at 49° 20′S. 'It is a country capable of containing a great number of inhabitants and which promises great advantages to those who might wish to come and settle, for everything which grows in Europe would do well there, and the animals would find abundant pasture.' Not only the land, but also the climate appeared to recommend it. 'The air is cold tonight but very healthy for strong men; I have not had my finger ache as yet; a man hath an excellent stomach here; I can eat foxes and kites as savourily as if it were mutton... Nothing comes amiss to our stomachs; not one man complains of cold in his head, or of coughs.' During some six months spent in this region, Narborough found time to take note of penguins, mussels, seals, birds and 'sweet smelling herbs like lettuce', he enquired repeatedly after gold to no avail, and described the Indians as beings of only medium stature, so discrediting the stories of giants that had for so long figured in sailors' journals.[7]

On the basis of these and many similar conclusions reached during the course of his visit, Narborough ended his journal by supporting the establishment of what he judged would become a profitable trade between England and the coasts of the Viceroyalty of Peru. In particular, he pointed out the high cost and shortage of European goods which reached Peru and Chile via the Isthmus of Panama, or illegally through the River Plate. And so he was to recommend as a source of profit, a trade in Dutch linens, silks and laces from Flanders, silk stockings, ribbons and linens from France, and looking glasses, all of which help us to understand the style of life and the tastes of the viceroyalty at that time, if his assessment of the market was correct.

However, putting to one side the public expression of peaceful objectives, we find also in the journal indications that more hostile action in the future could not be discounted. For although Narborough had no intention of using force on this occasion, he had already apparently considered it when he wrote:

> I am of the opinion that the most advantageous trade in the world might be made in these parts, if it were but follow'd, and that leave were granted by the King of Spain for the English to trade freely in all their ports and coasts: for the people which inhabit there are very desirous of a trade; but the governours durst not permit it without orders, unless such ships of force were to go thither and trade per force, and not take notice of the governours; which might be easily performed by four ships of twenty and thirty pieces of ordnance a ship.[8]

His observations on the position and firepower of Valdivia's forts, and on the strength of Spanish forces on Mocha and Santa María are further proof of a preoccupation with military matters.

Therefore, taking account of the above facts, it seems that the prime object of the enterprise was the systematic exploration and reconnaissance of the southern coasts of South America, probably as a first step in setting up an English trade in that region, and even beyond to the East Indies. This work consisted of pinpointing those sites most suitable for trade and settlement, but it concealed in addition a secret desire to estimate Spanish strength in the south of the viceroyalty. To stimulate interest in contacts with England on a commercial basis, and to judge the reaction of Spanish settlers, the two ships carried cargo valued at £300, composed of knives, scissors, mirrors, bracelets, axes, nails, needles, pins, tobacco and pipes.

On 15 May 1669, John Narborough received his commission giving him command of two navy vessels which were to be fitted out at the expense of Charles II. Due to some delay in the loading of provisions and cargo they were unable to leave the Thames until 29 September, heading for Madeira and the Cape Verde Islands. After taking aboard fresh supplies of cows, goats and fish on 29 October, they began the crossing of the Atlantic intending no landing on the coast of South America until they reached a point beyond the River Plate. However, amid storms and thick mists the two vessels became separated on 23 February 1670, and the *Bachelor* was not seen again during the course of the voyage. Narborough pressed on alone in the hope that she had somehow got ahead of him, but finally dropped anchor alone in Puerto Deseado, taking possession of the region in the name of Charles II during a ceremony held on 25 March.

The winter months were spent in the vicinity of Deseado and San Julián, where the Englishmen apparently developed a taste for the local fish, the meat of seals and penguins, and for penguin eggs. Doubtlessly bearing in mind the objectives of the venture, Narborough comments, 'Our men are all in good health and are lusty and fat; those which had the scurvy are got very well with eating of fresh meat, and such green herbs as they can get on the shore, as green pease leaves and such track; they mince it, fry it with eggs and seal oil.'[9] Indeed, apart from the loss of the *Bachelor*, the voyage so far had been a happy one. Narborough seems to have devoted time to the welfare of his men, and in this way avoided the unrest and disease which had been such a wretched feature of the earlier Dutch expeditions. He professed equality in the distribution of provisions, followed a strict regime in matters of cleanliness, ensuring that each man washed thoroughly before eating under penalty of the loss of a day's rations, and was prompt in dealing with the first signs of illness. Two favourite remedies seem to have been a weekly dose of vinegar to prevent scurvy, and bloodletting to forestall fevers in hot climates. His medical inclinations are further evidenced by his search for bezoar stone, found in the paunch of ruminants and at the time esteemed as an antidote to poisons.

Feeling the worst of the winter conditions behind them, and after collecting fresh supplies of penguins and their eggs at Puerto Deseado towards the end of September, the *Sweepstakes* began her approach to the Straits of Magellan. She rounded Cape Vírgenes on 22 October and emerged into the South Sea in mid-November, some 13½ months after setting out, the slowness of her progress due to the decision to winter at the approaches to the Straits and the painstaking collection and annotation of useful information. During the passage of the Straits this work of observation continued and the corresponding pages of the journal contain notes on bays, the existence or lack of wood, water and minerals, and descriptions of semi-naked Indians of average stature, 'well

limbed, and roundish faced, and well shaped, and low fore-
headed'.[10] The lack of evidence of gold is again duly noted.
Once in the South Sea, Narborough seems to have headed without
hesitation for the port of Valdivia, but on 15 December a little to the
south of the main entrance to the harbour, one of their number was
put ashore bearing a sword, a case of pistols and a selection of their
trading goods, apparently with the intention of establishing
contact with the Indians. For some time his progress could be
observed from the *Sweepstakes*, but suddenly he disappeared
behind a rock and was never seen again by the majority of the
expedition. For purposes of clarity we shall refer to him in future as
don Carlos, although there is some mystery as to his true identity.
In the journal, Narborough indicates that he served as guide or
interpreter but was undistinguished in the performance of his
duty.[11]

It was the disappearance of don Carlos which brought the first
direct contact between the Spaniards of Valdivia and Narborough's
expedition. Groups of Englishmen who landed seeking news of
their companion, and fresh supplies of bread and water, were
initially received cordially though with a certain reserve. The
discussions and the whole sequence of events in Valdivia were
recorded in a dispatch of the viceroy, the Count of Lemos. He
reports, 'he said that it was a ship belonging to the King of
England, en route for the Moluccas, and that in accordance with
the peace that existed between the two Crowns, their king had told
them that they could approach any port in this sea, if as a result of
some misfortune they were in need of provisions'.[12] In return for
their hospitality, a group of Spaniards were invited aboard the
*Sweepstakes*, where one of their party was even offered a change of
clothing since his own had become wet during the trip from the
shore.

Thus the early exchanges were polite and friendly, but a study of
the records of the events shows that each side was simply
appraising the situation and trying to gather as much information
as possible about the other. The Spanish were understandably
wary and inquisitive, unsure at first whether the *Sweepstakes* was
alone or merely the vanguard of a fleet, bearing in mind the fairly
recent stories that had circulated in Spain and Peru about English
plans to send eight ships to the South Sea. Therefore, on their
return to Valdivia, those Spaniards who had been entertained by
Narborough were able to report that the *Sweepstakes* carried 36

guns, a crew of about 90 men, and a cargo of trade goods. From the fact that they were offered only cheese and preserved food to eat, they deduced that the expedition was short of food.

For his part, Narborough did not waste the few days spent in the vicinity of Valdivia, nor in entertaining four of its inhabitants, for he collected valuable details of the site, its defences, wealth and commerce. Of the Spaniards who came aboard the *Sweepstakes* he observes that they:

> are as well-complexioned men as ever I saw in my days; and the people a-shore both men and women of the Spaniards are well-complexioned people, of a ruddy colour, and seem to be mighty healthy. Some of the men are very corpulent, and look as if they came from a very plentiful country, where there is a great store of provisions, and abundance of gold and silver.[13]

Ever attentive to the slightest evidence of mineral wealth, he records with obvious delight the reports of those of his men who claimed to have been served by the Spaniards from silver stewpots, eaten from silver plates, washed in silver basins and noticed that the hilts of officers' swords were made of gold. They were given to believe that the sources of such wealth were the hills and streams behind Valdivia, and the region of Osorno, Chiloé and Castro. Indeed, there seemed sufficient proof for Narborough to be able to claim boldly, 'the most gold in all the land of America is in Chile'.[14] Narborough's journal, therefore, in its turn adds to the lure of Peru and in particular echoes the tales we have traced of Chilean gold.

For those interested in prospects of trade, on Narborough's evidence Valdivia produced for export to Lima principally gold, but also bezoar stone, red wool and slaves. In return it received cloth, wine, tobacco and sugar. The island of Santa María was well provided with wood and water, and a producer of a wide range of fruits – apples, plums, pears, oranges, peaches, quinces, apricots, olives and melons. Perhaps of even greater interest were his fairly accurate and detailed descriptions of trading patterns along the entire coast of the viceroyalty, with a particular emphasis on the route from Manila to Acapulco and Callao, which brought silks, spices and calicoes across the Pacific.

Moreover, as further encouragement to those who backed this present venture, Narborough estimated that the Spanish had made no serious attempt to defend such an important asset as Valdivia.

The river entrance, one and a half miles wide, was inadequately protected by cannon, and once inside 'St. Peter's fort can do very little or no hurt at all to your ship, excepting it be accidental dropping shot'. He is equally disparaging about the ability of the Spanish to make use of what weapons they possess. 'The Spaniards have match-lock musquetons, but they are very ordinary ones, and they are as silly in using them.'[15] This is obviously a case of Narborough belittling defences he himself was in no position to challenge, because they were so vastly superior in numbers of men. The nominal complement had remained 600 to 700, comprised of one cavalry company stationed at Cruces to the north of Valdivia, seven companies of infantry distributed among the fortifications of the town and outlying forts, and one company of artillerymen similarly disposed in charge of a total of about 50 guns.[16]

The original down-river defences had been improved and a further site was in process of construction. The town itself had by this time seen its original adobe fortifications transformed into an encircling wall of stone. Nevertheless, there were signs that the maintenance of Valdivia was a dangerous as well as a costly undertaking, with reports in the post-Brouwer years of continuing Indian attacks, the difficulty of providing supplies overland from Concepción, and the shipwreck of vessels bearing provisions in 1651. These problems of isolation and the general harshness of conditions had not unnaturally produced the suggestion that the port should once again be abandoned, particularly in view of the lack of hostile activity from Europe in those years.[17]

Obviously, it was in the very nature of the early contacts in Valdivia that when one side had adequately assessed the motives and strengths of the other, it would be prompted into positive action. As it happened, the Spanish were to take this initiative. On 18 December, Lieutenant Armiger and three companions were sent ashore to negotiate for supplies and begin trading. Instead they were at once imprisoned. To understand this abrupt change in relations, we must take into account the fact that only now had local officials received instructions from the governor of Chile to detain any sailors who came ashore, until the *Sweepstakes* came under the range of the guns protecting Valdivia. Furthermore, all trade was prohibited.

Naturally Narborough refused to accede to the Spaniards' demand, for it would have placed his ship and the rest of his crew in jeopardy. A rather peeved comment in the journal would appear to indicate that their action was not entirely unexpected, for he wrote, 'it hath been a general practice with the Spaniards in America to betray all foreign interest in these parts: as I had read of their treacherous dealings with Captain Hawkins at Saint Juan de Ulloa.'[18] His reaction, therefore, came swiftly and was the decision to sail from Valdivia on 22 December, returning to England via the Straits of Magellan. Clearly, it was based on the shortage of food supplies and the unwillingness to risk an attack with his scanty forces, but Narborough must have realised that those he left behind – Thomas Armiger, John Fortescue, Hugh Coe, Thomas Highway, not to mention the fascinating don Carlos – would be very lucky to see England again.[19]

Such behaviour was not gallant and in another age, that of Drake and Hawkins might well have been different. The only other possible alternative might have been to have sailed the coasts of the viceroyalty in the hope of taking a Spanish ship off the Peruvian coast and arranging an exchange of hostages. Where Narborough failed was in trying to deceive the Spanish without realising that they had the same intentions, and perhaps with greater justification. But in spite of this the return to England in June 1671 was a cause of rejoicing, since the *Bachelor* had reached Penzance a few months previously reporting the *Sweepstakes* lost in a storm. But what of those whose fate it was to be held prisoner in Chile and later in Peru?

The most intriguing of these is the individual we have chosen to call don Carlos, and the mystery begins the moment he disembarked, according to those who were later to become his fellow prisoners, at his own request, shortly before the *Sweepstakes* reached Valdivia.[20] For it was only a week later, on the very day that Narborough sailed for home, that he delivered himself into the hands of the Spanish, claiming to be 'director of the ship'. For over a decade he was to startle, puzzle and confuse his captors, and at times his fellow prisoners, with revelations and allegations that seem to constitute so clever a fabrication of truth and fiction that they could not lightly be dismissed nor go unheeded.

The process naturally enough began in Valdivia itself during January 1671, when in response to interrogation he offered a general account of his background in Europe and his involvement in the Narborough expedition.

By birth I am from Alsace in Germany, and in inclination and religion I am Spanish . . . From tender infancy until 16 years of

age I was continuously under the protection of the Queen
Mother of England, and from 16 to 22 years of age I wandered
through various kingdoms and provinces to see and reflect on
the world and acquire the knowledge that is needed in youth.[21]

Subsequently, during the next 17 years he claimed to have served
the English crown, in fact being recalled in 1669 from Stockholm
where he had been engaged on official business, in order to advise
on a proposal for a voyage to the South Sea, an expedition which
he was eventually asked to lead. These early statements seem to
have been intended to invest his own position with some prestige
and authority, also to allay any doubts over his religious prefer-
ences, through his declarations of loyalty to the 'true church' and
his wish to seek shelter among the Spanish to reveal to them the
aims of the 'heretics'.

A month later at Concepción the declarations took another
intriguing twist, as don Carlos alleged a friendship with a former
governor of Chile, Francisco de Meneses, with whom he had
become acquainted at the siege of Valenciennes in 1656. He further
demonstrated some knowledge of the personal and family circumstances of the former governor, and at one point was discovered to have addressed a letter to his wife in Santiago. Puzzling
though these titbits might be, of more immediate concern to the
authorities were don Carlos' views on English commercial objectives in the South Sea. His disclosures in this respect recalled the
presentation to the English crown in 1663 of a project to establish a
viable trade route via the Straits of Magellan and the west coast of
America to the East Indies. Initially it had been suggested that 'a
reconnaissance should be made of the ports which there are on
each side, within the limits and surroundings of the said Straits,
safe for ships and suitable for population and fortification'.[22]
Although other preoccupations had forced the implementation of
this plan to be postponed, it is obvious that in essence it had been
resurrected in 1669 and became the Narborough expedition. But don
Carlos' swift summoning to Lima for further investigation was
assured by his comments on long-term English aims, namely having
acquired a settlement close to the Straits, then 'to take possession of
Valdivia and hold it against Spanish power, and sack and destroy the
port of Callao and swallow up shipping in the South Sea.'[23]

No sooner was don Carlos in Lima than the viceroy was unable
to contain his bewilderment. 'He says that he knows me, and the

governor of Chile, and that he is a Catholic of German nationality, although from some of his phrases and expressions that have been noticed, it has been deduced that he is Portuguese.'[24] This was soon to be intensified by additional revelations concerning don Carlos' family background. His fellow prisoner Fortescue declared that he believed don Carlos to have a sister in Peru, married to a person of some authority, and that don Carlos himself was the son of another powerful gentleman who was a prisoner in Peru 20 years ago because he refused to be 'King of the Indians'.[25] To the great amusement of some of his companions, don Carlos alleged that he was the illegitimate son of Prince Rupert, Count Palatinate of the Rhine. Although he had never received public recognition of this relationship, he had nevertheless benefited from financial support which had enabled him to study in several European cities, move in court circles and be employed in Lisbon in the negotiations for the dowry of Catherine of Braganza.

If this, and much more, were true then it is somewhat surprising that little seems to have been done to secure the release of the prisoners. Equally obvious, though, is the fact that the disclosures by don Carlos removed the likelihood of any precipitate action being taken against them. What finally motivated a change of attitude in Peru was the presence of buccaneers in the South Sea in 1680. Confronted by their attacks, the new viceroy, the Duke of La Palata, felt no longer able to remain indifferent and inactive with regard to those in prison. A process of judicial investigation concluded on 22 April 1682 that don Carlos be condemned to death as a pirate, spy and deserter. His final attempt to cheat these conclusions was the concoction of a story in which he insisted once more on his Catholic beliefs and produced documents which purported to prove that he was a Franciscan, once resident in Cuzco, named José de Lizarazo. In fact a priest of this name had been missing in Peru for some two years.

Evidently perplexed, the authorities in Lima decided to try to resolve the identity and role of their extraordinary prisoner through an investigation under torture, beginning on 5 May 1682. This concluded that don Carlos was really Olivier Belin of St Malo, France. Words in his defence which emphasised the lack of hostility in his behaviour, and the value of the information he had revealed, were set aside and the fascinating episode drew to a close with his execution by garrote, probably on 8 May.[26] It is not certain whether the remaining prisoners were executed at the same time, but what is known is that one of them, Thomas Armiger, had died in jail in 1674, 'unfortunately still professing the Anglican heresies'.[27] What the final interrogation in Lima had failed to clarify was don Carlos' true role in the Narborough venture and his motives for inventing the anecdotes we have recounted. Did he have something to hide?

In order to shed some light on these issues it is important to try to set don Carlos' alleged role in the Narborough expedition into the general context of proposals for English penetration into the South Sea at this time. In addition to the scheme of 1663, to which don Carlos himself refers, there are remarkable and tantalising links between him and two other persons of Peruvian origin also intent upon stimulating European interest in the area – Baltasar Pardo de Figueroa in France and Diego de Peñalosa y Briceño, who appears to have been in contact with the Duke of York and Prince Rupert in England. In reporting the worrying activities of the latter, the Spanish ambassador in London mentions the involvement also of a certain Carlos Henríquez.[28] While we are left wondering about don Carlos' relationship with one or all of these, a further project which offers a new insight into his mission is that of Simón de Cáceres.

It was in 1655 that Cáceres had presented his 'humble proposition' to Oliver Cromwell, basically a scheme to round Cape Horn, fortify the island of Mocha and from there launch an assault on Valdivia, with the intent of converting it into an English settlement or base. Recently misled by Thomas Gage with regard to Spanish defences in the West Indies, Cromwell treated the proposal unsympathetically, but again the destination, and the nature of the optimistic commercial outcome expected, bear considerable resemblance to the conclusions of Narborough.[29] More interesting, however, than this further confirmation of the growth of English attraction towards Peru in the 1650s and 1660s, is the identity of Cáceres, who for some years had been a leading figure in the Jewish community in London, his signature appearing on a number of petitions issued by that community. When he states in his proposals to Cromwell his intention to 'engage some young men of my owne nation', that is Jews, when we remember that don Carlos also claimed to have been involved in negotiations for the dowry of Queen Catherine, as were Jews, these and other scraps of information lead us to suppose that on the basis of the present evidence, the answer to the search for identity is that don Carlos was a member of the London-based Jewish community, which had been urging English participation in the South Sea for several years.[30] If this were true, the elaboration of a series of tales designed to prevent his captors reaching such a conclusion would seem plausible, but why he should have deliberately chosen to desert his companions in these circumstances remains a mystery.

Ultimately, then, a study of this fascinating personality does indirectly throw some light on the development of English expectations in South America, and more particularly on some of the sources of support for such proposed ventures. But although Narborough enthusiastically reiterates the opportunities for trade and settlement, his contribution in this specific sphere offers nothing radically new. Charles II was not persuaded to act on the basis of Narborough's reports and the English crown did not become involved in another similar enterprise until 1689. Narborough's journal was not published until 1694.

Nevertheless, the voyage represented a notable advance in one respect, for if England wished to pursue commercial goals in the South Sea, it needed to acquire accurate knowledge of the coasts and sailing conditions. The efforts of Narborough went some way towards fulfilling these requirements in providing descriptions of the coasts of Patagonia and of Chile as far as Valdivia, together with a detailed map of the Straits of Magellan.[31] The map is adorned with drawings of local curiosities such as penguins, ostriches and 'a savage man and woman'. The notes include practical instructions on sailing directions, anchorages, shoals and sandbanks, winds and depths of water, offering descriptions such as 'habitable land and good ground', 'mussels in this bay, much pearle in them', or 'a cursed rocky sound'. Altogether they help to rectify mistaken concepts about the Straits, some of which may have been invented and circulated by the Spanish in an attempt to discourage others. The ease of the passage both outward, and more significantly homeward, certainly helped dispel fears about a variety of perils, including the view that a return voyage by the same route was impossible. Therefore, although no immediate crown decision was taken to follow up the investigations and expectations of Narborough, he had nevertheless provided the precise information that might make such an enterprise just a little easier and surer of success. The work of Narborough and Wood was to become the standard English guide to the region for decades.

For the Spaniards of Peru and Chile the 1670s marked the commencement of a new era of concern about threats to their security, or at the very least their livelihood. This was especially so during the brief period from 23 January to 14 February 1671, when it was believed that not one but a dozen English ships were anchored off the Chilean coast. Lima and Callao became scenes of frenzied activity and some panic as hasty preparations were undertaken to gather and arm the maximum number of defenders. Cavalry and infantry forces underwent regular training, negro and mulatto companies were called up, university students and merchants formed their own companies and men were drafted in from neighbouring settlements. It is estimated that the alert brought some 7000 men under arms.[32] Obviously John Narborough and the *Sweepstakes* were not the menace that seemed imminent. The viceroy in Lima, the Count of Lemos, was reacting not only to false reports from Chile, but also in response to fears aroused by recent English expansion in the West Indies, and the rumours of recent years concerning their aims in the South Sea. However, even when the presence of only a single ship at Valdivia was substantiated, what did it represent? If it were the means of reconnaissance by which the English hoped to improve and update their knowledge of Peru before more powerful fleets were risked, then there was still cause for concern.

This worry was to a certain degree provoked by a recognition that during the last 20 years the defensive preparedness of the viceroyalty had declined in answer to the lull in foreign intervention. We have already seen some evidence of this at Valdivia. At the centre of the viceroyalty, the wall of Callao, which viceroy Mancera had claimed to be such a godsend to the security of the capital and its port, rapidly had become a burden and a liability.[33] Of the 240 000 pesos debt from the construction work bequeathed to his successor, over 76 000 pesos were still outstanding in 1656. At that time the extent of public and official neglect can be measured in a report that piles of rubbish thrown over it had been allowed to accumulate in some areas, to such a degree that they were almost level with the parapet.[34] The ongoing debt also meant that virtually no repairs were undertaken either to counteract the pounding of the waves and slow infiltration of the sea, or the effects of the earth tremor of October 1655, with the result that some sectors had collapsed. Moreover, the financial burden imposed by the wall had the effect of persuading the crown to reduce expenditure on regular forces in the vicinity of Lima and Callao, and criticise the high costs of maritime operations.[35]

Therefore, feeling that he had inherited a declining defence position at a time when the indications were of a renewal of interest in the South Sea, especially by the English, the Count of Lemos until his death in 1672, and then his successor the Count of Castellar, maintained a vigorous interest in ensuring efficiency and expertise amongst the potential defenders of Lima and Callao. Many pairs of eyes warily scanned the southern horizon in search of the ships which don Carlos had hinted would follow Narborough, and there were indeed sails to report that can only have added further to the apprehension.[36]

Firstly, there was an unnamed expedition of two vessels, financed by English and Dutch merchants, which sailed from Amsterdam in 1671. After reportedly taking aboard traditional cargo at Cadiz, and perhaps seeking some sort of license to trade, the ships passed into the South Sea via the Strait of Lemaire and Cape Horn, and seem to have done profitable business at Guayaquil and Realejo, before proceeding to Acapulco. Following their return to Holland by the same route, 'loaded with many riches,' two participants persuaded Antonio de la Roche, described as an English merchant, to organise a sequel which departed from Hamburg in 1674. Although its two ships sailed the entire length of the coasts of Chile and Peru, they failed to match the commercial success of the 1671 venture.[37] Finally, in 1673, a group of Bristol merchants led by Thomas Peche, who is reported to have had experience of sailing to the East Indies and China, also fitted out two ships under the pretext of trade with the Canary Islands. They rounded Cape Horn, crossed the Pacific to the Philippines, headed back to the coast of New Spain in 1676, and then progressed southwards along the coast of Peru, passing into the Atlantic via the Straits of Magellan in 1677.

The most one can say about these voyages is that they were very likely the result of efforts by enterprising merchants, eager to follow up the stories of rich profits to be made in trade with Spanish colonies in the New World. They attempted to do so by causing as little undue commotion as possible and without official sanction. They may be indicative of others which followed a similar route, but which by their very clandestine nature have not even enjoyed the vague memory shared by these three.

While the evidence is flimsy, there is indirect corroborative proof of the second of the above voyages from sources in Peru. For briefly in 1675, it was thought that don Carlos' forecast of further English intervention had been proved correct, following reports from a routine patrol sent out from Chiloé that Indians claimed to have glimpsed foreign sails. Although the governor of Chile, Juan Henríquez, was sceptical about the stories of Indians, who were in his own words 'children of fantasy easily led to any belief', in the context of recent events it was vital to pursue the veracity or otherwise of the statements. During close examination in Chiloé, two Indians further elaborated on their original tale, no longer limited simply to the description of foreign vessels but amplified to include mention of two separate settlements, populated by men, women and children and protected by a stockade with artillery pointing out to sea. Their evidence also contained physical descriptions of the governor of each settlement as well as a reference to windmills where they made flour.

Lima and Callao, again on the basis of rumour, were thrown into confusion and tortured by anxiety, with merchants again declining to commit their silver to the squadron preparing to sail for Panama.[38] In order to put these revelations to the test, an exploratory force under the command of Antonio de Vea and Pascual de Iriarte sailed south in September 1675, for a rare Spanish penetration into the remotest regions of the viceroyalty. Despite shipwrecks and appalling conditions, Vea and Iriarte managed to reconnoitre the islands of southern Chile and the entrance to the Straits of Magellan, but their search for intruders had borne no fruit by March 1676. A month later on their return to Lima, instructions were issued that the two Indians on whose testimony the rumour was founded should be whipped for giving false evidence.[39]

Ironically, as we shall see in the next chapter, when it did materialise the threat came not from the expected, traditional quarter, the south, but from the north across the Isthmus of Panama as a consequence of the greater presence of Englishmen and Frenchmen in the West Indies. The only other significant English venture into the South Sea in the seventeenth century, approaching through the Straits, was that of John Strong in 1689.

# 6

# Sharp and Company: The First of the Buccaneers (1679–82)

Before the 1670s had expired, a force was already gathering which would launch assaults on Peru from a fresh direction, the West Indies. Soon, and with greater justification, it would revive the alarm inspired by the initial rumours of Narborough's presence in the south of the viceroyalty at the start of the decade, as it ranged along the coasts and through the islands. The buccaneers, of which it was composed, were an identifiable group in the West Indies by the early seventeenth century, particularly in the north and north west of Hispaniola, where they found herds of cattle running wild in the dense forests after their abandonment by Spanish settlers who had followed the tide of discovery and conquest to the mainland. These cattle provided a means of sustenance and income for refugees from wrecked ships, runaway negro slaves, and a variety of rogues and villains who sought to escape the hand of justice, and whose livelihood came to be based on the selling of supplies to passing privateers and traders. Originally referred to as 'cow killers', they eventually were designated buccaneers from their manner of cooking and preserving strips of meat, Indian style, on a *boucan*, a hardwood grill or gridiron placed over a pit or hollow housing the fire.[1]

The consolidation of the buccaneers on Hispaniola, and their expansion to the small nearby island of Tortuga, seems to have occurred about 1630 following the expulsion of French and English settlers from St Christopher. Despite Spanish attempts to dislodge them, the two nationalities lived in uneasy proximity until the English were driven out in 1640, many taking refuge on Providence Island, another buccaneering base. A more definitive separation of home bases of operation followed the English capture of Jamaica in 1655, with the English settling at Port Royal and the French remaining on Tortuga and Hispaniola (St Domingue), although there was a considerable degree of intermingling and collaboration for actual assaults on the Spanish, as we shall see later in the South Sea.

The heyday of the buccaneers was in the decade beginning in 1660, although this was also a time when the English had begun to question whether a share of West Indian trade might be achieved by more peaceful methods. For the moment, however, both English and French colonial governors were authorised to support the buccaneers as guarantors of the security of their respective colonies, as well as for the income derived from the booty they unloaded in their ports. This was a new and urgent concern particularly for the English following their capture of Jamaica, and so Charles II was to initiate a policy by which the crown would officially renounce responsibility for illegal actions by its subjects in the New World, but which in practice was dependent on changing alliances in Europe. It was countered by those English settlers who already felt that buccaneering hindered peaceful settlement and the expansion of trade. The actual suppression of the buccaneers, therefore, was a policy only fitfully pursued with full implementation delayed for over 20 years. But ultimately there were increasing restrictions on buccaneering in the West Indies which persuaded some of its participants to seek more distant fortunes, in a South Sea whose riches were legendary.

Following the rebuff of Sir Richard Fanshawe's overtures for peace to Philip IV in Madrid, and at the same time, from 1664, the less than enthusiastic implementation by Governor Sir Thomas Modyford in Jamaica of his instructions to prohibit the granting of commissions to buccaneers, sceptical about conciliatory approaches to Spain and even less willing to lose prizes to the French at Tortuga, the pursuit of an accommodation between the two countries moved closer to fruition following the death of the Spanish king in 1665. An initial agreement of alliance and commerce was reached in May 1667 by the Earl of Sandwich and discussions concluded due to the diplomatic skills of Sir William Godolphin in July 1670, culminating in the Treaty of Madrid. Although there was little faith among either English or Spanish settlers that a treaty signed in Europe could be implemented in the West Indies, it wiped clean the slate of past hostilities and proclaimed the intention of each party to refrain from attacking the other in all parts of the world, revoking all commissions for reprisal in the West Indies. But of special significance for Peru, it allowed

England to retain sovereignty over those colonies held at that time in America, including the West Indies.

It was during the final phases of the peace negotiations that the English were to leave their West Indian bases for raids that were to open up access to Peru. Stating at first merely a fear that the Spanish were preparing to mount acts of reprisal against Jamaica, Modyford authorised Henry Morgan to undertake buccaneering actions which, in 1668, accomplished the dramatic capture of Portobello, terminus of the galleons from Spain. Following actual Spanish attacks, and despite his awareness of the progress of discussions in Spain, Modyford further sanctioned the assault on Maracaibo in 1669 and Panama late in January 1671.[2] Morgan had achieved what even Drake had failed to do. The Isthmus was crossed, Panama terminus of Peruvian silver fleets was burned to the ground, and the way was open to the South Sea and Peru. Although some of his men were tempted by this prospect, Morgan persuaded them to renounce the idea, a project which was to await realisation for a further decade.

We have seen that in Peru, also in late January 1671, viceroy Lemos was to receive exaggerated reports of an English presence in Chilean waters. On 8 March he was informed of the tragic loss of Panama. Later in the month he wrote urging his queen to permit the creation of a squadron of ships to clear the West Indies of foreign interlopers before the entire Spanish Indies was placed in peril.[3] At the end of July, after the public proclamation in Lima of the treaty of peace with England on the 17th of the month, he addressed his queen for a second time, warning of the potential dangers of English colonies so close to Cartagena and Portobello, and of the provisions of the treaty which would seem to allow English ships into Peruvian ports. 'The Indies are lost, since there is no defence in the ports of this realm to resist them if they want to make themselves masters of the region where they come ashore.'[4] By May 1672 he was again urging specifically the need to recapture Jamaica, to deny the English a base from which to take control of Portobello and the Isthmus of Panama, and then direct their offensives against Peru. Though his queen tersely replied that the articles of the Treaty of Madrid must be honoured, viceroy Lemos' only mistake was to be premature in his warnings.[5]

The 1670s did not witness the decisive enactment of a policy to suppress English buccaneers in the West Indies, but rather the continuance of the see-saw of support and check. Morgan returned to Jamaica to find that the treaty had been ratified and the text published in all parts of the Spanish and English world, and both he and Modyford were recalled to London under arrest. But in 1675, after an interval in which Sir Thomas Lynch tried to enforce the law and offered pardons to buccaneers who voluntarily surrendered, both returned to Jamaica as lieutenant-governor and chief justice respectively in the administration of Lord Vaughan. It looked as if Spanish viceroys and governors were right to place little faith in English overtures for peace, especially in the New World, and particularly in the West Indies where even during the moments of restrictions on English buccaneers, they maintained their raiding and plundering under French commissions, finding support on Tortuga and St Domingue with governors such as d'Ogeron until 1675, and then his successor de Pouançay during the next decade. The English did attempt to close this loophole in 1677 by forbidding service under a foreign flag and by offering pardons to those who had sailed previously under French commissions, but the arrival of the Earl of Carlisle in 1678 marked a period of laxity in the enforcement of anti-buccaneer legislation.

It was with commissions from the new governor, specifically to cut logwood in the Bay of Honduras, that the first of the buccaneers who for most of their voyaging along the Peruvian coast were led by Sharp, left Port Royal in December 1679. Since Morgan's exploits the pathways of the Isthmus of Panama seem to have been largely untrodden by intruders, with the exception of unsuccessful attempts by French buccaneers Lessone and Bournano to reach Chepo in 1675 and 1678 respectively.[6] However, an important consequence of these two episodes, and of the constant cruising of buccaneer craft along the northern coast of the Isthmus in search of Spanish prizes, was the establishment of friendly relations with Indian settlements in Darien. These Indians were to be of immense practical benefit to this and later buccaneer parties seeking the South Sea.

The group originally comprised John Coxon, Cornelius Essex, Robert Allison (or Alliston), Thomas Mackett (or Magott), and the Frenchmen Jean Rose and Bournano in addition to Sharp himself.[7] As had most certainly happened on previous occasions, once out of sight of port they forsook their avowed intent and turned their minds to privateering, setting course for the Isle of Pines at the eastern end of the Isthmus. While there they encountered for the first time Indians who invited them to march overland to the South Sea under their guidance, with the prospect of rich plunder. But for the time being this venture was postponed, and under the leadership of Coxon a no less dramatic plan was agreed for a repetition of Morgan's attack on Portobello.

Leaving their ships at Springer's Key, where they had been joined by Lessone, about 250 men set out in canoes for Puerto del Escribano, where they disembarked and began a six day march designed to bring them to the undefended rear of the town. And so the assault on 7 February 1680 took the Spanish completely by surprise, as one account relates.

> A boy came running into the town along the road from the slaughterhouse at ten in the morning, and shouting: 'To arms Christians, the English are coming.' Those who heard him were confused and refused to believe him, when they saw some five or six Englishmen coming towards them at a quick pace pointing their guns, which was sufficient to send them fleeing to Santiago castle to shut themselves in.[8]

Since they had time only to remove from their homes the more portable of their belongings, the greater part of the town lay open to plunder. Therefore, for the loss of 30 men according to Spanish versions, the buccaneers were to gain a booty of 50 000 pesos in silver, and cloth to the value of 20 000 pesos, causing damage that would cost 25 000 pesos to repair. When distributed the profits were £40 per man according to Exquemelin, or 100 pesos according to Coxon, with special allowances for those in command, carpenters and surgeons, as well as compensation for those who lost limbs or suffered other injuries, as was the usual buccaneer practice.

Heartened by this success, many began to view the prospect of crossing the Isthmus with greater interest and were soon to add fresh recruits to their number. First, as they were leaving Portobello they were joined by Edmund Cook, a privateer out of Jamaica whose crew included the surgeon Lionel Wafer, later to become famous for his account of his enforced residence among the Indians of the Isthmus.[9] Then, at Bocas del Toro, on the western side, they received further reinforcements in the form of the ships and crews of Peter Harris and Richard Sawkins, like Coxon and Sharp both privateers of some standing.[10] With their numbers strengthened in this way, they finally resolved to accept the aid of their Indian allies and undertake a privateering adventure in the South Sea. Thus the Ayres account commences:

> that which often spurns men on to the undertaking of the most difficult adventures is the sacred hunger of gold; and 'twas gold was the bait that tempted a pack of merry boys of us, near three hundred in number, being all souldiers of fortune, under command (by our own election) of Captain John Coxon, to list ourselves in the service of one of the richest West Indian monarchs, the Emperor of Darien.[11]

One could hardly ask for a plainer statement of what it was that lured buccaneers to Peru.

The Frenchmen among them, however, two of whose captains had direct personal experience of the dangers and trials of the overland crossing, were unimpressed by this carefree attitude and chose to stay in the Caribbean. Hence it was an English party that set out from Bocas del Toro on 23 March en route for Golden Isle. It was composed as follows:

| Captain | Tons | Guns | Men |
|---|---|---|---|
| John Coxon | 80 | 8 | 97 |
| Peter Harris | 150 | 25 | 107 |
| Bartholomew Sharp | 25 | 2 | 40 |
| Richard Sawkins | 16 | 1 | 35 |
| Edmund Cook | 35 | | 43 |
| Robert Allison | 18 | | 24 |
| Thomas Mackett | 14 | | 20 |

Guided by the Indian chief Andreas, they crossed to the mainland on 5 April 1680, leaving Allison and Mackett at Golden Isle to guard their ships pending their return.

Over the next few months during operations on the Isthmus, in the Gulf of Panama and off the coast of New Spain, the buccaneers were to display characteristic patterns of action, their strengths and their weaknesses, before the main nucleus of the party concentrated its efforts on the coast of Peru. Marching in companies, each bearing its own colours, they headed towards their first target, Santa María at the eastern end of the Isthmus. In launching their attack on 15 April 1680 they hoped to win a fortune in gold, but were disappointed, the site being mainly a defensive one against the Indians though producing some gold dust washed down by the river. At most they gathered 20 lbs of gold and some silver, but as ever in such cases as this were led to believe they had narrowly missed a shipment of three hundredweight, or four chests, of gold dust recently dispatched to Panama. Sharp echoes what must have been a general disillusionment. 'This was not so good a place as we did expect. It was a small pitiful place all thatched houses and but one church.'[12]

But apart from the failure to fulfil their general expectation of booty, two other features of the attack were to recur. The first of these is the undoubted courage, but also impetuosity and foolhardiness of Sawkins, who rushed into the assault with only 50 men before the rest were able to lend support, obviously hoping to secure the pick of the plunder. Then, when optimism had turned to disappointment, there occurred the first doubt about prospects in the South Sea. The lack of plunder at Santa María, but more particularly some lack of enthusiasm for the prospect of severing links with regular haunts and placing themselves in a situation where they must rely entirely on prizes captured and towns plundered for their subsistence, caused a few to have second thoughts. Coxon was the first to utter these, but for the time being was placated by being confirmed as overall commander.

Following two days residence at Santa María, the buccaneers resumed their crossing of the Isthmus by canoe, relying again on Andreas and his fellow Indians for guidance as to the best route. Because they were dispersed among 35 of these craft, one cannot with confidence unravel the sometimes conflicting accounts of their activities immediately upon arrival in the South Sea. However, it would seem that on 20 April, in the Gulf of San Miguel, they took control of a Spanish vessel of 30 tons which was put in the hands of Sharp and about 130 men. A smaller craft was taken on the next day and given to Peter Harris. These operations clearly scattered the canoe flotilla, and one party led by Coxon and Sawkins now headed for an agreed rendezvous at the island of Chepillo, arriving on 21 April, where it just failed to capture a bark making off hurriedly, it was presumed to warn the President of Panama of their presence. Therefore, when they reached the island of Perico two days later, preparations had already been made to forestall an attack by putting 250 men aboard the three barks which formed the *armadilla*, or squadron, which patrolled the waters off Panama. These now sailed to engage the intruders.

Again the buccaneers demonstrated their reckless daring in an encounter that must have been fierce and bloody at times, and despite their weariness from paddling and rowing and the fact that their numbers had been depleted to only 68, following Sharp's decision to head off in search of water in the vicinity of the Pearl Islands. Two of the Spanish barks were taken and the third put to flight. The Spaniards suffered 75 dead and 20 wounded, the buccaneers between 11 and 18 killed and 34 injured, including Peter Harris shot through the legs. He died soon after from his wounds. With the protecting squadron defeated, the buccaneers with no great difficulty took over five other vessels anchored at Perico. One of these, the *Santísima Trinidad* of 400 tons, was briefly to become a hospital ship for wounded buccaneers and then Sharp's flagship for most of the remainder of the voyage.[13]

Sharp, meanwhile, reached the rendezvous at Chepillo on 23 April only to find the settlement already burned by the canoe party. He rejoined his comrades off Panama on the next day, that is following the recent bitter engagement. However, rather than uniting into a stronger, combined force, disputes arose over the question of whether to remain in the South Sea or return to Jamaica. Coxon was the ringleader of those who favoured the return, could not be dissuaded on this occasion, and in unhappy circumstances departed with about 50 of his men, 'which I think will not redound to his honor for he left about 20 of his men here wounded . . . and carryed away with him ye best of our doctor's medicines', adds Sharp.[14] Charges laid against him of cowardice in the recent battle with the *armadilla*, appear to have persuaded Coxon that he could best seek his fortune elsewhere. He was replaced in command by Richard Sawkins.

Despite having defeated the force by which the Spanish had hoped to drive them from the bay, the buccaneers plainly lacked the strength to mount a frontal attack, without the element of surprise, on the new city of Panama. Therefore a blockade of the port was planned and executed on the basis of a rumour that a richly laden ship was due from Callao. Consequently on 29 April they sailed for Taboga Isle with this intent. The expected prize never appeared, but the two weeks in this fresh location provided them with the means and the encouragement to pursue their activities in the South Sea, for they captured other prizes more suited to this objective than the variety of canoes and boats in which many of them still sailed. The encouragement came from the seizure of a bark which must have caused considerable delight, since her cargo was 1400 jars of wine and brandy, 100 jars of powder and 50 000 pesos to pay the wages of the Panama garrison. When the spoils were shared out each man received on average about 240 pesos. Further income was derived from the sale of brandy and wine to a Spaniard on Taboga Island for 3000 pesos. Sharp also took a 100 ton prize with a useful cargo of flour and transferred himself and his crew into her. The buccaneer force now consisted of the *Trinity*, commanded by Sawkins, and two vessels of 100 tons each commanded by Sharp and Cook, together with a variety of smaller craft.

And so, within a matter of weeks through resolute and bold action and in spite of small and indeed decreasing numbers, Sawkins and Sharp were beginning to gather the prerequisites for a lengthy buccaneering expedition in the South Sea. Some basic food supplies had already been acquired, and they were now able to select from their prizes those ships most suitable for the remainder of the voyage. Apparently the only cause for concern was the lack of fresh meat, and in order to remedy this shortage Sawkins planned an assault of Pueblo Nuevo on the coast of New Spain. Unfortunately, once more his eagerness cast him prematurely into the attack, on 23 May, before the majority of his companions were able to render assistance. This time Sawkins was to pay with his life.

The death of Sawkins was now the cause of renewed disputes, for it deprived the buccaneers of their second leader. In his place, the 'ill-beloved' Sharp went aboard the *Trinity* as overall commander.[15] His unpopularity in some quarters, even at this early stage, is proved by the fact that soon after his appointment a further 70 men chose to follow those who had already set out to return to the Caribbean. Sharp gave them a small boat and some provisions for their journey, at the same time reorganising the remaining 146 men who were now to accompany him southwards to Peru and who included three well-known writers of published journals, Ringrose, Dampier and Wafer. Edmund Cook joined him aboard the *Trinity* after differences with his crew, and a certain John Cox became captain of one of the prizes, renamed the *Mayflower*, with a crew of 40 men.

They departed Coiba Isle, where the above arrangements were

made, on 6 June in search of a suitable spot to careen their ships
and replenish their stocks of fresh food. Both these needs were
satisfied at Gorgona Island between 17 and 25 July, where they
found plentiful supplies of rabbits, turtles, oysters, monkeys and
birds to vary their diet. Then began their steady and unhurried
progress along the Peruvian coast, past Cape San Francisco and the
port of Manta, arriving on 13 August at Isla de la Plata, so called
since Drake was reported to have shared his plunder there, but
now a source of fresh provisions in the shape of goats and turtles.
Their first encounter, in the Gulf of Guayaquil on 25 August, was
with a small vessel that had just left the port specifically to discover
their whereabouts. She was captained by Tomás de Argandoña
and carried, according to Ayres who mocks their bravado, 'a parcel
of merry blades, gentlemen, who drinking in a tavern made a vow
to come to sea with that vessel and thirty men, and take us'.[16]
Whatever the wisdom of the enterprise, from it the buccaneers
learnt that their arrival was expected.

Obviously Argandoña's impetuous response to the sighting of
the buccaneers off Manta was an example of purely local initiative,
but the presence of the buccaneers certainly drew attention to the
need for proper regard for the security of Guayaquil, its shipbuilding and cacao trade, now vulnerable to attacks from the north. The
viceroy, archbishop Liñán y Cisneros, had taken the precaution of
dispatching 200 muskets and as many arquebuses, together with
three small cannon, and a defence force of 800 men had been
collected from the towns of Quito, Cuenca, Riobamba and Loja.[17]
But he had not fulfilled a crown order to investigate the means to
build a fort at Guayaquil, at no cost to the treasury, claiming that
his efforts were interrupted by the arrival of the buccaneers. He
did, however, suggest that finance might be found by placing a tax
on cacao exports from the region.[18]

Information gleaned from Argandoña would certainly have
confirmed Sharp's suspicions that he must give Guayaquil, Callao
and Lima a wide berth as a result of their military preparedness,
but the lesser ports and their shipping were not so lucky. Before
seeking these, the buccaneers managed to collect 3276 pesos in
plunder from Argandoña and his 30 companions, and obliged
them to witness an act of cruelty which Ringrose ashamedly
records. 'We also punished a friar, who was chaplain to the bark
aforementioned, and shot him upon the deck, casting him overboard before he was dead. Such cruelties, though I abhorred very

much in my heart, yet here was I forced to hold my tongue and contradict them not, as not having authority to oversway them.'[19] Amid the language of adventure and reckless courage which often accompanies tales of buccaneer deeds, this is a reminder of the type of men involved, a breed as yet unknown in the South Sea, except by report. Ruthlessly, with allegiance and care for none but themselves, and this often strained beyond breaking point, they sought quick personal gain virtually regardless of the odds and the cost.

With this typical buccaneering business done, Sharp now continued his course southwards, passing Cape Blanco (26 August) and the port of Paita (31 August). A further prize fell into their hands on 4 September off Barranca, being the *San Pedro* en route from Guayaquil to Callao with a cargo of cocoa beans, cloth and timber. After taking from her all that they required, they put some of their prisoners aboard her and set her free, taking the usual precaution of cutting down her main mast.[20] But by now it was becoming increasingly clear that something rather more rewarding than the capture of an occasional trader must be attempted, despite their small numbers. Supplies of food and water were again becoming desperately low, hence the need to be rid of some of the prisoners. Cox comments that by 20 September they were each allowed a little more than a pint of water per day and five ounces of flour. Some were prepared to pay as much as 30 pesos for an extra pint of water.

Yet it was not until they were well past Callao that they decided to venture a landing, first at Ilo on 24 October and then at Arica a day later. These efforts were abandoned due to high seas, and so it was not until 27 October that they successfully put an initial party of 48 men ashore by canoe at Ilo. Then, after overcoming the slight resistance of some 60 cavalry and infantrymen, they were able to satisfy their immediate need for supplies of fresh water, flour, oil and some fruit. During a scouting expedition inland they discovered a small sugar mill which the local inhabitants begged them not to burn, offering 80 head of cattle as a ransom. In expectation of such a welcome supply of fresh meat, Sharp was able to stay the hand of some of his more hot-headed companions, but his efforts were not duly rewarded. On 2 November the Spanish revealed that the interval had been used not for the collection of the agreed ransom, but to gather some 300 horsemen who now prepared to drive the buccaneers out of the town. Though Sharp boldly asserts that 'in a little time they had their bellies full of us',[21] it is clear that he dare not risk a major confrontation and therefore withdrew on the following day, but not before setting fire to the sugar works.

Exactly one month later a similar series of events was to be repeated at Coquimbo. An advance party of 35 men were landed on 3 December only to be confronted by 150 Spaniards. Undaunted, they resisted attack until with the help of fresh reinforcements from the *Trinity*, as Sharp puts it, 'we soone cleared the field of them',[22] and proceeded to move to La Serena. During the next four days the town was wide open to plunder, enabling Sharp and his men to sample the delights of its vineyards, gardens and orchards, which produced apples, pears, cherries, strawberries and peaches. As at Ilo, fearing for the safety of their property, the local residents again offered a ransom, this time of 95 000 pesos, to dissuade the buccaneers from setting fire to the town. But again, instead of collecting the booty they busied themselves in organising a body of armed men positioned with the intention of blocking the retreat of the buccaneers to their ship. It was only after fierce fighting that the cordon was broken and Sharp and his men regained the safety of the sea, taking with them plunder amounting to 500 lbs of silver plate and a quantity of jewels, much of which must have come from the local Jesuit and Mercedarian churches which they sacked.

For the apparent ease with which the attackers were able to gain control of La Serena on the first day, the local inhabitants won the criticism of the viceroy. 'They took possession of the place without any opposition, because the inhabitants, either because they were unskilled or scared, withdrew at the first shot they received from the adversaries.'[23] This view appears to be confirmed by an unnamed eyewitness who, while he sets himself apart from the rest, also exaggerates the odds facing them all, suggesting that the buccaneers numbered 280 men. 'One of our men fell and like people who are unskilled and undisciplined they began to swarm about and move away, with the result that not even with the abuse and threats that it is lawful to use on such occasions, could I detain them, and thus I was left merely with the principal officers.'[24] The latter clearly sounds like a local official endeavouring to excuse himself from the blame of his superiors in Lima, but the viceroy's opinion is a somewhat uncharitable response (by one never exposed to such dangers) to the plight of ordinary people in a small community facing some of the most desperate and ruthless individuals of the time.

In reality, there was at least one bold attempt to harm Sharp's party which has not gone unrecorded by the buccaneers themselves, in a note sent ashore by one Samuel Gifford.

Honored Captaine. These may informe you that the last night about a 11 or 12 a clock their was an Indian with a pare of barkeloggs made of 2 seale skinns had gott tarr, brimstone, okeham with other combustable matter and stuck it between ye rudder and ye starne post & set it on fire with a brimstone match ... but some men leapt into ye canoes and others searching about for ye fire, at length found it before it had taken on ye shipp & put it out.[25]

Following this lucky escape, Sharp set sail on 7 December heading towards the Juan Fernández Isles. Most probably his intention was to refresh his men and restock his ship before returning to the West Indies via the Straits of Magellan. This is confirmed by several of those who kept journals of the voyage. They complain that Sharp had gathered a small profit, perhaps as much as 3000 pesos or £1000 as a result of the prizes taken, the death of Sawkins and from gambling, and so was willing to go back, whereas as many as two thirds had collected very little, or lost a lot, and wished to proceed with the venture in the South Sea. John Cox, therefore, illustrates the democratic manner in which Sharp was removed from his command by the majority. 'Now our men are come to be filled with water and victualls nothing will serve their turns now but a new commander, so a party of us refractory fellows went a shoare & signed a paper to make one John Wattlin Captaine, & turne Sharp out.'[26]

Indeed, it is Cox whom Sharp himself identifies as the ringleader of this plot against him, a man he describes as 'a true hearted dissembling New England man who I for ould acquaintance sake had taken from before ye mast and made him my Vice Admiral'.[27] Evidently this is another example of the fierce rivalries that could emerge in buccaneer groups such as this, exacerbated here by the general lack of material success and by the fact that Cox and his men had been for some time sailing in the same overcrowded vessel as Sharp, the *Mayflower* having been scuttled following an accident when she was under tow. And so it was under a new leader, John Watling, that they made a rather hasty departure from these islands on 12 January 1681, when three

Spanish ships were sighted making good headway in their direction. Dispatched by the governor of Chile, they were one of several squadrons that had been seeking Sharp since July of the previous year, and had come closest of all to a direct confrontation with him.

The first and the largest had sailed from Callao on 6 July 1680, under the command of Santiago Pontejos and Pedro Zorrilla, that is just over a week after the viceroy had received news of the sea battle off Perico in April.[28] It was a fleet of eight sail composed principally of privately owned merchantmen, since the crown armada in the South Sea had been allowed to run down in recent years as a result of the reduced frequency of sailings to Panama, and the costs of maintenance. Therefore, although they carried 727 men their total armament was only 30 guns. Rather belatedly, since it was unlikely that the buccaneers would return there, they were laden with a cargo of 1000 firearms, rope, shot and powder for the defenders of Panama, and a welcome gift of 50000 pesos in aid from the merchant guild in Lima. The job of the fleet was to confront the buccaneers before they reached the heart of the viceroyalty, but failing this the viceroy full of bravado states, to prevent their 'escape' back to the West Indies. Each task was denied it, since Sharp was already on his way to careen at Gorgona Isle.

Once he had received more positive news of the arrival of Sharp off the Peruvian coast, the viceroy dispatched the crown patax, *San Lorenzo*, with 20 guns and 150 men commanded by Manuel Pantoja, to reconnoitre bays and inlets to the south of Callao, but she too was always one step behind the buccaneers, reaching Ilo after their departure. Early in January 1681, a private vessel named the *San Juan Evangelista*, under Francisco de Salazar, sailed for the Gulf of Panama on crown business to commence another search. Sharp was still in the Juan Fernández Islands. But when the southerly track was reported in Lima, early in February 1681 Diego de Barasa was sent to Valdivia to transport the year's aid for the port, with further instructions to stay in Chilean waters exploring the islands and mainland coast. By this time Sharp and his companions had taken the decision to head back northwards following an assault on Arica.

This widespread movement of ships in pursuit of intruders recalls the efforts made at the start of the century to track down the earliest Dutch arrivals. Then as now it was to be fruitless and conflicted with the need to attend to the shipment of silver to Panama. Consequently, having been recalled from the Gulf of Panama, Pontejos' flagship and a *chinchorro* were sent to Arica early in February to offer protection to the port during the loading of silver there, but yet again arriving too late to deter the latest attack. They were joined by Pantoja in the patax, which had left Callao in March to guard the shipment of mercury to Arica. Thankfully, however, from the viceroy's point of view, although still in the vicinity the buccaneers in no way troubled these operations and the silver squadron finally sailed out of harm's way in September, when Sharp was already again safely back in Chilean waters.

But to return to January 1681, having been driven northwards by the governor of Chile's squadron, the buccaneers now under Watling's command fixed their attention on a target that had tempted others, Arica. Hoping for better conditions than those which had thwarted their attempts to land on the voyage southwards, they once more prepared to mount an assault on 30 January, although the date was evidently judged to be an inauspicious one by at least one writer, 'being ye martyrdome of King Charles ye first and a fatall day to ye English to ingage on'.[29]

Unaware that they were bound for their fiercest encounter on land since entering the South Sea, approximately 90 men approached the town at 8 a.m., the plan being to divide into two groups with the respective aims of putting down resistance in the town (Watling) and storming the fort with grenades (Ringrose and Sharp). In spite of being driven from their homes to seek refuge in the fort, the *ariqueños* managed to regroup and launch a strong counter attack. This, Watling and his men resisted for four hours, but hopelessly outnumbered by a force of six or seven hundred they were ultimately left with no other choice but to undertake a costly retreat during which Watling himself was killed. Of those who had disembarked at Arica, only 47 buccaneers were left able to fight, 28 were killed and 17 or 18 were wounded. The Spaniards for their part lost 23 or 24 killed and suffered 60 casualties.[30] A number of buccaneer wounded were also abandoned in a church they had plundered, in the care of two of their surgeons. The former it is recorded were 'knocked on the head',[31] but the latter spared for their precious medical skills. And so the ferocity and the hatred which accompanied episodes such as this at Arica, and one must suppose whenever confrontations took place on land or at sea, were not exclusive to the buccaneers. In fact it is an account composed in Arica which records that one of the buccaneer captains (presumably Watling) was killed and his head carried through the town as one of the spoils of victory.[32]

The first hand accounts of some of the buccaneers convey the impression that the odds were insuperable, in some cases exaggerating the Spanish force to over 1000 men. The reality seems to have been local resolve, effectively commanded by the *maestre de campo*, Gaspar de Oviedo, and a local force of six companies of militia, five artillerymen and their guns. Reinforcements of 200 men and a further six or seven cannon transported by Pontejos' squadron, intended to offer additional security during the loading of silver, arrived two weeks too late.

Yet despite the happy outcome from the Spanish point of view, the locally written report stresses the daring and valour of the skilled buccaneers, in contrast to the fear and indiscipline of Arica's defenders.

> The enemy marched with such daring and ferocity that the cavalry, terrified and fearful, took to flight before the battle so that our infantry lacked the protection of cavalry, and leaving two of the enemy dead in the field and several wounded, withdrew to the city. The wailing of women, and of those unfit to fight, the swiftness of the flight through the hills, the commotion in the port and the general confusion, although they are normal in times of war have been all the more noticeable on this occasion for being unusual and never before seen in these parts.

The buccaneers, on the other hand, rushed at the fort 'with superhuman effort and the valour and ferocity of lions, fighting recklessly with an unnatural disdain for all risks and making light of death'.[33]

The immediate consequence of their repulse from Arica and the death of their new leader was that the buccaneers turned again to Sharp. This at once reopened the debate on whether it was opportune to return home or remain in the South Sea, whilst at the same time putting to the test those whose loyalty to Sharp had never been ungrudging. There seems to have followed a lengthy period of indecision during which they sailed southwards to Huasco and north to Ilo, landing on 13 and 28 March respectively

:o obtain fresh supplies of food and water. The uncertainty was
finally resolved at Isla de la Plata on 16 April. When a vote was
:aken the anti-Sharp group, including Dampier and Wafer, was
found to be in the minority and opted for a return to the West
Indies. Forty-four or 45 buccaneers, accompanied by three Indians,
eft the next day to make their way to the Isthmus of Panama in a
ong boat and two canoes. It was during the march overland that
Wafer suffered an injury to his knee, scorched by some gunpowder
accidentally ignited while being dried, and he was forced to remain
among the Indians of Darien. The majority reached the north coast
on 23 May and were taken aboard a French privateer in the
Samballoes on the following day.

The months of May and June were spent, by the 70 or so who
remained in the South Sea, in the vicinity of the Gulf of Nicoya and
Golfo Dulce, where they rebuilt their ship and prepared for
another foray along the Peruvian coast. On 10 July, pursuing this
intention, they found themselves off Cape San Francisco in sight of
a possible prize. When it was overhauled it proved to be the *San
Pedro*, a ship they had taken the previous year. This time the cargo
vas cacao, cloth, some silver plate, 21 000 pesos in chests and
16 000 pesos in silver coins in bags. The latter were shared out at a
basic rate of 234 pesos per man. While off Cape Pasado on 27 July
hey seized the packet boat from Panama but discovered little of
value in her. She did in fact carry a ransomable personage, Rafael
Ascona, *Alcalde de la Real Sala del Crimen*, together with his wife and
amily.[34]

Two days later a prize of greater significance was sighted, a
merchant ship, the *Santo Rosario*, en route from Callao to Panama.
Her captain, Juan López, had seen the *Trinity* but noting her
Spanish lines had taken no evasive action. By the time that he had
realised his mistake, the only recourse was to join battle in which
he and several of his crew were killed. Plunder from the ship
amounted to several hundred jars of wine and brandy and silver
coins which produced a share of 94 pesos per man, but Sharp
appears to have been attracted more to one of the *Rosario*'s
passengers. 'In this prize we took a lady of about 18 yeares of age,
her name was Dona Jonna Constanta, a very comely creature, her
husband's name was Don John the Rosario.' Ringrose too is moved
to comment on one he calls 'the most beautiful woman that I ever
saw in the South Sea'.[35] Perhaps because they were both beguiled
by the young lady's beauty, they were the victims of a remarkable

oversight, for it is reported that they failed to remove from the ship nearly 700 bars of crude silver, 'which we (such was our dullness) supposed to be tin'.[36] The error only came to light much later when part of a bar, which had been kept for the purpose of making bullets, eventually was sold for £75.

Yet there was still another prize on the *Rosario* whose value Sharp did not underestimate, a collection of Spanish maps and charts of the South Sea. Such was their significance that all reference to them was suppressed officially save in one printed account of the voyage.[37] They were also to prove to be of considerable personal importance to Sharp himself, as we shall see.

The *Rosario* incident brought to an end the most active month the buccaneers had spent since their arrival in the South Sea some 15 months ago, and was also the last significant action of Sharp's party. After a visit to Isla de la Plata in mid-August and an abortive attempt to land at Paita on the 28th of the month, they set out southwards to return to Jamaica via the Atlantic, unaware of the changed attitude towards those of their kind since their departure. They had left Jamaica during the governorship of the Earl of Carlisle who had acted negligently in furtherance of legislation aimed at suppressing the buccaneers. But he had sailed for England at the end of May 1680, bequeathing his authority to Henry Morgan as lieutenant-governor. The latter quickly demonstrated little sympathy for those whose profession he had once enjoyed, for on 1 July 1680 he issued a warrant for the arrest of Sharp and his companions, together with any individual who might have dealings with them. Ironically, the warrant referred specifically to the attack on Portobello, only a decade ago a target for Morgan himself.[38]

Still untroubled by the hostile reception that awaited them, Sharp and his men sailed homewards. Their immediate concern was a safe passage through islands off the Chilean coast amid strong winds and storms. Failing to find the entrance to the Strait early in November due to bad weather, they were forced beyond 58°S, subsequently making the first rounding of Cape Horn by Englishmen and then continuing on an easterly course, as de la Roche is supposed to have done, beyond Staten Island before turning northwards. On 5 December a final distribution was carried out of the plunder reserved thus far, and it produced a share of 328 pesos per man. Continuing northwards, Christmas

Day was celebrated in due fashion as Sharp recalls: 'This day we eat ye hogg and drunck severall jars of wine and were very merry.'[39] Remarkably, their first landfall since leaving the South Sea was Barbados, on 28 January 1682, when they were approached by a boat from the frigate *Richmond* and invited to come aboard. This they declined to do, fearing imprisonment for their recent activities. They next sought harbour at Antigua on 31 January, desperately short of food. Although the local population were eager to deal with the buccaneers, clearly hoping to gain from the booty they carried, the governor forbade them to land. Thus, it was at this point that the decision was taken to distribute what remained of the plunder and allow each man to fend for himself. Consequently, a group of seven men who had lost all their booty through gambling were given the *Trinity*, others sought safety in Jamaica, Barbados, New England and Virginia, whereas Sharp, Cox, Ringrose, and other companions sailed for England arriving at Dartmouth on 26 March 1682.

Of those who found their way to Jamaica, four fell into the hands of Henry Morgan and were dealt with as he himself relates.

One whereof surrendered himself to me, the other three I with much difficulty found out and apprehended myself, they have since been found guilty and condemned, he that surrendered himself is like as informer to obtain ye fauour of the court, one of the condemned is proued a bloody and notorious villain and fitt to make an example of, the other two as being represented to me fitt objects of mercy by the judges, I will not proceed against till his Ma[ties] further commands. [40]

A subsequent order from Charles II approved of Morgan's decisions and advised the execution of the one prisoner who seemed justly to deserve it. [41]

Sharp and his shipmates John Cox, William Dick and two others were tried on 19 May 1682 at the High Court of Admiralty at the Marshalsea, following protests from the Spanish ambassador, Pedro Ronquillo. [42] The main charges were the robbery of the *Santísima Trinidad*, the death of the captain of the *Rosario*, Juan López, piracy against the *San Pedro*, and the plundering of towns along the coast of Peru. Despite the evidence of one Simón Calderón, a native of Santiago de Chile who had been taken from the *Rosario* as a prisoner, the outcome was that none was found guilty; a decision which brought further protests from the Spanish, but to no avail. The rest of Sharp's career is not always perfectly clear, though he seems to have operated both on the wrong, and like Morgan, the right side of the law, and briefly in 1688 was governor of the island of Anguilla.

The fact that Sharp did not suffer as a result of his buccaneering in the South Sea is in no small measure due to his intelligence, quick-wittedness and powers of observation. In his journal he had amassed valuable data about Spanish possessions, identifying the important ports, their trade and the agricultural produce of nearby towns, together with the state of their defences. Clearly this information could be used on his behalf in his defence, since it was of undoubted significance for any future enterprise in the region, and therefore of national interest. But his shrewdness is best demonstrated by his preventing the tossing overboard of the maps taken from the *Rosario*, realising their great value at a time when the only charts offering practical navigational advice for the length of the South Sea coast were Spanish, and consequently jealously guarded. These maps above all else enhanced his reputation and prevented firmer action being taken by the court, for Sharp was able to persuade William Hack to copy, decorate and add an English translation for a special presentation version of the charts, which were given to Charles II under the title *A Waggoner of the Great South Sea*, after the Dutchman Wagenaer.[43]

In splendid and unfaded colours, the maps portray major and minor ports from Acapulco to the Straits of Magellan. In many cases they are accompanied by advice to anyone seeking to enter them, with notes on the availability of water, timber, fruits and other produce. For the Bay of San Mateo, however, there is added a special warning, namely, 'you must observe these two following things: first not to jest with theire women nor debauch them, secondly not to threaten any native with armes or otherwise (for they are tuchy [sic]) but treat them with humility.'

Thus was concluded the first intervention of buccaneers into the South Sea. Its importance proved to extend beyond that of a series of piratical raids, because of the information contained in the journals of participants and in the Spanish charts fortuitously seized and by good sense preserved. Rather than rendering the service of security or protection, common in the West Indies, Sharp and his companions, perhaps unintentionally, performed a useful service of knowledge which could be used to support the interests of the crown and private merchants.

Furthermore, they confirmed the possibility not only of crossing the Isthmus of Panama, but of surviving for a considerable time, though not without hardship, on provisions gathered and plundered in the South Sea. When they entered the Gulf of San Miguel, Coxon, Sawkins and Sharp had little besides the canoes and small boats in which they travelled, but almost at once occasions arose on which larger vessels could be and were commandeered as prizes, and their cargoes used either as food or to purchase food. By calling at unpopulated islands, or by making sorties on land at weakly protected ports, adequate provisions of goats, turtles, cattle, sheep, oysters, fresh fruit and water were available. Although the prizes taken were never of a legendary nature, such as those of Drake or Morgan, they were nevertheless indicative of the profits to be made from buccaneering in the South Sea.[44] That they were not so great as expected in Sharp's case was due to an error of judgement in the matter of the *Rosario*'s cargo, and to two internal weaknesses in the organisation of the group.

If we consider the sources of the plunder taken by Sharp we find that it was derived largely from attacks on shipping. The reason for this was simply that for most of the voyage along the Peruvian coast their numbers were so scanty that during any attack on a port they were in immediate danger of being outnumbered. Originally over 300 had crossed the Isthmus, but a party soon returned under the leadership of Coxon, to be closely followed by a second group after the defeat at Pueblo Nuevo, so reducing the number to 146 when Sharp assumed command and began to approach the coast of Peru for the first time. With this number further depleted by deaths and weakened by injury they entered and briefly held Ilo and La Serena, but were unable to maintain their occupation long enough to enforce the payment of ransoms when Spanish reinforcements arrived. At Arica, where the resistance of the defenders was perhaps not so determined as some buccaneer accounts suggest, they put ashore less than 100 men whose hot-blooded courage could not match a force at least six or seven times as large. Significantly, following the departure of Dampier and Wafer's group, there was only one further attempt at a landing, at Paita, and that unsuccessfully.

This weakness was of course related to a second factor which narrowed considerably the margins of success. Throughout there was a lack of permanent, effective and generally accepted leadership to unite the various factions and produce a single combined effort. Coxon, the first leader, seemed reluctant to stray far from his usual sphere of operations in the West Indies and returned there amid charges of cowardice. Sawkins was killed in his rash assault at Pueblo Nuevo and Watling suffered a similar fate at Arica. Sharp, who was leader for the greater part of the voyage, seems to have been disliked by some from the very beginning, and his election and later re-election to the position of leader caused two separate groups to desert northwards. The precise motives for this are not clear, but at the very least Sharp lay himself open to criticism and envy as a result of his luck, or skill, in acquiring money at the expense of his companions during their frequent bouts of gambling.

However, although only appreciated later by men such as Hack, Sharp displayed more than creditable navigational skills in the South Sea, especially in bringing his men home via Cape Horn non-stop to Barbados. In assessing the repercussions of Sharp's entry, Spanish documents are also quick to note that the time taken from the last attempt to land at Paita to the arrival in Barbados, a distance of 9500 miles, was exactly five months. The surprise that is expressed comes accompanied with the urgent desire to discover the route. For example, the former viceroy of Peru, the Count of Castellar, by chance encountered at Cartagena en route for Spain, one of those formerly held prisoner by the buccaneers. Following an interview with him he expressed his amazement at their navigational skills, 'for never has it been known in all the regular sailings by pilots in the South Sea to reach the Straits of Magellan in such a short time from the port of Paita'.[45]

Once they had reached the South Sea, the buccaneers enjoyed their greatest successes under the leadership of Sharp, particularly during the last phase, and there seems little evidence to support the charge of cowardice from Dampier and Wafer who deserted him. Given the nature and the temperament of the buccaneers, it is to be doubted whether anyone else could have fared better.

Sharp had not directly threatened the principal centres of population in the Viceroyalty of Peru, nor placed in danger the bullion shipments to Panama, but his mere presence in the South Sea after the isthmian crossing, for longer than any previous intruder, compelled both the viceroy and the crown to survey the effectiveness of their defences. By reaching the South Sea from the north, Sharp had achieved what Morgan's raid on Panama had promised and viceroy Lemos feared nearly a decade ago. Viceroy

Liñán y Cisneros was confronted by the fact and the reality that intruders could be expected from two opposite directions, and that ports and islands in the north could now become the first targets for attack or sites for landings, as those in Chile had long been. By this time, the notion that a force of buccaneers such as this could even briefly threaten the security of Lima and its port was beyond the bounds of credibility. Even if the wall at Callao were neglected, unrepaired and crumbling, it still housed 50 pieces of artillery and the port still enjoyed the protection of a permanent garrison of between 400 and 500 men. Moreover, worries about the English presence in the West Indies and rumours of their intentions in the South Sea throughout the 1670s, had encouraged viceroy Castellar to train and exercise his militia forces. On 22 December 1675, 'the best day Lima has had', a special muster revealed that 8433 individuals, including Indians, negroes and mulattoes, were capable of bearing arms in defence of the capital. Repeating the exercise in face of what he considered to be a threat posed by Sharp, Liñán y Cisneros discovered that 8092 were still available to him in 1680.[46]

But what was not apparently appreciated was that the irruption of the buccaneers shifted the balance of the direction of attack in the viceroyalty. It was not their aim or intention to challenge Spanish supremacy, either on their own or as an undercover instrument of the English crown, nor did they seek to create permanent enclaves or trading posts. They came to plunder Peru of its legendary wealth and to get rich quickly, even if this meant great risk to themselves. As a result, more than ever before it was the average citizen who felt the pressures and experienced the fear – as owner or captain of a captured coastal trading ship, as a member of the crew held for ransom, as a defender of one of the lesser ports where the buccaneers need not fear that they could be overwhelmed by the advantage of sheer numbers, as owner of property, a business or farm in those coastal settlements. While Lima and Callao might be secure, the viceroyalty lacked the resources and the foresight to attend to these needs. Hence merchant ships were easy prey, and towns such as Ilo or even the strategically important Portobello were overrun. State and church were not immune, of course, to these raids, for the properties of both offered likely prospects of plunder, encouraged by nationalistic and religious rivalry. But the challenge to these occurred again in locations remote from the capital, where the consequences of Sharp's intrusion had to be faced by a local response.

The arrival of the buccaneers from the north, then, meant that existing resources were stretched further, with a resultant loss of overall effectiveness. For example, in addition to the patax *San Lorenzo*, the crown armada was now reduced to only two galleons of 825 tons. All of them had been built a long time ago, in fact on the orders of the viceroy, the Count of Alba de Liste, in the latter half of the 1650s. The galleons exceeded by their size the norms prescribed by the crown for such vessels in the South Sea (400–500 tons), following the experience with Mancera's 1000 tonners, which had proved costly to maintain and one of which had run aground in 1654 amid charges of unmanoeuvrability.[47] Viceroy Liñán y Cisneros seems to have inherited a squadron that was old and whose galleons, already once modified, needed further repairs and careening.

Therefore, when Sharp ventured into the South Sea the old galleons were under repair, and with the exception of the *San Lorenzo* the viceroy had no other alternative but to rely on hastily armed merchantmen. It is likely that only one of these, the *San Juan Evangelista*, which he had sent to Panama in January 1681, could have been easily converted for its new role. This was thanks to a prudent move by the Count of Castellar. In August 1676 he had received royal sanction for his plan to introduce procedures to ensure that merchant vessels built at Guayaquil should be capable of performing a military role. In exchange for positions as *corregidores*, the future owners of the *San Juan*, then under construction, agreed it should be built as a frigate of war, though remaining under private ownership.[48] Contributions to maritime defence by the merchant community of Lima and Callao was a trend viceroys would need to resort to increasingly during later buccaneer intrusions.

With these facts, it is readily understandable why the Peruvian armada, still theoretically the first line of defence, was unable to convey aid in time to ports in danger, to confront the buccaneers at sea or offer protection to coastal traders. Sharp again posed the old dilemma of whether expenditure should be authorised in expectation of others to follow, and if so whether this should be designated for warships, or arms and fortifications. Moreover, he created the new quandary of not knowing for sure from which direction a new invasion might come. His entry had, of course, been costly. One estimate claims that 200 Spaniards died, 25 ships were destroyed and damage worth four million pesos inflicted.[49] The cost of fitting out and arming the vessels used in the operations against Sharp, and in providing rations for soldiers and sailors, was put at 234 566 pesos by viceroy Liñán y Cisneros.[50] And so, after a decade's delay, when Henry (now Sir Henry) Morgan was playing a different game, the feared consequences of his crossing of the Isthmus of Panama were beginning to be realised.

# 7

# English and French Buccaneers: The Second Wave (1684–9)

The first successors of Henry Morgan's crossing of the Isthmus of Panama were relatively few in number for most of their operations off the coasts of Peru, but the years from 1684 to 1689 were to find the South Sea invaded by more intruders than at any time since the Nassau Fleet. Their origins were diverse but their attraction to Peru was a common one, namely the aim of acquiring some portion of the wealth of the region, whether it be through trade or buccaneering. They sailed, therefore, in pursuit of their own personal enrichment or that of their private backers. They were John Cook whose voyage started in Virginia, John Eaton and Charles Swan who embarked in London, and several groups of buccaneers who followed the route pioneered by Sharp and company at the eastern end of the Isthmus. Those setting out from London represent a further stage in the fitful fascination of the English with Peru, re-established by Narborough but more vividly revived by the return of Sharp and friends to London and their subsequent trial. The buccaneers found their way there in a climate of increasing opposition to their lifestyle in the West Indies.[1]

The year 1682 saw the reappointment of governor Lynch in Jamaica and the recommencement of stricter enforcement of legislation for their suppression, aided by an inclination among some settlers to consider the buccaneers a hindrance to the development of the local economy. Lynch could never have hoped realistically for total suppression, for there were too many on the island who for long had been accustomed to the profits of illegal trading with the Spanish and privateering against them. But the tide had turned and was already flushing some out of their old haunts towards new spheres of operations. Moreover, those who chose to try and swim against it, found from 1684 that they could no longer rely on the dubious legality of a French commission. For in that year the French governor of St Domingue, de Pouançay, was replaced by Tarin de Cussy bearing instructions to cease the granting of commissions. It can be no coincidence that so many of the buccaneers in this second phase of their entry into the South Sea were French.

The starting point for this new period of buccaneering was the abandonment by Dampier, Wafer and others of the Sharp expedition in April 1681. Guided by one John Cook, they had quickly established contact with buccaneers in the Caribbean and were eventually joined by Wafer, following his recovery from the gunpowder accident and his four months sojourn among the Indians. There followed a spell of rather aimless activity and much wrangling with new companions, but in April 1683 Dampier, Wafer and Cook were all reunited in Virginia where they began to plan a return to Peru via the southern route in Cook's ship, the *Revenge*.[2] Two other notable participants in the future enterprise also enlisted at this early stage. They were Edward Davis, who had accompanied Dampier and Cook during the return across the Isthmus in 1681, and a newcomer, William Ambrose Cowley, who was to keep a journal of the voyage and who signed on as navigator. The latter, however, wishing to set himself apart from any responsibility for future actions, claims that his objectives were more limited. 'I not knowing better but that wee were bound for the Island of Potigawoos [Petit Goâve], for I was hired by the Captaine for five hundred peices [*sic*] of Eight to carry the ship thither and no where else.'[3]

The *Revenge*, with her crew of 70 men and armament of 18 guns, left Chesapeake Bay on 23 August bound for the Cape Verde Islands, but it soon was apparent that a vessel of greater strength and seaworthiness would be required for the passage into the South Sea. Therefore, on arrival off the African coast their activities were directed principally towards this end. It was in November, off the Guinea coast, that the ideal vessel presented herself, armed with 36 guns and well provisioned for a lengthy voyage. However her capture, completely ignored by Dampier, was nothing short of piracy, for the ship was of Danish origin and in no sense could the buccaneers' dubious commissions be claimed to extend to hostilities against ships of that nation.

A little further along the coast near Sherbro the *Revenge* was burnt, 'by reason she should tell no tales', according to Cowley.[4] Perhaps, however, she was merely exchanged for 60 negro girls

taken aboard their new Danish prize, appropriately renamed the
*Bachelor's Delight*.[5] Their spirits doubtlessly raised by companion
ship that was to last until the cold climate of the South Atlantic
took its toll, the party headed for the passage into the South Sea in
November. Their route brought a sighting of the Sibbel de Ward
(Seebald de Weert Islands) on 28 January 1684,[6] and simultaneously
a report of 'great shoals of small lobsters, which coloured the sea in
red spots', an echo of the same phenomenon recorded by the
Mahu–Cordes expedition 80 years previously. They passed to the
east of Staten Island on 7 February, emerging into the South Sea
from Cape Horn about one month later, less than four months after
leaving the coast of Africa.

Their first encounter in the South Sea was of an unexpected
nature. It occurred on 19 March in the vicinity of Valdivia, when
glimpsing a sail ahead of them, they at once gave chase on the
assumption that she was of Spanish origin, but on closing
discovered her to be the *Nicholas* out of London, under the
command of John Eaton. She had been fitted out privately for a
piratical cruise under the pretence of trading intentions. The trail of
destruction left along the Brazilian coast and in the estuary of the
River Plate, and the capture of a Portuguese prize, since lost in a
storm, testify to the real purpose of the *Nicholas*. Nor was she
alone, for her captain, Eaton, was to give news of a second English
ship in the vicinity, also from London, which he had met at the
entrance to the Straits of Magellan and then lost during bad
weather. She was the *Cygnet* under the command of Charles Swan
with a crew of 60 men, armament of 16 guns and a cargo of trading
goods worth £5000. No stranger to the New World, Swan had been
with Henry Morgan at Panama, and some twelve years later his
interest in the region was re-awoken by his acquaintance in
London with Basil Ringrose, whose account of the Sharp voyage
had claimed great attention. After swapping experiences the two
had decided to pool their knowledge in a new venture, and to
protect his financial investment in the *Cygnet*'s cargo, Ringrose had
decided to sail in her and thus renew his acquaintance with the
South Sea. However, for the time being, her exact whereabouts
was unknown to Eaton and Cook.

Having taken the decision to join forces, Cook and Eaton sailed
for the Juan Fernández Islands, with which several of them were
familiar from their visit with Sharp. They were pleased to be
greeted by a former colleague, a Mosquito Indian called William,

left behind when Sharp's company (then briefly led by Watling) had been forced to make a hurried departure from the islands in January 1681. Since that time, as the original Robinson Crusoe, he had lived alone, cutting up his gun barrel to fashion it into a saw, fishhooks, a harpoon and a knife.[7] His diet had consisted of the fresh supplies that Cook and Eaton now sought, mainly fish, goats and their milk, and herbs.

It was only on 8 April, after attention had been given by the surgeons to those suffering from scurvy and refreshment sought by all, that the two ships put to sea once more. Their course had apparently already been the subject of some discussion, with some favouring an assault on an important town such as Arica, while others preferred action at sea in the north of the viceroyalty, lying in wait for a treasure ship bound for Panama. Cowley expresses his disappointment that the latter proposal won the day, lamenting the loss of a supposed prize, the sort that had lured them into the South Sea. 'But had we gone into Arica wee had loaded our Shipps with money and piggs of silver, for there was a ship att that time loading of silver and was near loaded when wee were there as wee understood afterwards by prisoners that wee taken.'[8]

Sailing northwards, then, at a good distance from the land so as not to warn the Spaniards of their presence, they took their first prize on 3 May. She was a vessel of little value to them, carrying a cargo of timber from Guayaquil to Lima, but from her crew Cook and Eaton learned the unwelcome news that despite their precautions the whole coast was alerted to their presence, as a result of news recently dispatched from Chile to Lima. One cause of this alarm was Swan, who had openly sailed into the port of Valdivia, in the manner of Narborough, in the hope of trading peacefully, while Cook and Eaton were refreshing in the Juan Fernández Islands. Perhaps in an attempt to gain favour, he had warned of the presence of other Englishmen with less peaceful intentions, but again like Narborough lost a number of men as prisoners to the Spanish. He failed completely, then, to stimulate any commerce, and as a result of his action Peruvian ports were closed, defences manned and provisions and articles of value withdrawn inland.

During the coming period of a little over a month, as Cook and Eaton continued to keep company, their actions were governed by a number of important factors. First, although they maintained their chosen northerly course, it was recognised that it was now unlikely that any treasure ship would put to sea. A second implication of the news that the coast of Peru was alerted to their presence was the realisation that they must avoid unnecessary contact with the mainland. Therefore, when they wished to clean and repair the ships they anchored at the islands of Lobos de Afuera (9–19 May). This decision was further dictated by a factor which had also affected their buccaneer predecessors in the South Sea. They numbered only 108 fit men, and one of their captains, Cook, was already sick. Their one piece of good luck at this time came on 18 May, when three sails were sighted and eventually overhauled. They proved to be carrying mainly cargoes of flour, being dispatched by the viceroy to Panama to prevent supplies there running short in the event of a prolonged interruption to trade. Other miscellaneous items aboard these vessels, seven or eight tons of quince marmalade, an image of the Virgin Mary carved in wood to adorn a new church in Panama, a letter containing further news of 'enemies lately come into that sea', and to quote Dampier, a 'stately mule' for the president of Panama – constituted plunder of somewhat mixed and dubious appeal, but the value of the flour was at once appreciated.[9] This is indicated by a shift of course towards the Galapagos Islands, even more remote from the danger of Spanish attack, and a site they had selected in which to unload their prizes and lay up the flour in store as a reserve for possible future emergencies.

While most seem to have been engaged from 31 May on unloading the packs of flour, Cowley busied himself on what must have been the earliest survey of those islands, noting harbours and bays and ascribing to them and the islands themselves the names of famous living persons in England.[10] Dampier too, as whenever there was a pause in buccaneering action, fills the pages of his journal with descriptions of his surroundings, in this case the characteristics of land and sea turtles, the latter 'so sweet that no pullet eats more pleasantly'. With the important manual labour complete, they now headed north for the coast of New Spain on 12 June, hoping that news of their presence had not yet progressed so far since they had intercepted at least one dispatch with that objective. Sadly, as they approached Nicoya with the expectation of gaining fresh supplies of beef, Captain Cook died, his place being taken with common consent by Edward Davis.

Effectively at this point the partnership of the *Bachelor's Delight* and the *Nicholas* was ended due to friction between the two crews, reportedly caused by Davis' insistence that his men should have the major share of any future booty since they possessed the better ship, the *Bachelor's Delight*. The journalist Cowley on this occasion elected to join Eaton in the *Nicholas*, 'to be ridd of my slavery, I having brought that shipp and the other which they burned from Virginia into these seas without the assistance of a mate'.[11] In fact, after spending the month of August refreshing and careening on the coast of New Spain, both ships sailed independently for the coast of Peru and anchored in close proximity at Isla de la Plata on 21 September. But after failing to win a ransom for two prizes containing negro slaves and a cargo of sugar off Paita, Eaton finally headed out across the Pacific where his crew disbanded. Both he and Cowley returned to England, the latter reaching London on 14 October 1686.

Despite being numerically weakened by the departure of Eaton, Davis approached land at Santa Elena and Manta in search of supplies. Both sorties were unfruitful and discouraging, for he discovered that the Spanish had begun to implement a policy they would use extensively against the buccaneers, having persuaded the local Indian population to withdraw stores of food inland, destroy crops under cultivation and burn boats to prevent them falling into enemy hands. Dampier, nevertheless, still found topics to exercise his pen, for though unimpressed by the general barrenness of the area, he was fascinated by tar bubbling from natural springs, important to the nearby shipbuilding industry, and further recorded the sinking of a rich treasure ship in the vicinity. The chance of locating sunken silver would soon attract John Strong to this region.

Having returned to Isla de la Plata, the prospects for Davis and his crew seemed improved when they were joined on 2 October by Charles Swan in the *Cygnet*. Moreover, he was not alone, for after his failure at Valdivia he too had progressed as far north as the Gulf of Nicoya, where the future nature of his venture was transformed by an encounter with Peter Harris (nephew of the Peter Harris who had accompanied Sawkins and Sharp), and a party of buccaneers who had recently crossed to the South Sea. Being fewer than 100 in number, they had left Jamaica in January 1684 to follow the path of Sharp's crossing of the Isthmus, seized a booty of gold at Santa María, fought a force of five vessels sent out against them off the Pearl Islands on 21 July, and finally met up with Swan on 3 August.[12]

As a result of the encounter with Davis, Swan abandoned any

further hope of trading and threw in his lot reluctantly, and he claims under coercion, with the buccaneers, selling off some of his cargo to them but keeping the silks and muslins. His agreement with them also accepted that ten shares of any prize taken were to be reserved for his owners in London, whose investment he earnestly strove to defend.

Assure my employers that I do all I can to preserve their interests, and that what I do now I could in no wise prevent. So desire them to do all they can with the king for me, for as soon as I can I shall deliver myself to the king's justice, and I had rather die than live skulking like a vagabond for fear of death. The king might make this whole kingdom of Peru tributary to him in two years time but now I cannot tell but it may bring me to a halter.[13]

Leaving Isla de la Plata on 20 October, despite their increased strength, something closer to 200 men, the combined force of Davis, Swan and Harris were still to be indifferently rewarded for their efforts during the remainder of 1684. A warning from a captured Guayaquil timber ship that the viceroy was planning to send out a fleet of 10 sail against them, did not dissuade them from plans to raid the mainland, returning to the islands to recuperate. A landing was made at Paita on the morning of 3 November, nothing of value nor of use acquired, and since demands for a ransom were not met, what Dampier describes as 75 or 80 low and poorly built houses were set on fire. Then, early in December, during difficult progress through marshes and mangroves towards Guayaquil, a captured Indian guide effected his escape thereby frustrating their intended surprise attack. Moreover, whereas in the interval between these two episodes they had sought refuge at the Lobos Isles, where Swan encouraged his own men to partake of the food at hand, 'comparing the Seal to a roasting pig, Boobies to Hens, and the Penguins to Ducks',[14] following their return to the favourite haunt of Isla de la Plata after the Guayaquil incident, they were dismayed to find that the usual stocks of goats had been destroyed on orders from Lima.

Some slight recompense for their exertions was the seizure off Guayaquil of a vessel carrying Quito cloth to Lima, and later three others bearing 1000 negro slaves, men and women, 14 or 15 of whom were added to the buccaneer crews.[15] These prizes furnished Dampier with material with which to speculate on the wealth and opportunities that still beckoned. His introduction to Guayaquil commences with a description of the port's trade (cacao, wollen cloth, hides, tallow and sarsaparilla), but more significantly alludes to its links with Quito, 'the place in all the Kingdom of Peru that abounds most' in gold. Having been denied the chance to put this to the test, even more remarkably he discloses a plan to transport the newly captured negroes to Darien, where they could be employed in the gold workings at Santa María. The project envisaged the fortification of the mouth of the river, 'so that if all the strength the Spaniards have in Peru had come against us, we could have kept them out', and the export of gold dust and the import of necessary supplies via buccaneering allies on the north coast of the Isthmus. He concludes, 'we might have been Masters not only of those Mines . . . but of all the Coast as high as Quito.' These were, as Dampier himself rightly states, 'but Golden Dreams' of the sort that enticed men to Peru.[16]

The reality was their realisation that their options in terms of attacks against the Spanish were still limited by their numbers and firepower, as proved by their having sent out a bark in the vain hope of finding Eaton and persuading him to rejoin them. To remedy this weakness it was decided to steer for the Gulf of Panama. Two further reasons contributed to this decision. First, they already suspected correctly that fresh arrivals of buccaneers were making their way across the Isthmus. And secondly, as they were sailing northwards at the end of December, off Gallo Island they took a packet boat en route from Panama to Callao. Packets of letters tossed overboard were quickly retrieved and yielded a further incentive, the news that the galleons from Spain were already at Portobello and a request that the Peruvian silver fleet should put to sea at once. As they 'jogged on' towards the Pearl Islands to careen and lie in wait, another small prize, the *Santa Rosa* of 90 tons, fell into their hands on 8 January 1685, with the result that the buccaneer force was now in possession of six vessels, the *Bachelor's Delight* and the *Cygnet*, two tenders, a fireship and their most recent acquisition.

The period from February to April was passed awaiting the fruition of these two reasons for their having chosen to head north once again. It saw the gathering of a formidable assembly of buccaneers, and their formulation of a detailed strategy to confront the expected Peruvian armada. The first to arrive, on 14 February, were Captain François Grogniet and Captain Lescuyer, leading a

party of 200 Frenchmen and 80 Englishmen in canoes. Grogniet
and the French were offered the *Santa Rosa*, while the English were
accommodated on board the *Cygnet* and *Bachelor's Delight*. To
repay the gift, Grogniet presented Swan and Davis with blank
French commissions issued by the governor of Petit Goâve.
Dampier explains:

> It hath been usual for many Years past, for the Governour of
> Petit Guavres to send blank Commissions to Sea by many of his
> Captains, with Orders to dispose of them to whom they saw
> convenient. Those of Petit Guavres by this means making
> themselves the Sanctuary and Asylum of all People of desperate
> Fortunes: and increasing their own Wealth, and the Strength
> and Reputation of their Party thereby.[17]

Davis readily accepted the offer to replace the commission he had
inherited from Cook, already secondhand in the latter's possession.
Swan, however, desperately clinging to the last strands of legality,
declined commenting that:

> he had an order from the Duke of York, neither to give offence to
> the Spaniards, nor to receive any affront from them; and that he
> had been injured by them at Baldivia, where they had kill'd
> some of his men, and wounded several more; so that he thought
> he had a lawful Commission of his own to right himself.[18]

Since Grogniet had also brought the good news that another
group of buccaneers was engaged in crossing the Isthmus at that
moment, a party was sent to await them in the Gulf of San Miguel.
On 3 March they met Captain Townley with a group of 180 men,
mostly English, in two captured barks. On 11 April a further band
of mainly French buccaneers completed the crossing. They were
264 men under the leadership of captains Rose, Le Picard and
Desmarais, and included the more famous Raveneau de Lussan
who has left us a detailed account of his travels.[19] In the meantime,
a bark bearing about a dozen Englishmen had entered the Gulf of
Panama from the west, having separated from a party led by
Captain William Knight who for the time being remained off the
coast of New Spain.

Therefore, after some reorganisation and removal from one ship
to another, the buccaneer fleet shortly before the attempt to seize

the silver squadron from Peru was composed of 960 men, distributed as follows:

| Command | Vessel | Guns | Men |
|---|---|---|---|
| Davis (admiral) | *Bachelor's Delight* | 36 | 156 |
| Swan (vice-admiral) | *Cygnet* | 16 | 140 |
| Grogniet (rear-admiral) | *Santa Rosa* | | 308 |
| Townley | | | 110 |
| Harris (Knight's bark) | | | 100 |
| Townley's bark | | | 80 |
| Branly's bark | | | 36 |
| Davis' tender | | | 8 |
| Swan's tender | | | 8 |
| Fireship | | | 14 |

Although this fleet represented a formidable challenge in terms of the numbers of men it carried, there was an obvious weakness in that only two vessels were of medium size, bearing guns, the remainder being small, coastal craft.[20]

Since their arrival in the South Sea a little over a year ago, that is early in 1684, Davis, and Swan had never been deliberately challenged at sea by ships armed and fitted out for this specific purpose. And so they had been able to wander freely to New Spain, return southwards to the Lobos Islands and head northwards again to their present location near the Gulf of San Miguel, now much strengthened in numbers. This was because the viceroy, the Duke of La Palata, at first had found himself powerless to react offensively, and then lacking the support to do so, despite being kept regularly informed of the buccaneers' movements.[21] His first public announcement of foreign ships in southern waters came on 12 March 1684, following a report from the governor of Chile, José de Garro, of sightings of three or four vessels on 10 February close to Mocha. This was followed by news of contact with a ship putting in to Valdivia on 2 April, claiming to be a merchantman en route to trading factories. Obviously this was Swan. The usual procedures were at once enacted, namely the calling up of men for service in Callao, the exercising of cavalry and infantry, the distribution of warnings along the coast, and the posting of lookouts. But the duke's main worry was that he had no forces available to offer a challenge at sea, hence the freedom to roam the buccaneers had enjoyed for over a year.

The crown squadron which he had inherited was the same as that proved to be unsatisfactory at the time of the Sharp intrusion, namely the two galleons built by viceroy Alba, the *San José* and the *Nuestra Señora de Guadalupe*, plus the patax *San Lorenzo*.[22] Although repairs had been carried out by viceroy Liñán y Cisneros, the three ships had returned from Panama in 1682 in need of further repairs and refitting. The *capitana*, for example, lacked a rudder and her hull was seriously damaged by shipworm, a common problem with vessels returning from Panama. But the work had proved impossible in Callao because of the shortage of wood and other materials. Therefore, the decision was taken to send the patax to Guayaquil on 26 July 1683, so that she could be careened there and then return with the required timber and other items to enable work to commence on the galleons at Callao. In practice the repairs to the *San Lorenzo* lasted about 11 months, so that the ship did not return to her home port until June 1684, almost totally rebuilt. Consequently, although viceroy Palata reports that work had started on the *capitana* (*San José*) on 22 March and on the *almiranta* (*Guadalupe*) on 10 April, it was not until the return of the *San Lorenzo* that substantial repairs could be completed. This work lasted until 23 September, during which time Davis and Eaton had proceeded to New Spain and back to the Isla de la Plata.

Unfortunately, by the time that the crown squadron was in seaworthy condition there were other problems to solve. The first was the usual dilemma of whether it should be used to try to rid the South Sea of buccaneers, or else to carry the next silver shipment to Panama. The latter was becoming urgent since the viceroy had already received instructions by a crown dispatch of 13 February 1684 that the galleons would sail from Spain in August that year. Since he estimated that a thorough search of the coasts to the north and south from Callao would take nine months, using the few ships available to him, and then assuming no contact was made, the proposal to do so was untenable in view of the expected arrival of the galleons. For the crown would not tolerate their delay on the Isthmus of Panama, exposing the vessels to deterioration, the crews to disease and the crown itself to the possible loss of a silver shipment from Peru.

However the alternative, the immediate transport of crown and private silver to Panama encountered an immovable stumbling block, the unwillingness of the merchant community to participate while the buccaneers were at large. Discussions between the viceroy, his advisers and the merchants were long and obviously bitter, with the viceroy talking about 'obstinacy and stupidity born of fear', and making the general observation that the problem in Peru was that 'everyone wants to be in charge and they all want to be in charge of the viceroy'.[23] He does, nevertheless, find one strong defender who contrasts the 'weak imaginings of the many' with the viceroy's 'unfailing and matchless moderation, stout, sound, zealous and unyielding heart'.[24] In the end his determination almost paid off, when supported by the news on 3 March 1685 that the galleons had indeed arrived on the previous 28 November. With the promise that the silver armada would leave, further reinforced by arming three private ships, the merchants seem to have come close to having been convinced that it would be to their detriment not to be involved. Then additional reports reached Lima of the recent arrivals of fresh groups of buccaneers, joining their companions in the Gulf of Panama. This shattered any hope that Palata had come to cherish concerning the departure of a full silver fleet.

Therefore, the squadron which finally left Callao on 7 May 1685 carried supplies of flour and other foodstuffs, arms and men to strengthen the defences of Panama, together with a small amount of private silver and the crown quota amounting to 533 434 pesos. It was still a tempting target. The commanders were Tomás Palavicino, brother in law of the viceroy, and two individuals who had already gained experience in the pursuit of intruders, Antonio de Vea and Santiago Pontejos. Its composition was as follows:

| Vessels | Tons | Guns |
|---|---|---|
| *Crown ships* | | |
| San José (galleon) | 825 | 24 |
| Nuestra Señora de Guadalupe (galleon) | 825 | 24 |
| San Lorenzo (patax) | 80 | 20 |
| small tender | | 6 |
| *Privately owned* | | |
| Pópulo | | 20 |
| Rosario | | 20 |
| 1 fireship | | 6 |

A total of 1431 men were enlisted, all paid in advance for eight months service.[25] They were soon to prove a measure of truth in the viceroy's boast that the buccaneers 'are pirates who do not

come to fight for their honour, but to benefit from furtive opportunities and flee from those which may entail risk'.[26]

By early May 1685, the buccaneers' vigil in the waters between
Panama, the Pearl Islands and the Gulf of San Miguel must have
become tedious, the monotony relieved only by chasing the odd
trader trying to run their blockade and by mounting a canoe-borne
expedition to Chepo. But as the morning rain cleared on the 28th of
the month, they caught sight, off Pacheca Island, of the fleet that had
united them with a common purpose. What they did not realise was
that by carefully and intentionally following a more westerly course
than was usual, the armada had already eluded them and un-loaded
its valuable cargo. After taking on fresh reinforcements, it had set sail
again with the single aim of driving the intruders from the South Sea.

During the months of relative idleness, the buccaneers had
formulated a plan whereby Grogniet would support Davis in his
attack on the Peruvian flagship, and Townley would back Swan
against the vice-admiral. When the time came, however, it proved
impossible, for on the first day Grogniet found himself so far away
from the rest that he was unable, or unwilling, to lend assistance.
Action, therefore, was reduced to an ineffective exchange of shot
from a distance. That night the Spanish commander employed a
stratagem of extinguishing and rekindling lights on his flagship
and other craft which induced the buccaneers into believing that he
had changed station. Consequently, on the next morning, whereas
the Spanish force was in good battle order, the buccaneers seem to
have been somewhat scattered as a result of the confusion. A
running fight ensued with the buccaneers being chased around the
Gulf of Panama, and ending with their flight to the safety of Coiba
Isle in the west. Though they were merely driven out of the gulf, as
viceroy Palata had forecast, being unprepared to face up to unfavourable odds in terms of guns, the Spanish claimed their flight as a
victory and were content with that.

Dampier, on the other hand, expresses the bitter disappointment which he and his companions felt at the failure of a project
which had for so long dominated their lives.

> Thus ended this days work, and with it all that we had been
> projecting for five or six months: when instead of making
> ourselves Masters of the Spanish Fleet and Treasure, we were
> glad to escape them; and owed that too, in a great measure, to
> their want of courage to pursue their advantage.[27]

De Lussan, however, prefers to console himself with what might have happened.

> If we had met up with the fleet, as we had hoped, before it had been reinforced in Panama, or if we had simply gained the wind over it when we were attacked, I do not doubt that things would have looked rather different, and that we would have taken some of their ships to return in them through the Straits with sufficient riches to place us at our ease. [28]

But these expressions of disillusionment in no way matched the deep despair soon to be felt in Lima. On 4 September it was reported that the military aid and silver had been safely delivered to Panama and the buccaneers subsequently routed. This caused a popular outburst of rejoicing and jubilation. There was a general air of celebration and a *Te Deum* was sung in the cathedral, all of which served to disguise the fact that the armada had really failed to follow up its gaining of the upper hand by not pursuing the buccaneers. Worse than this, on 19 September the news began to circulate that the *San José*, on her return voyage, had suffered an explosion and fire in the port of Paita two weeks previously. Palavicino had escaped injury by being ashore due to illness, but 241 persons died, including Santiago Pontejos. [29]

As for the buccaneers, the unexpected culmination of their carefully laid plans became the source of friction and discontent, which initially was to stimulate Anglo-French rivalries, with each party seeking to lay the blame on the other. The English, for example, criticised Grogniet for having failed to take a decisive part in the recent encounter. 'As for Gronet, he said his Men would not suffer him to join us in the Fight: but we were not satisfied with that excuse; so we suffered him to go with us to the Isle of Quiboa, and there chashier'd our cowardly Companion.' [30] But certainly there had been some fault of overall leadership which had failed to detect the first approach of the Peruvian squadron to Panama, and then was easily duped on the first night of the engagement.

The tension between the English and the French reached breaking point after the failure of a joint force to win fresh supplies from an attack on Pueblo Nuevo on the coast of New Spain, during the third week of June. The French had two major criticisms, according to Raveneau de Lussan, which point to religious as well as nationalistic motivations for their rivalry. Since there were more Englishmen, they tried to make themselves masters of the affairs of the fleet, but more than this they upset the French by a lack of respect for religious objects. 'For when they entered churches they had no scruples about cutting the arms off crucifixes with their sabres, and shooting them with their guns and pistols, with these same firearms breaking and mutilating the images of saints, and mocking the fact that we Frenchmen worshipped them.'[31]

And so a mainly English party of Davis, Swan and Townley set sail to follow an independent course, having been joined also by William Knight with a crew of 40 Englishmen and 11 Frenchmen, of whose existence in the South Sea they had been aware for some time. In all they were about 640 men in eight ships, but despite destructive attacks against Realejo and León during the first two weeks of August, there were few financial rewards.[32] Eventually the continuing disappointment prompted a division within the English group, with Swan and Townley (12 barks and 340 men) preferring to remain on the coast of New Spain, believing that there were gold and silver mines close to the coast which they might raid, and tempted by the prospect of intercepting the Manila galleon. When neither of these goals had been achieved by the New Year, 1686, Swan concluded that he would rather head for the East Indies. He died in what was possibly an arranged accident on Mindanao, but the *Cygnet* continued to Madagascar, where she proved to be completely unseaworthy. Dampier, who had transferred to the *Cygnet* to join Swan on the coast of New Spain, finally returned to England on 16 September 1691. Less fortunate was his former shipmate Ringrose, who was killed in an ambush in February 1686, that is before they had abandoned the coast of New Spain. Davis, however, was by now attracted again to the coast of Peru by the news which Knight had brought, probably from the crew of a prize he had taken off Guayaquil and in which he now sailed, that only half the bullion had been embarked in the recent armada, and that all the merchant ships which should have accompanied it lay fully laden at Paita.

During 1686 it is increasingly difficult to plot with certainty the tracks of those who remained in the South Sea, but fortunately we are able to utilise Spanish records of their activities which clarify details or fill in gaps in the English and French accounts.[33] Following Swan's departure early that year, there were basically three groups still active in the South Sea: the original band which had set out from Virginia, now under the command of Edward

Davis and including Harris and Knight, Frenchmen under the leadership of Grogniet, and the Englishmen led by Townley. In all they still numbered over 600 men. It is the first of these, little more than 250 men, who were to hold the entire coast of the Viceroyalty of Peru in a state of alert and trepidation throughout 1686. Before doing so they were detained in the Gulf of Amapala during the first weeks of September 1685, while some struggled to overcome what Wafer calls 'spotted fever', refreshed on coconuts at Cocos Isle, from where Harris possibly departed in turn for the East Indies,[34] and then headed for the Galapagos Islands in order to take aboard several hundred packs of the flour they had judiciously stored there in company with Eaton.

Although glimpsed for the first time attempting to land at Huanchaco close to the important city of Trujillo, at the end of February 1686, they were frustrated most probably by hostile weather and conditions, and renounced the idea. During the remainder of the first half of the year, their assaults were directed mainly at the smaller settlements along the coastline north of Callao. Saña was the first to suffer the effects of this new phase of Davis' operations during the first few days of March. The hamlet was ransacked and a booty of 300 000 pesos in jewels, silver coin and plate collected, together with 400 jars of wine and a quantity of indigo. The clergy and other non-combatants had already sought refuge inland before the buccaneers arrived in response to warnings from Lima, but those who remained – a defence force of 130 militia on foot and horseback – were no match for over 200 buccaneers who landed at Chérrepe, a few leagues distant, and were unopposed as they marched over sands and through exposed country. Nor was access to Saña itself denied them by destroying its wooden bridge. With the plunder complete, on 6 March, Davis and his men withdrew to the Indian village of Motupe to await a reply to the ransom demand for 50 000 pesos, 'with the same safety as if they were in England'.[35] However, this latter attempt to enrich themselves failed, and they set sail on 15 March before reinforcements could arrive from Trujillo.

On 21 March it was again the turn of Paita, where bales of cloth were broken open and sold off cheaply to Indians, and Indian women raped. Two prizes were also taken – the *Nuestra Señora de Aranzazu* with a cargo of sugar and arms, and a frigate from Panama with a cargo of 350 negroes, 39 of whom were taken aboard the *Bachelor's Delight* to augment her crew. The *Aranzazu* was incorporated into the buccaneer fleet and participated in later raids, although on occasions she may have acted independently of Davis. These exertions were followed by a period of rest at Colán until 6 April. Although the reasons are not explicitly stated, Richard Arnold and 38 companions abandoned Davis at this point to return to the West Indies. He reports that some 250 men remained loyal to his former leader, and hence mounted the coming attacks on Huacho, Huaura, Chancay, Huarmey and Casma, where stories of buccaneer greed and brutality ceased to be matters of rumour and were translated into a vivid and terrifying reality.[36]

On 14 May, off Huacho, they overhauled, retained and crewed the *Nuestra Señora de la Asunción*, out of Chancay for a cargo of guano, and then entered and burnt the town.[37] A second possible prize eluded them, but only after being run aground on rocks off Huaura with the loss of her cargo of wine, brandy and flour. This town too was taken by a mere 50 buccaneers who ransacked its churches for plunder. According to the Provincial of the Franciscans, Diego Felipe de Cuéllar, they selected, by casting lots, a priest named Francisco Fernández and later shot him in his own church as a reprisal against the clergy in general who had refused to reveal the whereabouts of valuable sacred objects. The eminent Franciscan also describes the scene he witnessed during a routine visit of his province. 'I found it [Huaura] desolate, the houses closed and the inhabitants in the hills, since the pirates had only recently sacked it, and although I have tried to encourage them to return to their homes, I have achieved very little, such is the fear that burdens them.'[38] A different source informs us that in the same raid the buccaneers captured the *alcalde provincial*, Blas de la Carrera, and slit his throat when his ransom was not paid.[39]

At Chancay, negotiations with a local resident for the payment of a ransom of 8000 pesos to secure the release of prisoners, were interrupted by the arrival of reinforcements from Lima. The buccaneers vented their anger on two captives whom they beheaded. At Huarmey it took a second assault to gain control and then plunder at will, and finally in this series of attacks in May and June, at Casma the local priest was to die as a result of a beating inflicted in a vain effort to persuade him to disclose hidden valuables.

One can well understand the terror of the ordinary inhabitant of these and similar ports and harbours, as tales of buccaneer atrocities were circulated, as they learnt that not only their livelihoods but their lives were threatened, their fate crudely decided by a game of chance. Moreover, it was plainly evident that the viceroy did not possess, nor had he devised, the means to offer them protection, and perhaps was not even inclined to do so. In general reinforcements from larger towns arrived belatedly, when the buccaneers had already occupied a port. The local population, therefore, stood or fell by its own initiative, took its own decisions on whether to destroy property and produce likely to be of benefit to the enemy, whether to dispatch inland only those unable to fight, with whatever that was portable, or whether to opt for a total evacuation.

At dawn on 11 July it fell to the people of Pisco to face up to these dilemmas, but in fact they had already made some decisions of their own in a desperate attempt to protect themselves and their properties, not only against Davis on this occasion but against proposals from Lima which they considered to endanger their safety. For viceroy Palata, faced with this new wave of raids against small coastal towns, had decided to equip a squadron to seek out Davis, but in order to do so required guns from those ports to arm his ships. The request to Pisco for its five pieces of artillery was rejected by its *corregidor* Juan de Villegas, who eventually found himself removed to Lima as a prisoner for his insubordination. His successor, Ventura de Isasiga, was also unable to comply with the instruction, but for what was then an unusual reason, joint action by the women of the community. Some 300 of them, 'taking on the role of Amazons', [40] occupied the fort, took control of its weapons and finally gained the backing of a further 200 women from Ica.

The viceroy's squadron was thus denied its guns, at least from Pisco, but unfortunately the efforts by its women were in vain, for a force of 123 buccaneers landed at Paracas, marched on the town and quickly overcame resistance when the untrained defenders somehow contrived accidentally to explode their own powder. Hostages were taken, including the governor, priest and several women, to be followed by celebrations much enlivened by the consumption of large amounts of the renowned locally produced wines and brandies. Even when reinforcements of 200 infantry and cavalrymen arrived from Chincha and Cañete, the buccaneers through greater resolve, daring and firepower were able to retain the advantage, killing 32 defenders – 16 Spaniards (three of them priests), and the rest negroes or mulattoes. Their own losses were

probably as little as three or four dead. It was this second engagement which prompted the handing over of a ransom of 20 000
pesos and 20 jars of wine to secure the release of the captives.

Before proceeding further southwards, where they would spend
the remainder of the year, Davis and his companions dallied off
Callao (19–20 July), 'full of military bravado and scorn for our
forces, from the safety of their ships taunting like a bullfighter the
main port of these seas, where they knew two galleons and a patax
were being fitted out to pursue them'.[41] In this vicinity they were
to capture a total of four traders, two with loads of wheat, before
continuing towards Huarmey to careen, 'as if it were England'.[42]
Saña, revisitted later in the month, proved to be deserted. Here
there seems to be firm evidence that disputes over the share out of
booty and ransom were reflected in a temporary division of the
party on 14 August, one group in the *Aranzazu* heading towards
Trujillo and then back beyond Callao to Ica, Caballas and Nazca,
and the largest led by Davis turning southwards to the Chilean
coast for the first time.

This latter party landed in the bay of Coquimbo on 17 September
but was unable to maintain its slender foothold, losing seven or
eight of its number in its efforts to do so. As we have seen before in
respect of the Chilean coast, it was gold that had attracted them
southwards judging by Wafer's comments.

> The Sands of the River by the Sea, as well as the whole Bay, are
> all bespangled with Particles of Gold; insomuch that as we
> travelled along the Sandy Bays, our People were covered with a
> fine Gold-dust; but too fine for any thing else, for 'twould be an
> endless Work to pick it up.[43]

Apart from a brief visit to Ilo, 'the Noblest [valley] in all Peru',[44] to
collect timber, this was the last sighting of the buccaneers for some
time, allowing the Spanish to breathe more easily and consider
future action, but unfortunately encouraging the belief that Davis
might have sailed for the Straits and the West Indies.

Indeed, as he headed for the Juan Fernández Islands in the
*Bachelor's Delight* it may well have been his plan to re-fit his ship
before undertaking the long and hazardous voyage, satisfied with
profits gained, which Raveneau de Lussan estimates at 5000 pesos
per man. However, as had occurred with Sharp, hard gotten gains
were sometimes frittered away in the bouts of gambling that filled

idle moments, and so finally it was only a group under the leadership of William Knight who decided to follow this course, most probably sailing in the *Asunción*. Davis, supported by those who were not content with what they had managed to amass and keep so far turned the *Bachelor's Delight* towards the island of Mocha, where in mid-December they restocked with fresh water and provisions. Wafer became preoccupied with the peculiarities of llamas, relating how they rode them two to an animal and killed them in search of bezoar stones. Early in the New Year, 1687, it was, therefore a diminished force of under 100 buccaneers which departed northwards, ultimately to meet up with those from whom they had separated well over a year ago.

After a fruitless landing at Copiapó, Arica seems to have been caught completely by surprise on 2 February, delivering up spoils which the Spaniards themselves valued at 40 000 pesos. This was a trifling amount in comparison with the loads of silver which still passed through the port (if less regularly) on their way to Panama, but Wafer must surely have been satisfied with his share as he pondered on the fate of his fellow surgeons who had been abandoned there in January 1681. Ilo, clearly one of his favourite places in the South Sea, 'the finest Valley I have seen on all the Coast of Peru',[45] likewise saw some of its excellent local produce fall into the buccaneers' hands, notably sugar, figs, fruit and oil. But a potentially more profitable venture was to follow at Cañete on 14 February, where a landing at 3 a.m. by 60 men ensured that they found the *corregidor*, Martín de la Cueva, and his family asleep in their beds. Like their counterparts at Arica, it would appear that they had prematurely assumed that all the buccaneers had already taken the southern route home. The sum of this assault was a ransom of 5000 pesos paid for the *corregidor* and his wife, daughter and several priests.

Regular action of this sort continued for several weeks but the rewards were slight – at Chincha a prize, the *San Jacinto*, with the customary wine and brandy, an unfulfilled plan to plunder some rich hacienda near Paracas or Caballas, another prize at Huacho (17 April), the acquisition of materials to make gunpowder at Huarmey (19 April), and the investigation by Wafer of an Indian burial ground. But on 23 April, also at Huarmey, the *Bachelor's Delight* was forced into a rare engagement with one of a squadron of vessels fitted out in Callao to drive them from the South Sea, the first such encounter since that of May 1685.[46]

The three ships had left port on 9 July 1686 in fulfilment of the
first part of their mission, which was to deliver aid and supplies to
Panama. They were the *San Francisco de Paula* (12 guns), under the
*maestre de campo* Francisco de Zúñiga, the *Santa Catalina* (6 guns),
commanded by a captain of the Callao garrison, Gaspar Bernabeu
de Mansilla, and a patax under Pedro García de San Roque. It was
for this squadron that the viceroy had unsuccessfully attempted to
withdraw artillery from the port of Pisco. Their voyage to Panama
was executed without incident, but during the subsequent search
for Davis the *Catalina* became separated from the rest. It was as she
put into Huarmey for fresh supplies that it proved impossible to
avoid him and a battle ensued. Although carrying 145 men, the
*Catalina* was outgunned, lost her captain early in the fight and was
run aground by her crew. Spanish losses appear to have been
heavy, as many as 50 drowned, seven or eight killed and another
10 or 12 wounded. The fitting out of this squadron represents the
viceroy's recognition that in response to the demands of those
subjected to raids during the first half of 1686, he must offer some
tangible evidence of retaliation.

This episode was followed by a return to excursions on land at
Santa, for more flour, and at Colán (3–4 May). At this point the
pattern of Davis' operations was abruptly transformed by the
seizure of dispatches which sent him hurrying northwards, for
they contained the news that his former comrades, led by
Grogniet, had launched an attack on Guayaquil.

Since the English and French elements of the buccaneer force
had elected to go their separate ways in July 1685, some 300
Frenchmen had cruised off the coast of New Spain and in the Gulf
of Panama, raiding Pueblo Nuevo, León and particularly Realejo,
deserted in consequence with its shipbuilding and repair facilities
in total disorder. Townley, meanwhile, on his way southwards
from Acapulco following the failure to intercept the Manila
galleon, had briefly joined them in April 1686 for an assault on
Granada, and then proceeded alone to the Gulf of Panama.[47] His
return there proved profitable, though at cruel cost to those who
fell into his clutches. A landing at La Villa on 22 July yielded
merchandise estimated to be worth 1½ million pesos (subsequently
lost in an ambush), 15 000 pesos in silver and gold and 300
prisoners. After demonstrating his callous resolve by cutting off
the heads of two of his captives, Townley received an undertaking
from the president of Panama to supply him on a daily basis with

cattle, sheep and flour. An exchange of correspondence with the president eventually also contained Townley's bloodthirsty threat to behead a further 50 prisoners if five buccaneers in Spanish hands were not released.

While continuing to negotiate, however, the Spanish had not as yet succumbed completely to these bullying tactics and on 22 August sent out an armed force of three ships and 240 men from Perico to resolve the matter. Disastrously, two of the ships were captured and only 65 Spaniards escaped injury or death. The ensuing defiant correspondence of both parties was now complemented by a more placatory letter from the archbishop of Panama, excusing the brusqueness of the president on the grounds that he was merely obeying orders, and offering the news that 'all the English were [now] catholics'.[48] Townley's reaction was to send to Panama the heads of a further 20 of his prisoners. 'This measure was in truth a little violent but it was the only means of bringing the Spanish to reason', adds de Lussan.[49] Eventually an additional 10 000 pesos was delivered to Townley on 4 September, but he was not to enjoy his gains for long, for on 8 September he died from wounds sustained in the recent naval battle. His body was cast overboard, as he had wished, near Otoque Island close to the scene of his atrocities.

After lying in wait for prizes at sea during the rest of the year, in order to maintain stocks of provisions, Townley's party, now commanded by George Hout (or Hutt), was joined on 23 January 1687 by Grogniet and some 60 Frenchmen. The remainder of their group had chosen to head north for California or else return to the West Indies by an overland route. It was after a joint excursion to Nicoya in the first half of February, that the more ambitious project was devised for an attack on Guayaquil. This produced a resurgence of the old religious and national rivalries, exacerbated by disputes over the share-out of possible plunder, and so it was an uneasy alliance of French and English which turned southwards on 24 February.[50]

Boats and canoes used by the buccaneers were first detected on 16 April as they studied their best approach to the city, for they must have been aware of the difficulties Davis had encountered three years earlier. On 18 April a lookout paddled hurriedly into Guayaquil claiming to have seen lights on the Isle of Puná. Yet despite these warnings, which seemed to confirm previous sightings from Manta and Santa Elena, the *corregidor*, Fernando Ponce de León, reacted in a fairly desultory fashion. Additional lookouts were posted and the defence force of 200 men put on the alert. Two days later, with no further news of intruders, it appears that many, including the *corregidor*, had reached the conclusion that it was a false alarm. In reality the buccaneers were approaching in good order and with a careful plan, by which Grogniet would advance through an *estero* or marsh to take the heart of the city, Hout would aim for a small fort and Le Picard would enter through the shipyard to capture the main, wooden fort of San Carlos.

The attack commenced under cover of a heavy shower between 3 and 4 a.m. on Sunday 20 April, and the city was not taken until 11 a.m. with isolated encounters continuing in the outskirts until 8 p.m. The defenders, who were outnumbered as well as out-classed as fighters, were pushed back from a 4½ ft high defensive wall and a ditch along the river side, yielding ground both at the *estero* and the shipyard and retreating towards the main fort on the hill where a further struggle ensued.[51] Both Spanish and buccaneer sources agree that this failed to offer strong resistance because its seven or eight guns were poorly positioned. The surrender of the fort of San Carlos marked the end of the assault on the city, with sporadic ambushes and sniping being maintained in the countryside until the evening. Estimates of losses vary considerably, but reflect the victory of the buccaneers who seem to have sustained 9 dead and 12 wounded, compared to losses of from 34 to 60 Spanish dead by their own accounts. De Lussan estimates that plunder collected during the first attack included pearls, precious stones, silver plate and at least 10 000 pesos, but once more dreams of what might have been as he laments the loss of 3 million pesos which he believes were successfully smuggled out of the city during the battle.

There still remained, though, the chance to increase the rewards by bargaining over ransom payments for the city and its buildings, for 13 or 14 assorted craft and 600–700 captives, male and female, among whom was the family of the *corregidor*. After his earlier negligent attitude, the latter had taken an active and courageous part in the defence of the city, suffering serious injury as a result of a beating from the buccaneers in an attempt to force him to disclose the hiding place of valuables. Several notable figures in the city were threatened with being shot for the same purpose, among them as usual a number of priests, one of whom Lorenzo de Sotomayor was finally killed. According to Spanish sources, the ransom demanded was 300 000 pesos. De Lussan typically exaggerates this to 1 million pesos in gold and 400 sacks of flour. In any case, the Spanish claimed it would have to come from Quito and therefore involve a delay.

In the interim, de Lussan passed his idle moments by taking an interest in some of the female captives. He records that 'the women of the town are perfectly beautiful: but most of the priests and friars who live there behave in a lax manner, and with freedom in sexual matters, which is not a very good example'. To blacken the name of the clergy further and reduce them to ridicule, he also recounts an amusing tale which he states they told the womenfolk when the attack was imminent. 'These priests hate us so much that they persuade women who have never seen buccaneers that we do not resemble men in any way: that we do not even have the same shape as men; and that in fact we eat women and little children.'[52] Although the exaggeration in this story may be such as to produce laughter, we are soon reminded of the brutality which gave rise to it, when on 9 May four prisoners were decapitated to hasten the payment of the ransom. Five had originally been selected by lots but the fifth was spared when the musket aimed at him failed to fire.

By this time, in fact on 26 April, the buccaneers had retreated from the city to establish their base on the Isle of Puná, taking with them 250 prisoners and the ships they had seized. There are good reasons for this – fear of counter-attack using forces sent from Quito, the danger of disease as a result of unburied bodies lying in the streets, and a fire which burnt out half of Guayaquil, started according to one account by a careless buccaneer roasting a chicken.

One other event of note soon after the removal to Puná was the death of Grogniet, on 2 May, from wounds sustained during the initial attack. He was succeeded as leader of the French by Le Picard. But the loss of the former chief did nothing to prevent the continuation of the good life, guaranteed by ample supplies of food, music provided by the town band who had fallen prisoners, and the company of women. Again de Lussan comments on this aspect of their stay. 'All our men were so delighted with that life that they had forgotten their past miseries, and no longer dreamt of the Spanish, as if they were safe in the middle of Paris.'[53] He claims also to have been tempted to accept an offer of marriage.

It was while the parties of Hout and Le Picard were savouring

such rare luxuries that Edward Davis arrived on 16 May in the
*Bachelor's Delight*, bearing the news gleaned from a dispatch he had
intercepted recently, that the Spanish were delaying the ransom
deliberately in expectation of help by sea from Callao. Addressed
to the viceroy, it began:

> I give your Excellency notice, for the second time, that the
> English and French are still at Puná. Several days ago the time
> which they have granted to us for the ransom of the prisoners
> expired . . . They have just sent me the heads of four of our
> people. I will amuse them with several thousands of pieces of
> eight from time to time . . . If it pleases your excellency, hurry . . .
> And when they must needs send me yet 50 heads, I judge that
> that loss is less detrimental to us than if we were to allow to live
> persons of such evil intentions.[54]

This is again a chilling insight indeed into the conduct of ransom
negotiations. It naturally provoked further threats to kill more
prisoners, followed by the handing over of 20000 pesos and 80
packs of flour in 23 May. On the next day, agreement was reached
to pay another 22000 pesos and more flour as the final amount.
    However, during these last days of May the buccaneers became
aware of a squadron of ships off Guayaquil bent on their destruction.
Therefore, feeling that there was little hope of squeezing more
plunder out of the city, and afraid of remaining too long in the
same waters, Hout, Le Picard and Davis resolved to put to sea to
face the challenge, leaving behind the majority of their captives
with the exception of the *corregidor* and other notables. These were
now obliged to watch from the bridge of one of the buccaneer ships
as the sea battle unfolded on 27 May, continuing intermittently
until 2 June. This was no buccaneer victory, for they failed in their
efforts to board the Peruvian ships and lost one of their prizes, the
*San Jacinto*, which they were forced to abandon. Nor was it really
the victory it might have been for the Peruvian squadron, for it
allowed the buccaneers to disperse to Isla de la Plata, rather than
pressing home its advantage, a repetition of the outcome of the
battle in the Gulf of Panama just two years ago.
    The Peruvian ships, fitted out by a company known as *Nuestra
Señora de Guía*, were another instance of private finance coming to
the aid of the beleaguered viceroy.[55] In truth, of course, although
the merchants who supported it claimed their zealous desire to be

of service to the crown, their action served their own personal interests in wishing to be free from intruders and free to pursue their normal commercial activities unmolested. Three ships were armed, provisioned and put under the command of two Biscayan merchants – the *San Nicolás* under Nicolás de Igarza and the *San José* under Dionisio de Artunduaga, together with a patax. By agreement with the viceroy, they retained the right to keep any plunder or prizes resulting from their operations, handing over only captured guns. They had sailed in mid-May shortly after news had reached Lima of the fall of Guayaquil.

Whereas Artunduaga subsequently pursued a group of French buccaneers as far as New Spain, bringing them to a confrontation late in December 1687 in which they were worsted, the *San Nicolás* went aground on a sandbank off Atacames, though her crew and guns were rescued. Albeit less disastrously, this loss repeats that of the flagship of the crown armada, again following the 1685 sea battle off Panama. Somewhat prematurely, the company's action was hailed as the liberation of the South Sea from buccaneer infestation. Its founding members were proposed for honours by the viceroy and were awarded them as a measure of the gratitude of the crown. To this extent the crown was prepared to back local initiative, but when petitioned by the company for a regular grant of 250 000 pesos per year for four years, to maintain its ships and pay their crews, it was refused.[56] Therefore, although the company responded to the loss of the *San Nicolás* by the purchase of a replacement, it drifted slowly towards total extinction in 1693 because of this lack of support. As on land in some of the coastal settlements, so now at sea the question of security from attack and the protection of trade was becoming one which increasingly the citizens of Peru would need to solve themselves.

After returning to the mainland to put their remaining captives ashore near Cape San Francisco, on 12 June, Davis, Hout and Le Picard planned an equitable distribution of their recent booty. This was not an easy task given its great variety and the desire of every man to possess the most readily portable items in view of the probable difficulties to be confronted during the return to the West Indies. Burney describes the procedure by which the silver pesos were divided first, then the more bulky items put up for auction and paid for in pesos. When all items had been disposed of in this way, the silver from the sale was redistributed. De Lussan states that each share amounted to 400 pesos. If there were about 350 buccaneers in the combined force, possibly as Burney suggests as many as 500 shares taking account of special payments to officers and the wounded, this would suggest a distributable plunder of 200 000 pesos.[57] Spanish estimates of the booty range from 150 000 to 300 000 pesos.

Final sightings of this lengthy period of intrusion were made about mid-June off Cape Santa Elena, after which all parties agreed that it was time to return to the West Indies by a variety of different routes. Only Davis, still sailing in the trusty *Bachelor's Delight*, had a vessel capable of withstanding a voyage through the Straits or around Cape Horn. For the others, largely Frenchman, about 280 remnants of the Grogniet, Townley and Le Picard parties, it was necessary to head for the coast of New Spain. During the remainder of the year they engaged in further buccaneering actions, met up with 30 of their colleagues who had deserted Grogniet to stay off California, and were finally persuaded to commence the march overland on 1 January 1688, following a second encounter with Artunduaga in the *San José*. De Lussan finally returned to the French colony at Petit Goâve in May 1689.

Davis meanwhile had collected fresh supplies at the Galapagos Islands before heading south for the voyage home. It was while in the vicinity of 12° 30' that the *Bachelor's Delight* suddenly shuddered as if striking a rock and the sea all about foamed and swirled. This they were to learn was the effect of the earthquake that struck Lima and Callao on 20 October 1687. Later off the Chilean coast at 27° 20', Wafer reported the sighting of land 500 leagues west of Copiapó, firstly 'a small, low, sandy island', and 12 leagues beyond that 'a range of high land'. This has frequently led to speculation that the latter could have been Easter Island, traditionally discovered by Jacob Roggeveen in 1722 when trying to locate what Wafer himself had first believed was Terra Australis Incognita.[58]

The Juan Fernández Islands were reached at the end of the year, but now found to be almost totally deserted apart from a handful of goats which had escaped the wild dogs let loose by the Spanish to kill them in furtherance of the policy of destroying food supplies for intruders into the South Sea. Nevertheless, five crew members still dissatisfied with the outcome of their buccaneering chose to stay behind rather than return to the West Indies. They managed to survive until taken off by John Strong in October 1690. The rest of the party, after finding Mocha and Santa María similarly devoid of human habitation and fresh supplies, headed for the Straits of Magellan. Stormy conditions, however, prevented their entry and instead they rounded Cape Horn on Christmas Day, reporting many icebergs and consuming the provisions of flour, salted turtle and turtle oil brought from the Galapagos. They made their next landfall to the north of the entrance to the River Plate and there recuperated on a diet of ostrich eggs.

It was in the spring of 1688 that they reached the West Indies in time to hear of a pardon offered to buccaneers who, under certain conditions, surrendered to the authorities. This was in fact a renewal by James II, on 22 May 1687, of a proclamation issued three years previously by Charles II, which had also included a clause declaring the confiscation of the property of those buccaneers then in the South Sea. Unwisely, Davis, Wafer and John Hincent (or Hingson), a companion of Wafer on the Isthmus of Panama, rejected the offer of a pardon and continued northward to Philadelphia, where they anchored in May 1688. A month later they had the bad luck to be spotted by a vessel belonging to the squadron of Sir Robert Holmes, sent out specifically in 1687 to bring in buccaneers. Subsequently under cross examination at Jamestown, they all denied privateering and claimed to be West Indian traders, but were betrayed by the evidence of a negro, Peter Cloise, who had accompanied them since being taken by Davis from the Spanish some nine years previously.

Imprisonment in the town jail lasted, despite constant litigation, until the late summer of 1689. A year later the three were free to sail for London. However, their property was not returned until a royal order of March 1692, less £300 to be used to build a college in Virginia. The contents of their sea-chests holding all their belongings at the conclusion of the voyage were itemised at Jamestown and are a revealing comment on the fortunes of buccaneers. John Hincent had 800 pesos, silver plate weighing 106 lbs, pieces of linen and ribbons. Wafer possessed '37 silver plates; two scollops; seaven dishes, silver Lace, some cups broken', weighing in all 74 lbs, 'three baggs of Spanish money marked L.W., containing 1100 dollars or thereabouts. In a chest marked L.W., a peece of cloth and some old things, with old broken Plate and some little Basons, weighing in all 84 lbs.' Davis' tally as a result of all his efforts was three bags of Spanish money, a parcel of broken silver in a chest, weighing 142 lbs, four pairs of silk stockings, 'fowle lynnen', and pieces of 'Damnyfied ribbon'.[59]

As far as Wafer was concerned, this was the conclusion of his buccaneering experiences. He was subsequently engaged, as we shall see, as an adviser to the Scottish Darien venture, saw the publication of his book in 1699, and lived in London, probably amongst fellow privateers and adventurers in Wapping, until his death in 1705. Davis may well have been the same Edward Davis who later was a companion of the notorious Captain Kidd.[60]

This four year intrusion into the South Sea was certainly the most directly damaging to the Viceroyalty of Peru of all such occurrences in the seventeenth century, the large numbers of individuals involved raising serious questions about the security of most maritime operations, and of all ports with the exception of Callao. In fact we cannot be so sure, as during the Sharp era, that even the latter would not have been temporarily endangered if the full force of this second wave, almost 100 men, had dared challenge it. However, although the principal groups led by Davis, Townley, Grogniet, Le Picard and others only managed to act in unison on a single occasion, the individual units seem to have suffered less from constant internal unrest and rivalry. Furthermore, a consequence of the dispersal of this large force was that during 1686, while some ranged along the Peruvian coast and as far south as the Juan Fernández Isles, others threatened shipping in the Gulf of Panama and yet more raided ports of New Spain.

The Duke of La Palata as viceroy, therefore, found his inadequate forces thinly stretched in a struggle to defend coastal zones, offer reaction at sea, and maintain vital commercial links with Chile, Panama and the ports supplying Lima. Moreover, it was all too brutally apparent that his officials who came face to face with them at sea or on land, could rarely expect to appeal successfully to the sympathy, humanity or sense of honour of their opponents. Any expectation of an adherence to some vague concept of proper conduct between adversaries was fruitless.

We may value the contributions to scientific and geographical knowledge contained in the journals of a few, but in the main the buccaneers were lured to Peru for what they could plunder. Therefore, they ransacked and pillaged, holding captives and buildings to ransom under threat of destruction. Negotiations for the release of hostages were, then as now, a chilling game of bluff and bargain with the lives of innocents at stake. But equally the buccaneers knew perfectly well that if any of them were to fall into Spanish hands they would not survive for long.[61]

Nevertheless, while abhorring the cruelty which frequently accompanied their actions, few commentators in Peru fail to record their reckless daring, their superior military skills in terms of tactics and the use of weapons, and their firm determination amid all manner of adversities and hardships. Although he is ever prompt to recount a tale of buccaneer atrocities, particularly with reference to fellow members of the church, González Suárez typifies this point of view after describing the terrible damage suffered by Guayaquil. 'We are led to admire the buccaneers' daring in the attack, their patience in enduring all manner of hardships and suffering, their perseverance despite the most terrible setbacks and their indomitable courage; we could call them heroes if for true heroism virtue were not indispensable.'[62]

If we try to be more specific about the cost of the intervention by Davis and company, there can be little doubt that they dominated the sectors of open sea and coastal waters in which they chose to operate, where no trading vessel engaged on the day-to-day commerce of the viceroyalty, whatever its cargo, was safe from plunder or else was commandeered for the buccaneers' own use. Some individuals saved their own lives at the cost of running their ship aground and only the very lucky outsailed them to the security of a nearby haven. As a result of the damage to merchant ships during the Sharp intrusion, viceroy Palata had been instructed to order that no vessel should leave port without the protection of guns and armed men. Obviously this had been impossible to achieve by 1684, not simply due to the cost but due to the shortage of guns and of ships capable of carrying and using them effectively. Palata also pointed out that there were barely enough skilled gunners and crew available for service in crown ships, so that most shipowners were grateful to hire a Spanish or mestizo master and a crew of Indians or negroes.[63]

One can but speculate on the precise extent to which trade was curtailed, and on the hardships felt by those whose livelihood it was. The wealthiest of merchants involved in imperial trade with Spain were, as in the past, reluctant to take any risks, some of them doubtlessly hoping to use the shortage of goods as an excuse to raise prices. But the owners of small trading ships, and those who supplied them with their cargoes of flour, wines, fruit, sugar and timber, could not afford to wait for their profits. We can perceive that the loss of a ship or two, transporting a season's produce for sale in Lima, could be a tragic blow to a small coastal community.

Nor did Lima itself escape the effects of the disruption, with food shortages resulting from the unreliability of supplies coming in from the valleys to the north and south. Furthermore, the reduced levels of trade implied a loss of revenue through taxes levied on it by the crown. One consequence of this was the need to direct sales taxes to pay mercury miners at Huancavelica, whose remunerations formerly had been drawn from impositions on commerce.[64]

A report written at the height of Davis' raids in 1686 lists a number of specific results related to the new pressures on trade: Panama was isolated from its usual sources of supplies which came from Guayaquil, Callao, Trujillo and Nicaragua. Shipbuilding and repair was interrupted because the trade in pitch and tar from Realejo was halted, as was that in rigging, oakum and copper from Chile. Wines stored in tarred jars were spoilt. And lastly the garrison at Valdivia was put in danger by the inability to guarantee regular food supplies.[65] At the time early in 1685 when almost 1000 buccaneers patrolled the waters of the Gulf of Panama and raided haciendas close to the shore, its president bitterly complained of his misfortune. 'I see myself abandoned by Peru, it being over 14 months that the aid for this kingdom has not been sent.'[66]

The buccaneers were challenged at sea of course, by the crown armada in 1685 and the private *Nuestra Señora de Guía* in 1687. The jubilation aroused in Lima by such encounters is understandable, for it was the buccaneers who were pursued rather than the pursuers. But it should be remembered also that only the *Bachelor's Delight*, with her 36 guns, was really fit for the privateering action she was to see, the remainder of the vessels (with the exception of Swan's *Cygnet* in the early months) being captured barks, traders or large canoes. In fact, therefore, in these two battles, when the chance to come in close to board against more powerfully armed ships was remote, the wisest course of action was to disperse. Little damage was sustained and one suspects that few of the buccaneers were intimidated by the opposition.

As regards their sorties on land, this second wave, even when scattered into various units or weakened by departures, had sufficient manpower for the targets it chose. Davis' raids throughout 1686 are the best evidence of this. Furthermore, this was not simply because only weak targets or tiny hamlets were selected. Arica, which had withstood previous attacks, was caught by surprise, and the two principal shipbuilding centres of the west coast, Realejo and Guayaquil, were overrun. Occupation of these and the many other coastal settlements can rarely have been unaccompanied by deliberate acts of wanton vandalism. Such was the upset and the fear that there appears to have been a considerable movement of people inland to more secure sites, for example at Saña and Huaura. This was certainly the case at Arica, at least on a temporary basis, where the flight of its Spanish population interrupted the usual process of shipping mercury via the port to Potosí.[67] Like Panama following Morgan's attack, Guayaquil was transferred to a new site in 1693, although this was a less radical move in the latter instance to a new adjacent location. But significantly, in answering charges arising out of his defence of the city, *corregidor* Ponce de León had claimed that the old location was difficult to protect.[68]

The buccaneers also controlled the islands close in to the shore, such as Gorgona, Gallo, La Plata, Coiba and the Lobos. They were able to use as bases for blockades or attacks, islands close to important ports, such as Puná and Taboga, and they were at liberty to come and go as they pleased to islands at a greater distance from the mainland, such as the Juan Fernández and Galapagos. Although the Spanish may have had some success in reducing the number of animals they themselves had introduced to islands close in to the mainland, for example the goats of Isla de la Plata, there were seals, turtles and tortoises elsewhere, and in the Galapagos the buccaneers were even able to store packs of flour they had looted for future needs, unmolested except by the birds.

Accurate statistical facts on the depredations of the buccaneers are not easy to compile granted the possible prejudice and hidden motives of those making the estimates. There may be personal motivation behind reports seeking to blacken the reputation of the viceroy for his handling of the intervention, or else a desire to render more grave the damage and the ineffectiveness of the defences in order to present a better case for crown financial support should there be future attacks. Nevertheless, a few sources help us to establish a general picture. Looking first at the repercussions for merchant shipping, it was initially calculated that by early May 1685 some 34 vessels had fallen into the clutches of Davis and company, a figure which had risen to 62 by the end of 1686, according to the Marquis of Los Velez, out of a total of 100 such ships normally operating in the South Sea. Davis subsequently visited eight or nine ports in which there must have been shipping, and certainly took at least three prizes at sea.

Another account, which we have used to trace the buccaneers' movements during 1686, claims that the waters of the viceroyalty were cleared of 170 vessels, large and small, but this would seem rather excessive unless every canoe and boat were accounted for. One should also remember that although ships might be destroyed in port, or as a result of having been run ashore in desperation, at sea the buccaneers invariably released those which they did not require for their own purposes. This second source of information suggests that the Spaniards lost 400 men, exclusive of those killed in the accident to the *San José*, that 3000 were at one time or another prisoners of the buccaneers, and that the booty gathered by them was probably worth 500 000 pesos.[69] Our own research has been able to document landings at some 30 sites, at some more than once, the capture of 28 prizes at sea (not including the 13 or 14 canoes at Guayaquil), booty worth over 400 000 pesos, and the murder of 29 individuals.

Without a doubt, from its officials in Panama and Lima, from former viceroys and advisers in Spain, from witnesses of the events and those merely eager to comment upon them, the crown was presented with a comprehensive set of reports on the occurrences in Peru. There was a crumb of comfort for the future in the evidence that English authorities in the West Indies were more critically aware of the damage done to their interests by the buccaneers. In 1686, Lieutenant-Governor Molesworth of Jamaica referred to the actions of those buccaneers 'who have soe much disturbed y$^e$ trade of all Europe'.[70] A year previously, he had already pointed to the wider implications of interruptions to Spain's silver trade from Callao to Portobello, stating that 'this damage will not onely befall y$^e$ Spaniards but all Europe that are concerned in y$^e$ trade of these seas, —Besides w$^{ch}$, it will be a meanes of draining many people from this island, in Spight of all the Preventions that can be used here'.[71] And again in 1686, a further letter reveals that because of the buccaneers' presence in the South Sea, Spain had cut short plans to trade with Jamaica.[72]

At the same time, French governor de Cussy had, not without regret, worked hard to control his compatriots and claimed in 1689 that he had put an end to buccaneering in the French colonies. Interestingly, recognising that the will to suppress the buccaneers was becoming stronger, Pedro Ronquillo, Spanish ambassador in London, had advocated that the time was perhaps now opportune for a joint Anglo-Spanish effort to eradicate them. The *Consejo de Indias* was not impressed.

> For no cause nor reason does it feel that it may be suitable for the forces of His Britannic Majesty to join and mingle with those of Your Majesty for the operation that is proposed, because of the serious disadvantages that it could cause in America, both with regard to commerce through the introduction of cloths, and also the very freedom with which it is appropriate that the maritime forces of Your Majesty should operate.[73]

Bearing in mind views such as these, it is clear that the events of 1684–9 mark not the commencement of a new era of intrusion into the South Sea by buccaneers, but the end of the heyday. Davis and his French counterparts were not the last buccaneers to trouble the viceroyalty in the seventeenth century, and those who came later reinforced the belief that some action was needed to prevent their arrival, but they were never again to attain the numbers and scale of activity of this earlier intrusion. Even so, the 1680s had seen a dramatic rise in the presence of interlopers in the South Sea and the consequence was a broad discussion of the means to bring this to an end.

Like Sharp, most of those who had joined up with Cook and Davis were arrivals from across the Isthmus of Panama, and therefore much of the debate concerned the means to close that route and remove the danger to ports in the northern sector of the viceroyalty, which were suddenly more vulnerable. Broadly speaking, this involved action in the Caribbean to attack the root of the problem, and on the eastern side of the Isthmus through more effective occupation and defences. For example, an anonymous view counselled fortifications on each side of the Isthmus, close to the route frequented by buccaneers, and a roving force of 12 ships in the Caribbean to seek them out in their usual haunts amongst the islands and on the Main.[74] The former viceroy of Peru, the Count of Castellar, in 1683 felt that the root of the problem could be wrenched out by military conquest of the 1500 or so Indians judged to be allies of the buccaneers. Then, by using maritime patrols along the north coast from Cartagena to Portobello, and in the Gulf of Panama, with watch towers on the island of Chepillo to give early warning, the movements of potential attackers could be controlled.[75] A special *Junta Particular sobre la Defensa de América* in

1685, prompted largely by the recent events in Peru, also proposed solutions along similar lines, using a force of four galleons and an equal number of frigates to roam the Caribbean, and a flotilla of six canoes or similar craft to guard the exit from the River Darien.[76] None of these proposals found the immediate favour and support of the Crown.

The Duke of La Palata who faced the experience of having to deal with the latest irruptions from the north, was of the opinion that 'there will always be pirates in the [South] Sea', due to the loss of Jamaica, Curaçao and islands of the Lesser Antilles, and looked to a longer term solution.[77] Initially he suggested that Darien might be populated using people from Galicia or the Canary Islands, as a means by which Spain could take more effective control of the region, but expressed doubts almost at once about the rigours of the climate and the dangers of establishing a trade between the two oceans which it might prove difficult to control. His final idea, therefore, was the creation of a new viceroyalty, transferring to it administration for the area from Panama in the west to Cartagena, and hopefully attracting a greater population into the eastern zone of the Isthmus. His plan in answer to buccaneer intrusions awaited permanent implementation, as the Viceroyalty of New Granada, until 1739, when other factors were also prominent.

As regards the immediate future, as one who had found himself unable to respond at once to news of the presence of intruders because of the poor condition of crown ships in the South Sea, viceroy Palata put forward the desperate need for four frigates of war whose purpose would be to operate in pairs to the north and south of Callao on the lookout for foreign sails. Until these could be built, he wondered whether he might be able to purchase the two *navíos de permiso* at Buenos Aires which, coming through the Straits fully armed and crewed, would be in a position to offer immediate assistance. However, both on the occasion of the first request in 1685, and again in 1687, treasury officials in Lima were unwilling to agree to the expenditure of 160 000 pesos. An alternative answer to the dilemma of a viceroy who was left from September 1685 with only one crown galleon and a patax to ship silver to Panama, mercury to Arica and aid to Chile and Valdivia, to scour the coasts north and south for intruders and if necessary engage them in battle, was to return to the question of the viability of building and sending a fully armed and crewed naval force from Spain, first raised following l'Hermite's intervention and now re-examined by the *Junta Particular*.[78] Nothing in fact was done in September 1685 because of reservations expressed about the dangers of the route and doubts concerning the most appropriate season for the voyage. Two years and many more buccaneer raids later, the *Junta de Guerra de Indias* continued to advance the view that access to Peru via the Straits of Magellan or around Cape Horn was a route, 'today so unused and even unknown by the Spanish, that there is no pilot who knows how to sail it without probable risks and with great difficulty and delay, in addition to the great cost'.[79] It was resolved, therefore, that sailors, artillerymen and shipbuilding experts be sent to Peru to join vessels built there, and only tentatively mooted that one, or two, ships of appropriate size and strength might be constructed in Spain 'able to endure such a long voyage and its seas'. The crown, of course, was not prepared to finance a Peruvian squadron in Spain, nor did it prove possible for Palata or his successor to build in Peru any more vessels for the *Armada del Mar del Sur*, at crown expense.

In addition to drawing attention to gaps in his defence requirements, viceroy Palata repeatedly adopts an unsympathetic, metropolitan attitude, alluding to what he perceives as inferior expertise and equipment in Peru.[80] He criticises those who leave Spain to improve their lot in life by engaging in commerce, and whom he finds resistant to militia training, discipline and duty. He condemns the shortage of artillery especially after the loss of the flagship in 1685, but equally finds fault with techniques of construction in Lima, feeling that under expert guidance a better job could be done in Coquimbo, close to the source of copper. In respect of shipping in the South Sea, this critical tone is maintained, particularly in a letter from Antonio de Vea which Palata passes on to the crown. This claims that any intruder could easily outsail the galleons available, for theirs are like 'light cavalry' and ours 'infantry', adding, 'not only is there no one in the entire kingdom who has ever built a warship, there is nobody who has ever seen one'.[81] Such comments obviously overlook the fact that necessarily the major part of shipping used by the buccaneers was what they captured in the South Sea, and thus of Peruvian origin, suggesting if not greater skill on their part, at least greater determination.

But when we recall the negative response in Spain to the various proposals for improvements in the security of the viceroyalty, it is quite plain that the crown's unwillingness to commit extra

expenditure to this aspect of administration was the most significant factor limiting the reaction. Indeed one can fully understand
the lack of enthusiasm for military service in Peru, when one reads
a report of the *Junta de Guerra* recording that wages due were at
times 30–40 months late, with the result that those who served in a
military capacity lived on charity, begged from door to door, or else
abandoned their posts to find others in mines or on estates.[82]
Consequently, there had been occasions when as many as 200 men
were missing from their posts in the garrison of Callao, out of a
total complement of 500. Similarly, it was a concern to reduce
expenditure which led to the introduction of the policy of releasing
sailors and gunners from service when the armada was in port.
The result, as Palata found, was that in an emergency it was
impossible to find adequate experienced crews since many men
had drifted off to new occupations.[83]

Therefore, despite the gravity of the implications of the buccaneer incursion from 1684 to 1689, the only features of the defensive
and offensive response which saw any positive advance were
those financed from Peruvian sources. Such is the case of the
company of *Nuestra Señora de Guía*, which we have already
described, and also of two major works of fortification, namely the
encirclement of Trujillo and Lima by protective walls.

Trujillo itself had hitherto escaped direct assault by buccaneers,
although Davis had been attracted towards it early in 1686. Its
reputation as one of the oldest Spanish cities in Peru, at the centre
of an important zone of agricultural production, most certainly was
understood by them from their seizure of flour ships from the port,
making their way to Panama or Callao. Whether they had also
picked up tales of hidden pots of gold in Indian *huacas* close to the
town we do not know. It was first of all the arrival of Sharp from
the north which demonstrated the potential danger to Trujillo, and
occasioned an examination of its military strength.[84] Due to lack of
arms, powder and equipment in general, the citizens on that
occasion agreed to finance the purchase of two cannon. But it was
the second wave of raids on northern ports which led the *cabildo* to
place before the viceroy a formal proposal for a wall in 1686.

The plan was drawn up by an Italian engineer, Giuseppe
Formento, luckily at the time in Trujillo. The viceroy applauded the
local initiative, gave permission for the work to begin and informed
the crown that he personally would finance the construction of one
bulwark, having given an undertaking that a second (of the 15)

would be supported by crown funds. Apart from this, the remainder of the total cost of 84 000 pesos came from local sources. Work commenced on 5 April 1687. In January 1689 it gained the approval of the crown and was apparently nearing completion by the end of 1690. Later commentators have not been so uncritical of its usefulness, one pointing out that since it lacked ditches, other external defences and terreplein, 'it serves more for decoration and prestige than as a true defence'.[85]

A wall for Lima had been discussed seriously on at least three occasions in the first half of the seventeenth century, each of them coinciding not unnaturally with a period of Dutch activity.[86] With the construction of the wall of Callao, the matter was laid to rest until 1673 and the renewal of threats both from the north and the south. The detailed scheme produced in that year by Jean Raymond Coninck, for an encircling loop from river bank to river bank, was not at once implemented due to referral to the *Consejo de Indias* and the lull in actual incursions in the late 1670s. This first project traced outer and inner walls 28 000 ft long, about 15½ ft and 10 ft high respectively, with 25 bulwarks. There was an additional delay in later years due to the conflicting opinions of viceroy Liñán y Cisneros, who was opposed to it, and Luis Venegas Osorio, the crown's inspector of defences, who was a supporter. Two events finally swung the balance in favour – receipt of news in Lima in October 1683 that Vera Cruz, terminus of the *flota* from Spain had fallen to buccaneers several months earlier, and the notification from Chile, in March 1684, that foreign ships had been sighted off that coastline.

With the unanimous support of the local *cabildo*, the first stone was laid on 30 June 1684, practically a full year before the royal decree granting its authorisation with modifications suggested by experts in Spain. But the completed structure in 1687, increased to 39 000 ft and 34 bulwarks to avoid the need to demolish buildings in its path, probably owes more to the direct intervention on the spot of Venegas Osorio. Viceroy Palata had estimated the total cost at 700 000 pesos, but in the account of his administration quotes an actual expenditure of 400 000 pesos. The saving is not so significant as it might seem, since this latter figure does not include the contribution of the merchant community to finance a section of wall 8400 ft long, and worth 200 000 pesos. The remainder of the funds required were obtained without burden to the treasury, by gifts from the ecclesiastical community and the viceroy, a general fund throughout the viceroyalty, and through a series of taxes and impositions (e.g., on meat, wine, white paper, the import of negroes, Indian tribute and *encomienda* income). The fund collected 163 348 pesos, of which only 17 348 pesos came from beyond the immediate vicinity of Lima, an eloquent response to the demands of a capital from those feeling immune to the danger inland, or accustomed to having to fend for themselves elsewhere along the coast.

There can be little doubt that the second entry of buccaneers into the South Sea produced a more detailed scrutiny of the viceroyalty and its defences, than any undertaken since viceroy Mancera's responses to the presence of Brouwer. The latter, however, had posed a threat in one specific area, far from the administrative heart of Peru, and at a site then unpopulated by Spaniards. In addition to the vastly broadened sphere of operations engaged upon by Davis and Grogniet, what is particularly noticeable is the shifting of the responsibility for defence to the private owners of shipping and to settlers along the coastal fringe. They now committed themselves to measures which they might once have expected the crown to support, and which it patently did not. The measures were, of course, undertaken out of loyalty to the crown, as well as in defence of personal interests, but they do offer some indication of the greater need, and the freedom, to act alone if not independently.

# 8

# The End of an Era and the Onset of a New Phase: The Last Buccaneers, John Strong Privateer and the Arrival of the French (1686–1701)

The buccaneer presence in the South Sea was not quite over when Davis and his former French companions set their separate courses for the West Indies, for the dispatches of the new Peruvian viceroy, the Count of La Monclova, indistinctly trace the comings and goings of a small band from mid-1689 through to the early days of 1694. The information provided by these letters, recording their encounters with shipping and entries into ports as narrated by eyewitnesses, may be supplemented by a two-part French journal, initially anonymous but completed by one F. Massertie.[1] Like Davis, this party originally sailed from the coast of New England for the Guinea coast of Africa. They departed thence on 11 December 1686, three months later entered the Straits of Magellan and on 11 April 1687 emerged into the South Sea. Their most likely initial aim was to meet up with those French buccaneers already there, for after briefly putting in at Casma (21 June) and Tumbes (27 June), they headed for Coiba Isle (20 July) and the Gulf of Panama (4 August). From then until April 1689 they cruised the shores of New Spain, their total complement recorded by the anonymous journalist as being 41 men.

While accurately dating this fresh arrival of intruders, Spanish documentation does not begin to follow their progress until their arrival at Isla de la Plata in June 1689.[2] For almost exactly one year they were to use the Galapagos Islands as their main base for careening, refreshment and repairs, mounting occasional expeditions towards the coast from the Gulf of Guayaquil to Trujillo, taking three or four prizes but failing to disembark on the mainland. At Trujillo, the journalist mockingly notes in one of his few asides that preparations had been made to oppose them, as if 40 men could take 300 behind the town's new wall, adding that its best protection was the stormy sea, as Davis too had discovered.

The most detailed source of information at this point is Juan Martín Ibáñez, pilot of a merchant ship, the *San Francisco Javier*, captured by the buccaneers en route from Puná to Callao on 15 October 1689, and who was to remain a prisoner until December 1691. It is Ibáñez who reveals that the total complement of men was in fact 89, 34 of them French, 4 Dutch and the pilot English, the remainder being negroes and Indians. Their captain is named as Franco, variously described in Spanish documents as French or Dutch. During one of their visits to the Galapagos Islands in April 1690, they chose to burn their original ship (the *urqueta* in Spanish texts) and transfer to the prize *San Francisco*, which was to carry them for most of their stay in those waters.[3]

Following an interlude on the coast of New Spain from July 1690 to August 1691, Captain Franco retraced his course to the Galapagos Islands to repeat the pattern of activity of a year ago, before turning slowly southwards for the Juan Fernández Isles, where they anchored on 31 October. Three prizes in particular are recorded in the viceroy's letters – the *Santa María y Hospital de los Pobres* with a cargo of cloth, sails, ropes and 70 negroes, taken off Isla de la Plata on 25 August, the Jesuit owned *Santo Tomás*, carrying timber, seized on 2 September off Punta Pariñas, and on 3 November the *Begoña* en route for Valdivia with a welcome cargo of flour, biscuit, cheese and wine. Her pilot, Joseph Ventosilla, replaced Ibáñez at this juncture, perhaps because of his greater familiarity with ports in the southern reaches of the viceroyalty, which Franco briefly investigated in the latter days of the year.

Leaving their southern base on 1 March 1692, the remainder of the year was filled with coastal cruising northwards as far as the Galapagos. The round trip to the Juan Fernández Isles was complete by the end of December. After a particularly lean year in terms of prizes and plunder, Captain Franco had apparently been persuaded to abandon the South Sea and by March 1693 they were close to the island of Chiloé. However, without explanation, they headed northwards again for a repetition of the previous year's cruising, particularly favouring Iquique, Arica, Ilo, Nazca and

Pisco, and with greater profit. The *Santiago de Mendía*, taken at Iquique in March was sailed to Arica and burnt when the ransom demand for 7000 pesos was not paid, but when Franco returned in June with the *Magdalena*, and the *Nuestra Señora del Rosario* with a cargo of wheat from Chile to Lima, the merchants of Arica were now disposed to hand over payments of 4000 and 9000 pesos respectively. In vain, in the case of the latter, for she was sailed to the Galapagos and prepared for the return voyage to the Atlantic, in preference to the *San Francisco* which they abandoned.[4]

With plunder from a further three prizes taken in the vicinity of Pisco, mainly wine, they passed the Straits of Magellan during the first half of December, set course for Brazil, sought refreshment and provisions at Cayenne, only to conclude their voyage by running aground at La Rochelle on 4 September 1694.

The postscript to buccaneer intrusion into the South Sea was written by Franco's former quartermaster and 22 companions, who had chosen to part company from the rest in the Juan Fernández Isles in December 1692, after Franco's premature announcement of their return to the Atlantic. Since there is no journal of their adventure we are forced to rely on references in viceregal correspondence, which does not record their existence until November 1693. Then the reference is an important one, for it recounts how they overhauled the *Santiaguillo* which had been loading wheat at Yerbabuena, secured 17 000 pesos for her ransom and then retained her for their own use. We next hear of them near to Concepción in January 1694, where they were disappointed in a demand for a further ransom for a new prize, the *Santo Cristo*. It was presumed that they later returned to the Juan Fernández Isles before undertaking the passage of the Straits. The last news reported by viceroy Monclova was to the effect that the *Santiaguillo* had foundered at the mouth of the Straits. Four of her crew, with their share of booty amounting to 8000 pesos, reached Valdivia six months later in a canoe.[5] Unlikely though it may seem, more fortunate comrades constructed a bark from the timbers of the *Santiaguillo*, passed the Straits, made a landfall at Cayenne and reached France in 1695.[6]

Therefore, from the first arrival of Sharp, buccaneer intrusion into the South Sea lasts some 15 years. Captain Franco and his companions, however, represent the decline of that era, never able to mount even a minor assault on coastal settlements, relying entirely on uninhabited islands at the northern and southern extremes of the viceroyalty as bases, and preying on loan merchantmen for booty and provisions. In the latter respect they were doubtlessly a troublesome hindrance to safe commerce, particularly during 1692 and 1693. Ultimately of more long-term significance, was that their tales of adventure and their practical knowledge helped to swell the growing enthusiasm in France for enterprises in the South Sea. But before we move on to discuss briefly the new generation of Frenchmen who were to follow, we must examine a rather different type of venture which was present in the South Sea at the same time as these last buccaneers.

By the latter months of 1689, England (along with Holland and Spain) was in conflict with France in the War of the Grand Alliance, and because of hostilities committed against English ships, letters of commission were issued to enable them in future to attack and legally seize vessels belonging to subjects of Louis XIV. The voyage of John Strong to the coasts of Peru was undertaken under the protection of just such a commission from William and Mary. It read:

> Know ye therefor that we by these presents grant commission to and doe lycence and authorize the said John Strong to sett forth in warlike manner the said ship called the *Welfare* under his own command and therewith by force of arms to apprehend seize and take the ships vessells and goods belonging to the ffrench king and his subjects or inhabitants ... and to bring the same to such port of this our realm of England as shall be most convenient in order to have them legally adjudged in our high court of Admiralty.[7]

Although Strong attaches considerable importance to this aim of privateering against French ships, since it grants him an identity quite distinct from that of buccaneer or pirate, his financiers surely cannot have expected to obtain rich rewards from such vessels taken off the Peruvian coast which would have been limited to the sort of buccaneer we have been discussing, nor would they have been prepared to back the venture simply in the hope of achieving a profit from ships by chance encountered on the long voyage. The obvious reason for such a commission was that it allowed them to throw a mantle of legality over the expedition and involve in it other hopefully lucrative, but from the Spanish point of view, illegal aims. Richard Simson who sailed in the *Welfare* elucidates these in his account of the proceedings.[8]

First, like Narborough, Strong intended to test the market for trade with a cargo thought suitable for the purpose, including 'Bayes, Stockins, Arms and other Iron Work as Hatchets, Hows etc'.[9] In fact the expectations of potential profit in Peru went rather further than this, for Simson alleges that some believed a return of 1600 per cent was possible. Granted the folly of such hopes at this time, it causes little surprise to learn that others also dreamt of uncovering a Spanish treasure ship which was thought to have run aground in the vicinity of Santa Elena. Dampier, of course, had already recorded in his journal reports of two such wrecks close to the Gulf of Guayaquil. But although the entertaining of such prospects for gain would appear to be beyond the bounds of reason, in some ways Strong's enterprise was an endeavour to emulate the success of Sir William Phipps, who two years previously had found a sunken Spanish galleon off Hispaniola, recovering booty to the value of £300 000, of which his own share was £16 000, with each investment of £100 bringing a return of £10 000.[10]

In his dealings with the Spanish, Strong followed a similar approach to that used by Narborough. On the occasion of their first meeting in the Bay of Herradura, south of Coquimbo, he instructed his interpreter to reveal only the peaceful and hopefully acceptable side of the expedition, adding in a casual fashion that he would like to trade. Such is the report of the meeting in Spanish documents.

> He comes sent by King William and Queen Mary of England to carry out privateering acts against the ships of French pirates in these seas. He bears a warrant as evidence of the peace and alliance between the English Crown and Your Majesty, requesting that he be given provisions which he needs, and stating that if they wanted to trade he had brought merchandise from his country.[11]

Again, as was the case with Narborough, at a later point in the voyage, some Englishmen captured by the Spanish reported that Strong also intended 'to establish a trading factory on one of the islands in these seas'.[12] Although Strong had not come prepared to use force on this occasion, the possibility of some future action is borne in mind by Simson, specifically with reference to the Juan Fernández Islands. 'If these two islands with Mocha were fortified by the English, they would be capable in case of a Breach with

Spaine of doeing them a great deal of mischief.'[13] These, then are
the aims of the venture, let us consider its achievements.

John Strong was placed in command of the *Welfare*, a ship of 270
tons, with 40 guns and a crew of 90 men and boys. Sailing alone,
she left the Downs on 12 October and Plymouth on 1 November
1689, heading for Madeira and the Cape Verde Islands. Early in the
New Year they reached the coast of South America, but were
unable to refresh at Puerto Deseado because of strong winds.
These finally drove them, on 27 January 1690, into a sound
between two islands to which Strong attached the name Falkland,
after the Treasurer of the Navy, and where they made the first
indisputable landings. Eventually Cape Vírgenes was passed on 10
February 1690, but due to the lateness of the season they were to be
delayed further in the Straits by bad weather, the usual rain, snow
and gale force winds. Even so, in contrast to Narborough who had
left England a month earlier in the year and wintered on the
Argentine coast, taking over 13 months to reach the South Sea,
Strong emerged from the Straits on 21 May, less than seven
months after departure, his time bettered only by that of Brouwer
who followed a course through the Strait of Lemaire. The first
landfall was made at the island of Mocha on 10 June.

Finding the island deserted save for a few horses and dogs, and
the two settlements in ruins as a consequence of the Spanish policy
of depopulation, Strong set out for the mainland on 18 June,
approaching at Punta de la Galera a little to the south of Valdivia
on the 23rd of the month, under cover of a flag of truce. However,
when a boat was lowered to take some men ashore it was fired
upon, obliging Strong to take refuge again at Mocha. Although
sufficient to persuade the English not to press ahead with efforts to
come ashore, the guns at Valdivia fell far short of Simson's
estimate of 100 in a fort to the north, and three other fortified
positions with 80 guns each.

With one-tenth of their number already dead and fifty ill,
probably as a result of the enforced stay in the Straits, and
discouraged by this first attempt to contact the Spanish, they sailed
northwards putting in at the Bay of Herradura on 8 July. The
Spanish again appeared openly hostile, according to the English
firing on their flag of truce, but Simson's claim that 500 cavalrymen
occupied the shore must be another exaggeration. On this occasion,
Strong was not deterred by the preliminary exchange of shots and
a boat was finally sent ashore bearing a letter for the local

*corregidor.* This revealed the nature of the commission granted by William and Mary, underlined the state of peace between the two nations, and requested some trade. With all courtesy the Spaniards promised a reply on the following day, but when the interpreter, Anthony Bose of Ostende, was sent ashore to receive it, he failed to return and those who had accompanied him were informed that no trade was possible without the authorisation of the governor of Chile. Strong in the journal at first relates that Bose was forcibly detained, but later reveals that the Spanish declared his stay among them to be a voluntary one. Such a version is supported by Simson, who discloses that several of the crew were won over by the 'feigned kindness' of the Spanish, and particularly by a Scotswoman.

After the failure to win any trade in Chile, the *Welfare* departed northwards on 10 July, due to a fog missing Copiapó where they had hoped to take on fresh water, and still looking for refreshment in vain off Paita and Cape Blanco on 4 and 5 August. They were now close to the location where they intended to begin exploration for the wreck of the treasure ship, but all the time kept a lookout for likely prizes. While finally taking aboard food and water in exchange for merchandise at Río Tumbes on 12 August, they sighted two sails and immediately gave chase. The slower of the two ships was taken and found to be carrying a cargo of timber from Guayaquil to Paita. Simson justifies their action in these terms. 'The reason this Spanish shipp was taken by ours was because she was unknown, or must before our close meeting be reckoned so to be; ffor a ffrench Privateere ... might command a Spanish prize or set up Spanish colours.'[14] To atone for their error, the Spanish captain, Alejandro de la Madrid, and his officers were entertained by Strong all that night before being sent ashore to inform others in the area of the peaceful intentions of the *Welfare* and her crew. Consequently, on 14 August a small group of Spaniards came aboard and a little trading took place, the value of which Simson estimates at 7000 pesos. Conversation with his visitors led Strong to record the existence of gold in the Río Tumbes, but the river was disappointingly 'full of alligators and other ravenous fish'. There was mention too of a visit six weeks previously by a French ship, probably Franco or an associate, which had destroyed local commercial shipping. However, when Strong enquired about the wreck off Santa Elena he was told that the only one of which they were aware was a vessel sunk three or four years ago with a poor cargo of cloth, most of which had been salvaged.[15]

Despite this unwelcome and perhaps deliberately misleading news, Strong set out for the supposed site of the wreck. A boat sent ashore at Santa Elena on 21 August could find no trace, but on the next day the captain of another vessel which they had chased, again they alleged under the impression that she was a French privateer, was able to offer more precise but still discouraging news. According to Strong the wreck had been buried in the sand over 25 years and some 12 million pesos lay securely hidden within her. Simson describes her as the vice-admiral of the South Sea, gone aground in 1659 and from which only about 20 000 pesos had been salvaged.

The incident which most closely tallies with these details is the foundering of the *Jesús María de la Limpia Concepción* on the night of 26 October 1654, in the Bay of Chanduy on the northern side of the Gulf of Guayaquil, while transporting silver to Panama.[16] She was one of the often criticised 1000-ton galleons built by viceroy Mancera at the time of the Brouwer intrusion. As is often the case, tales of sunken treasure and the dream of rapidly acquired riches seem to have distorted the reality, for the ship was most likely carrying three to four million pesos, over a third of which was unregistered bullion, and almost all of which was salvaged during the following six or seven years.

The failure to establish any significant trade, the absence of prizes of value, French or Spanish, and now the impossibility of realising their aims with regard to the treasure ship, made it increasingly unlikely that any profit would be derived from Strong's venture. Furthermore, settlers in the Gulf of Guayaquil who had originally responded, if only to a small degree, to his peaceful overtures, were now becoming anxious about their own position. For dealing with the English they could bring down the severest of penalties upon their heads, and so they now took action to persuade them to depart, warning of the impending arrival of a fleet of four men-of-war and 20 merchantmen, and claiming to be able to obtain goods at Portobello and Cartagena that were cheaper than those carried by the *Welfare*. Yet Strong continued to search for the wreck or the prize that could still turn his enterprise into a success. On 26 August he caught sight of a ship without colours, supposed her to be French and gave chase. Her crew in panic ran her aground and then fled, but when Strong discovered them to be

Spanish he welcomed them to return and take possession of her intact. Presumably there was nothing of value in her.

This fresh disappointment, added to the pessimism which by now must have replaced the enthusiastic optimism at the outset of the venture, was sufficient to drive Strong southwards for the return to England. Initially, course was set for the Juan Fernández Isles with the main aim of gathering some essential supplies before grappling again with the rigours of the Straits, but where on 12 and 13 October they embarked four buccaneers left behind by Davis on his return to the West Indies in 1687.[17] Reluctant still to accept defeat, Strong decided to try his luck for what was to be the last time, by inviting Spaniards on the Chilean coast to trade. With this intent a boat went ashore near the mouth of the River Bío Bío close to the city of Concepción on 11 November, bearing a letter for some people seen there on the previous day. Their reply was that no trade could be commenced without them obtaining prior approval from the governor of Chile. This Strong tried to do by sending ashore 14 men to deliver his request, although, doubtlessly expecting some trick, with precise orders not to land. However, when the Spanish brought out fresh food and water, 12 of them could not resist the temptation, but once on land were swiftly surrounded by 50 horsemen. Only one of the 12 succeeded in returning to the *Welfare* and he was shot in the leg. The episode is neatly, if bitterly, summarised by Strong. 'We lost eleaven of ye lustiest men we had Aboard by ye treachery of these false hearted Spaniards.'[18]

As far as Strong was concerned this was the last straw. He had made every effort to fulfil the aims of his expedition, but each time had met with little or no success. The Spanish were clearly unwilling or afraid to have anything to do with him, regardless of the state of peace between the two nations in Europe. Many of his men were ill, the remainder tired, weary and short of food, and Strong himself was unwilling to lose any more as prisoners to the Spanish. To resolve the dilemma of whether to abandon the enterprise and return home, or remain in the South Sea to be revenged on the Spanish, a council meeting was called. Taking into account that just six months provisions were left, sufficient only for the voyage home, the decision was that a letter be sent ashore requesting good treatment for their companions who were captives. Once this was done the remainder would indeed sail for England.

They departed the coast of Chile on 13 November and entered the Atlantic after passing the Straits of Magellan a month later. On 16 February 1691 they reached Barbados and were delayed for some time by being pressed into service to search for a French privateer, whom they failed to apprehend. After loading a cargo of sugar they left for London on 4 April. Ironically, it was only as they approached home waters, to be more precise the north west of Ireland, that they finally took two prizes: the first a Dutch flyboat called the *Crown Prince Frederick*, seized on 29 May with a cargo of French wine for Copenhagen, and the second a smaller craft from Norway transporting pickled salmon and other fish and provisions to France. They were both sailed, along with the *Welfare* into the River Tyne, where Strong anchored close to North Shields from 14 to 18 June. Although Strong's own journal ends at this point, Simson reveals the near loss of the *Welfare* close to Yarmouth as they sought their final destination, London. The two prizes after assessment in the Admiralty Prize Court were probably judged to be worth less than £1800.[19] Simson this time concisely sums up the feelings of himself and doubtlessly many others. 'A traverse of near 4000 miles might have promised more, we for a long time, and to little purpose, convers'd with monsters of both men and beasts.'[20]

Strong's venture marked another failure for those Englishmen enticed to the South Sea for commerce, and now also as the hunters of sunken treasure as well as seekers of French prizes. Since the recent uniting of Spain and England under the Grand Alliance some had presumably been encouraged to believe that the reception for an English ship would be rather more amicable than that accorded to Narborough. But Strong had the bad luck to arrive, like Charles Swan from London, at a time of continuing buccaneer activity which, though much smaller scale than in the past, nevertheless still maintained the coast on a state of alert and disrupted shipping. Naturally, therefore, the Spanish opted for precautionary measures when he appeared off Chile and treated offers of contact warily. The first reaction was defensive, as we would expect, but later developed into a sense of perplexity when the English released undamaged the vessels they had overhauled in the Gulf of Guayaquil, claiming they had originally believed them to be French buccaneers or privateers. But the presence of an English ship on the Peruvian coast, receiving a relatively hospitable reception from some settlers eager to trade, was certainly a novelty, and soon an embarrassment when local officials were informed that it amounted to a disregard of their proper duty to allow such proceedings to take place.

Viceroy Monclova initially shared the uncertainties about Strong's precise motives, but after consideration concluded that in spite of his lack of hostility he must be treated as an unwelcome intruder, since lack of success in trade or a shortage of food might compel him to turn against the coastal communities and shipping of Peru. Moreover, the viceroy felt that Strong must have passed into the South Sea from the Straits of Magellan during the months of May and June, 'the harshest of winter in this hemisphere', which was also of concern for it seemed to contradict the established belief that the viceroyalty was safe from incursion via the southern route at that time of the year.[21] Strong had in fact reached the South Sea towards the end of May, but still much closer to the winter season than any of the other expeditions we have described, with the exception of van Speilbergen who reached the South Sea during the first week of May.

As regards Strong's proposal to trade in the South Sea in view of the improved relations between Spain and England in Europe, and under the authority granted by the commission from William and Mary, Monclova made it quite plain that despite any treaty of peace, Spain still reserved for itself the sole right to trade with its colonies in America, and neither the treaty nor the commission offered any relaxation of that basic principle. 'And so I presume', he wrote:

> that this Captain Strong has believed that he would be able to trade with his goods in these waters, as in fact others of his nation have done in the islands and along the coast of the Caribbean; . . . if John Strong were to seek a conversation in this port of Callao, and with the flagship of this South Sea during the voyage she is going to make to Panama or during her return, I will order that he be disarmed, for there is no clause in the peace that gives permission to any nation to sail these waters.[22]

Although acting above in recognition of instructions from Madrid on 24 January and 30 September 1689, Monclova at the same time sought to question this policy. In accordance with it, English ships which strayed into the South Sea or were driven there by storms or by the need for fresh supplies, were to be

disarmed, and if they carried letters of commission from William
and Mary, were to be escorted to the Straits of Magellan and
provided with supplies for a return voyage to Jamaica. The result
of Monclova's request for a clarification of this policy was a series
of discussions by the *Junta de Guerra de Indias*. One of the findings
of this body concerned the terms under which an English ship
might receive aid in a Spanish American port.

> It is only stipulated that if as a result of a storm, or if pursued by
> pirates, or because of some other disaster, the subjects and ships
> of either of the two allied parties were cast into the ports, rivers
> or inlets of America, they should be reciprocally treated in a
> humane and kind manner, providing them with food and what-
> ever they might require to continue their voyage.[23]

Hence, intervention of a deliberate nature, for example for the
purposes of trade, was excluded by this provision. But of more
resounding consequence with regard to the Viceroyalty of Peru,
was a further restriction on the above facilities.

> The Council considers it to be without doubt or argument that it
> only extends to, and must be interpreted with regard to, ports
> and coasts in the Spanish Caribbean, where the English also
> possess territories and have settlements, but not in the South Sea
> where they have none, and no right to have any, and even less
> right to set course thither on their voyages.

Therefore, the English had no right to be present in the South Sea,
and any such intervention on their part would be treated as a
hostile act. Thus the *Junta* recommended that no Spanish official
should be allowed to trade nor have dealings of any sort with foreign
ships that reached South Sea coasts, even in cases of emergency.

> Your Majesty must order that viceroys, presidents, governors of
> ports or coastal towns, or any other officials or persons should
> not hold discussions nor engage in trade, nor admit any foreign
> nation or nations which try to enter port, but effectively close the
> door to them regardless of whatever reasons or pretexts they
> allege, acting in a hostile manner towards them if they should
> attempt to do this, treating them as if they were fully declared
> enemies.

Such a statement comprehensively answers any questions about why Strong was not accorded a lasting, hospitable reception even though he acted without hostility, and provides the evidence for rendering understandable the response of the authorities in Chile shortly before he departed for England. Viceroy Monclova was commended for the measures he had taken and was allowed to proceed with the cases of those Englishmen who had become prisoners. Two of these, who had been sent to Lima, were part of the group left at the Juan Fernández Isles by the buccaneer Davis, and so in view of their piratical actions on the coasts of Peru and Chile were sentenced to death. A further eight prisoners who had formed part only of Strong's expedition were retained in Chile, where they were to be detained far from the coast.[24] The nature of the viceroy's response to Franco and Strong was tempered by the realisation that they represented the end of a phase rather than a new challenge, that they presented no serious threat to coastal towns or even villages, and that the cost of any defence must be consistent with these realities if it were to be acceptable to the crown.

Therefore, although he admired the speed with which his predecessor had reacted to the clamour of the *limeños* by encircling their city with a wall, Monclova numbered himself among those who expressed doubts about whether there were resources in the city sufficient to arm and man the entire perimeter. Furthermore, while accepting that there would always be 'pirates' along the coast of Peru, he supported the view which others had expressed throughout the century that attempts to fortify every likely landing site were fruitless, particularly when many areas of the viceroyalty were protected 'by their own barrenness'.[25] Hence, he concentrated his labours on the maintenance of the usual maritime operations to defend commerce and to seek out the intruders wherever they might be, bearing in mind the 'need to counterbalance the costs of seeking them out, at a time when the Royal Treasury is in such a ruinous condition, with the uncertainty of finding them, so as not to incur expenditure in vain'.[26] In practice this meant that small coastal traders were easy prey for Franco and company, with Monclova 'disillusioned that there is not strength in the viceroy nor in anyone else to persuade them to arm and crew their ships with some means of defence',[27] while his patrols ranged from the Juan Fernández Isles to Panama without apparently a single reported contact with either Franco or Strong between 1689 and 1695.

During the period up to 1693, with the crown squadron reduced to the 30-year-old *Guadalupe* and the equally venerable patax *San Lorenzo*, now fulfilling the role of vice-admiral, Monclova had relied on at least one vessel provided by the private company *Nuestra Señora de Guía*. As this drifted towards insolvency with the lack of crown funding, the effect of a continuing, nagging foreign presence in Peruvian waters was to encourage the increasing dependence on private, local sources for the maintenance of these operations. Consequently, by 1695, thanks to contributions from the merchant community of some 300 000 pesos, the *Armada del Mar del Sur* comprised two new galleons, the *Santísimo Sacramento* and the *Nuestra Señora de la Concepción*, of 845 tons and 701 tons respectively, a new patax, the *Santa Cruz*, of 252 tons partially paid for by the sale of the *Lorenzo*, a secondhand galleon, *Jesús, María y José*, bought from merchants, and a frigate presented as a gift by merchants. The total complement of this force is listed on one occasion as 1238 men and 144 guns, which represents a remarkable reversal in the declining fortunes of crown ships in Peru.[28] In the end it was neither Franco nor Strong who were to justify the generosity of local merchants in rebuilding the fleet, but the first rumours of a French interest in the South Sea which was to point the way to the trading ventures of the early eighteenth century.

The sources of French attraction towards the South Sea can certainly be traced back to the involvement of buccaneers from that nation in the wave of intrusions across the Isthmus of Panama, which began with Sharp and company in 1680. Yet, as we have seen, even earlier Baltasar Pardo and Diego Peñalosa, whose obscure background and undercover dealings have much in common with those of Narborough's don Carlos, had presented Peruvian projects to the French crown. In 1684 the Spanish crown was still receiving and circulating information which referred both to the presence of Peñalosa in France, where he had been seen 'handling money', and also to the fitting out of ships whose destination might be the New World.[29] But as long ago as twenty years previously, the *Compagnie des Indes Orientales* enjoyed the right, which it had not exercised, of fitting out expeditions for the South Sea.

Now, during the early months of 1695 when Spain and France were still at war, the former buccaneer Massertie, who had recorded the final stages of Captain Franco's venture, had begun to seek support for a privateering expedition. Subsequently, a force of six ships (one of them a naval vessel) carrying 126 guns and 720 men was gathered at La Rochelle for a semi-official voyage placed under the command of a naval officer Jean-Baptiste de Gennes.[30]

They set sail on 3 June for an experience that was to instruct them in the harsh realities other nations had already learnt of fitting out a successful expedition to the west coast of South America. Although their slow rate of progress ensured that they did not enter the Straits of Magellan until the second week of February 1696, eight months after leaving France, this time is broadly consistent with that achieved by the Dutch in the first half of the century. But de Gennes, his crews already ravaged by illness on the African coast, chose neither to find a safe harbour in which to winter nor to pursue a late and turbulent passage into the South Sea as did Strong, admittedly after a much shorter voyage. The project to reach Peru was thus abandoned and the expedition set course for Ilha Grande near to Rio de Janeiro to refresh, before continuing first to the West Indies and then France. In the words of the journalist Froger, 'it may be easily imagin'd in so lamentable a Conjuncture, how great a Mortification this Disappointment was to Persons who hoped to make their Fortune by so noble an Enterprize. There was not one Mariner of the whole Squadron who did not choose rather to perish with hunger, than to be diverted from the right Course.'[31] Even so, he urged that the court should not be discouraged by an undertaking which failed only for want of experience.

Whereas the de Gennes venture signifies the desire of another European power to challenge Spain directly in the South Sea, it was through a course of action, privateering, which had been common throughout the seventeenth century. His successor, however, was to appear in a role which points to a new era of relatively peaceful French activity which dominated the first two decades of the following century. In 1698, following the signing of the Treaty of Ryswick, there was created the *Compagnie Royale de la Mer Pacifique* which sought to exploit the new climate of friendly relations. In actual fact, although the initial scheme for a second French expedition to Peru envisaged reconnaissance and trade, in the manner of Narborough, it also went much further, revealing to what extent the French were succumbing to the lure of the South Sea and of Peru. For example, there were the usual references to islands famous for their gold and silver mines, to the possibility of colonies in Patagonia or Chile (again like Narborough), to settlements in the Straits of Magellan producing their own wheat and wines, the likelihood of mounting a trade in furs and skins and even prospects for whaling. These grandiose dreams were to be realised by an initial fleet of seven ships and 700 men.

Ultimately, however, a sense of moderation and reality prevailed as backers and would-be participants, including de Gennes, withdrew from the grand project. The force which left La Rochelle on 17 December 1698, therefore, comprised the *Phélypeaux* (44 guns and 150 men), the *Maurepas* (50 guns and 180 men), together with two smaller vessels which did not even cross the Atlantic. They were commanded by Jacques Gouin de Beauchesne and enjoyed the services as pilot of a former buccaneer, Jouan, possibly the quartermaster who had left Franco at the Juan Fernández Islands. Like their numbers, the objectives of the force had also been reduced to the more attainable commerce and reconnaissance.

The two ships entered the Straits of Magellan on 24 June 1699 but did not debouch until 21 January 1700, thirteen months after leaving France. The local authorities on the coast of Chile seem to have been successively wary, welcoming and finally hostile, which encouraged Beauchesne to proceed northwards. But in the Peruvian ports of Ilo, Pisco and even Callao he managed to dispose of some of his French textiles. Following an only moderately rewarding visit to the Galapagos Islands (7 June–7 July) for water and fresh supplies, his further offers of trade were rejected at Guayaquil, Paita and Yerbabuena, and so the remaining merchandise could only be traded at Ilo in October after threats to use force. On return to La Rochelle, 7 August 1701, significantly via Cape Horn, it was calculated that the entire cargo produced a return of 400 000 *livres*, which amounted to a loss on the voyage of 100 000 *livres*.

Nevertheless, in comparison with his English counterpart Narborough, he not only increased his nation's practical navigational and cartographical knowledge of the South Sea and its approaches, making detailed observations and drawings, but by disposing of even damaged cargo pushed ajar a door to a new trading market that his compatriots would soon fully open in the changed political and commercial climate of the eighteenth century. His pioneering effort is remembered in the attachment of his name to an island he discovered south of East Falkland, and that of the seafaring community of St Malo which would back many of those who followed him, in the term Iles Malouines, Spanish Malvinas, for the Falkland Islands in general.

And so, for the Viceroyalty of Peru, the seventeenth century came to a close as it had begun, with the intrusion of the Dutch, amid uncertainties created by the arrival of ships from a European power making its first irruption into the South Sea. For it was the expeditions of de Gennes and Beauchesne sailing directly from France and with a measure of official support, that most troubled both viceroy and crown, rather than Franco or Strong. Indeed, what one can only term alarm at the likelihood of a French challenge had already been expressed a decade earlier, when Pedro de Ronquillo, the Spanish ambassador in London, had written urging an investigation of plans then being made in Brest to send ships to the New World. The *Junta de Guerra* after deliberation resignedly commented that 'it considers it impossible to oppose the forces of a crown such as that of France in any enterprise that it would wish to attempt in the Indies'.[32]

Viceroy Monclova had first heard of the preparation of the de Gennes squadron in a letter from the President of Guatemala, which he received in Lima on 10 January 1696. The transmission of the warning was the result of deliberations in Spain by the *Junta de Guerra* in April 1695.[33] Subsequently, Monclova set in motion the full panoply of defensive precautions available to him, distributing his own warnings to ports north and south and particularly to Valdivia, sending a vessel to the Juan Fernández Isles to seek out signs of intruders, ensuring the readiness of the garrison at Callao, drawing up new lists of those available for militia service, levying an additional 100 cavalrymen in Lima and attempting to improve familiarity with equestrian skills by decreeing that no Spaniard between 18 and 50 years of age, capable of wielding a sword, was to ride in a carriage or on a mule.

During the first half of 1696, fairly accurate details of the French force and its precise date of departure had been delivered to Peru through royal dispatches, along with news from Rio de Janeiro, via Buenos Aires and Chile, of the actual presence of de Gennes' ships off the Brazilian coast the previous December. Thus, the rhythm of preparations in response was maintained in Peru, with the viceroy convinced that he could call on 3000 Spaniards for the defence of Lima, which number could be raised to 8000 men by the inclusion of Indians, mulattoes and free negroes. These figures tally very closely with those quoted by his predecessors the Count of

Castellar and Archbishop Liñán y Cisneros in 1675 and 1680 respectively.

Gradually, as the estimated time of de Gennes' arrival in the South Sea passed without incident, to be followed by confirmation that he had abandoned his plans and been seen once more off the Brazilian coast, Monclova prepared to stand down his militia and announce an end to the alert in Peru. No sooner was this done than, on 26 July 1697, he was in receipt of the tragic news that Cartagena had fallen to a French naval force over two months ago.[34] Without delay aid of men, materials and money was shipped to Panama in case this port were to be the next under threat. At the heart of the viceroyalty, a new force of cavalrymen was raised, this time 500 strong, a fund created throughout Peru to collect financial support for defence measures, and discussions held concerning the most effective means of defending Lima, obviously now felt to be in danger of some sort of assault. The opinion which prevailed was that of Monclova himself, reflecting his scepticism over the usefulness of the wall, namely that a space should be cleared and levelled on the exterior of the perimeter, in which cavalry and infantrymen could manoeuvre with ease.

Although the worst fears of 1697 were not translated into fact, the confirmation of French interest in Peru that was provided through the Beauchesne expedition implied that at least in the early years of the coming century Peruvian viceroys would continue to be troubled and preoccupied by foreign intrusion.

# Epilogue

None of the expeditions whose exploits we have followed seem at first sight to have left any lasting trace of their presence on the shores of the South Sea coast of the Viceroyalty of Peru, beyond the survival of a few names of geographical locations. Mostly they came to explore, to reconnoitre and to chart, to trade, to plunder and occasionally with some vague proposal to lay the foundations of a future settlement which a few were rash enough to believe might one day flourish as a base from which to launch an attack on Spanish power in the region. Without ever remotely fulfilling this latter objective, the Brouwer expedition to Valdivia progressed further than any other towards the idea of permanency, but only by simply clearing the ground in preparation for the construction of a fortified stockade. None of the rest advanced far beyond the acquisition of skills which enabled them to live for brief periods off the land, or more particularly the islands of the South Sea coast, whose individual characteristics soon passed into the store of European knowledge of the South Sea, and where they enjoyed some immunity from counter-attack. With the benefit of hindsight this failure to achieve permanent trading or colonial outposts is not surprising, for despite the general claims that defences were weak, Spain was to lose relatively little territory to foreign interlopers at this stage of its colonial enterprise. If it were already difficult to challenge and dislodge Spain's possessions in the more accessible waters of the Caribbean, then to do so in the South Sea would have required remarkable good fortune and an enormous degree of negligence on the part of the Spaniards themselves.

Another Dutchman, van Speilbergen, came close to combining his own good luck with the negligence of his opponents, at a time when even the defences of Callao and Lima could not have withstood for long a determined assault mounted from a powerful maritime squadron, with access to provisions and reinforcements and supported by well-armed soldiers. In reality, it was virtually impossible at that time to lead such a squadron to the South Sea intact, without suffering losses due to disease, desertions, climate and violent disturbances of the weather, and there maintain such a force at the peak of its original effectiveness. L'Hermite's Nassau

Fleet was drained of its power in this way, as well as being further undermined by indiscipline and unrest.

Similar circumstances also confronted the lone trader, once in the South Sea obliged to live on his wits or take the dangerous risk of appealing to the goodwill of local authorities and settlers by attempting to barter for fresh water and supplies. For until the latter years of the century, it would appear that the commerical exigencies of the viceroyalty were never so unfulfilled, and hence the demands for goods so great, that they were considered of such a magnitude as to override the normal prohibitions on commerce with foreign vessels.

Only the buccaneers, generally arriving after a shorter voyage, reinforced at times by new recruits from the West Indies, seeking personal gain with bold and reckless resolve and unrestricted by the niceties of proper conduct for the sake of future good relations, succeeded in maintaining a relatively lengthy presence and deriving some worthwhile spoils. In the final analysis, the remoteness of the South Sea, the dangers of the passage and the inhospitability of the Spanish were Peru's best defence, although they were never a total deterrent to the determined adventurer nor to the starry-eyed.

But, remarkably perhaps in these circumstances, the experiences we have related do not have a negative effect in the sense of deterring or curtailing interest in the South Sea. Therefore, as we stand at the end of one century looking back and turn to gaze ahead into that which followed, there is a broad consistency with regard to the components which comprised the attraction of the South Sea and lured men there, whether one speaks in terms of the acquisition of bullion, trade prospects, the location of future settlements or the draw of exotic lands and people. Indeed, by the end of the seventeenth century, Europe stands indebted to those whose suffering with scant rewards facilitated the dissemination of practical knowledge concerning the most favourable routes, safe anchorages, sources of food and fresh water and the most appropriate seasons for embarking on the various phases of an expedition. Without these fundamental labours, often accompanied it is true by a tendency to magnify or distort the rewards that by and large eluded their seekers in the seventeenth century, the continuing speculation of merchants and adventurers alike would have appeared doubly foolish, and without them the increased frequency of visits in the following century would at the very least have been less easy to realise.

Therefore, despite the generally unfavourable returns on investments in the case of the ventures we have discussed, the attraction remained as tantalising and as persuasive as ever, capable of launching the wildest of dreams and luring those bent on rapid financial gains. As an example of the former, before the century was out, William Paterson embarked on what was to become the disastrous Scots' Darien enterprise (1698–1700), whose origins can be traced directly to the inspiration provided by buccaneers who traversed that region after they came ashore from Golden Isle to the Isthmus of Panama.[1] For it was an acquaintance with Dampier, perusal of the manuscript of Wafer's forthcoming book and finally an invitation accepted by the latter to visit Scotland in order to provide in secret the final confirmatory information, which strengthened the determination to create a New Edinburgh in such an unwelcoming location. Despite the aid of other companions of Sharp and of his Indian allies, the adventure succumbed tragically to disease, starvation, the climate, mismanagement and finally Spanish opposition. That the proponent of the scheme was the same Paterson who had only recently formulated the sound ideas which had led to the creation of the Bank of England, and that he was so easily persuaded to overlook, or at least minimise, the obstacles of which Wafer was very much aware, once more demonstrates the alluring nature of the South Sea.

As regards the approaches from the south, the eighteenth century was to witness a marked increase in the volume of traffic, and in some cases in the profits acquired, as a result of the changed or changing political and economic climate. The death of the Spanish king Charles II in 1700, and the recognition by him of Philip of Anjou as his successor, provoked a *rapprochement* of Franco-Spanish interests and almost as inevitably the opposition of England through the War of the Succession (1702–13). Initially illicitly in 1701, but gradually with some degree of official support in Madrid and Lima, especially when the Frenchmen averred their ultimate aim to be China (not Peru) or offered their services as a naval force in support of the Peruvian squadron's pursuit of English interlopers, French traders proved the economic viability of voyages to the South Sea. At first using the route through the Straits of Magellan, and finally establishing Cape Horn as the standard track, they returned with profits from their visits to the coasts of Peru and Chile.[2]

The indication that a changing commercial situation was beginning to favour the intrepid intruder had already been proved by Beauchesne, who although at first opposed on the Chilean coast was in the end to dispose of all his damaged cargo further to the north. The reason was necessity, namely the shortage of goods in circulation in the viceroyalty as a consequence of the interruption to normal traffic via the isthmian route to Panama and Callao. The Dutch and Narborough (if not Strong) had sought to unload their merchandise at times when Peru was supplied, imperfectly though at least fairly regularly, by this traditional route. But the Spanish themselves had already reduced its frequency to triennial sailings from Callao in 1666. The buccaneers had rendered Peruvian merchants more disinclined to risk their bullion even when less frequent Portobello fairs were held in the 1680s, and when they enjoyed the backing of the English and French crowns they proved a threat to any Spanish fleet daring to approach the Caribbean. It was this continuing interruption of the links and the resulting isolation of Peru from Cadiz during the War of the Succession, that is commercial necessity rather than any genuine feeling of amicability towards the French, which enabled the latter to achieve for a time the commercial returns that had eluded their predecessors.[3] This French presence lasted beyond the theoretical re-establishment of the Spanish monopoly after the Treaty of Utrecht, and even beyond the bankruptcy of the *Compagnie de la Mer du Sud* in 1720.

Talk of financial disaster brings us back to the English. Privateering, which had first attracted Drake, Cavendish and Hawkins over a century ago, still continued to tempt Englishmen to sail for Peru where, though perhaps less brutally, they sought to repeat the buccaneers' tactics of waylaying merchantmen or bullion vessels and blockading and even attacking ports which their compatriots had already identified as being worthy of attention. Dampier appropriately was the first in 1703, and the least successful, in what has recently been termed a 'fumbled tragicomedy, a bad replay of the buccaneer exploits some twenty years earlier'.[4] One of its failures was the attempt to realise his dreams of controlling the mines of Santa María on the Isthmus of Panama. He returned to England in 1707 after crossing the Pacific, as did Woodes Rogers (1708–11) and Shelvocke and Clipperton (1718–22) following their respective cruises in the South Sea. Of these Rogers is the most fascinating in the present context, quite apart from the fact that his account of the rescue of Alexander Selkirk, voluntary deserter in

the Juan Fernández Isles of the troubled Dampier expedition, was
to be refashioned by Defoe as the story of Robinson Crusoe. For
Rogers was the first to return from the South Sea, since the age of
Drake, with a respectable dividend for his backers in Bristol.[5]
Moreover, he did so at a time when English enthusiasm was about
to burgeon forth into a project that would ultimately, by its
dramatic collapse, upset an entire system of finance and credit,
namely the South Sea Scheme.

Against the background of renewed English hostility towards
both France and Spain, the South Sea yet again appeared to offer
tempting commercial prizes through the exchange of manufactures
such as cloth and ironmongery, for dyestuffs, cochineal, logwood
and even bullion. Furthermore, there existed practical English
experience of the routes, sailing conditions and most likely
localities in which to pursue a trade. In this respect it is pertinent to
note that one of William Hack's copies of the charts taken by Sharp
off the Peruvian coast was bought by the South Sea Company in
1711. As one writer comments, 'doubtless this volume played an
important part in the beguilement of the public during the rise of
that great speculative failure, the South Sea Bubble'.[6]

The rebirth of English optimism can be viewed, for example, in
the words of Robert Allen who in 1712 surveyed the history of
South Sea trade until the recent French penetration by the direct
Cape Horn route, as a prelude to pleading for a replacement of
their initiative by English merchants. As throughout the seventeenth century, the prizes were still listed as 'gold and silver in vast
quantities, costly pearls, emeraulds, amethists, and several other
sorts of precious stones, copper and other metals'.[7] In the previous
year, Thomas Bowrey had recommended Valdivia as a site for the
location of a commercial base, estimating that the port could be
taken by 1000 men or less, but, as had the Dutch nearly 70 years
earlier, trusting to an alliance with the local population, who 'may
profitably joyn with us against them [the Spanish]'.[8] Yet again the
main incentive was the claim that 'Baldivia produces ye most gold
of any place in ye S° Seas', though its southerly location and cold
climate also offered an opening for English woollens, together with
manufactured items. Clearly aware of the work of Narborough, in
a further proposal he maintained the need for a settlement en route
to the South Sea, probably in the vicinity of Puerto Deseado or San
Julián, advising that a frigate be dispatched with men and
equipment before the end of the following November 1711.

These ideas are a good indication of the climate of opinion in which the South Sea Company was instituted in that very year, the culmination of a process of dogged faith in the seemingly inexhaustible resources of Peru and its trading potential, which following the Elizabethan era was again outlined in the 1650s by Simón de Cáceres and finally deposited don Carlos at Valdivia. Although like these predecessors, the South Sea Scheme was floated on the notion of achieving access for English merchants to lands southward from the River Plate to Tierra del Fuego and along the west coast through the South Sea to North America, it ironically symbolises unrealised aspirations. For when the bubble of dream and speculation burst in 1720 with the collapse of the company, it had not yet managed to send a single ship to the Viceroyalty of Peru, as a result of restrictions imposed through the *asiento* of 1713, following the declaration of peace with Spain.[9]

Despite the failure of this particular venture, the commencement of the eighteenth century is marked by the intrusion of a much larger number of foreign vessels into the South Sea via the southern routes, a process that would radically alter the patterns of South Sea trade. But although Peru would be in more regular contact with a greater number of European countries, from then virtually until the present day what attracted them has not changed. From the arrival of the Spanish and throughout the century we have discussed, the single common objective of all comers was to plunder its wealth or seek the means to do so. In part the present economic condition of the republic is a legacy of that which we can see today, and the seventeenth century but a single link in a long chain of exploitation.

When considered through Spanish eyes, although foreign incursions were fewer and less regular than they were to be in the following century, the consequences were such in the seventeenth century that viceroys were obliged to assign an increasing proportion of their administrative labours to the development of measures for defence and retaliation. Even periods of relative calm, such as the governments of viceroys Chinchón (1629–39) or Alba de Liste (1656–61), were disturbed by the rumour of foreign intentions, the report of presumed sightings of hostile ships or news of the enemy's success elsewhere in the Indies. As the century advanced, what had originally been perceived as a potential threat to Spanish wealth and power, following the tentative probings of Mahu and van Noort, was transformed in later years into the innocuous entry of lone traders or voyages of reconnaissance, and the fiercely hostile presence of buccaneers in the main directed at shipping and the populations of smaller coastal communities. An evaluation has been made, where the evidence exists, of the precise repercussions of individual intrusions. But the belief that vast quantities of silver and gold fell into the hands of piratical and privateering ventures such as these has long been rejected, however, and it is more instructive to look elsewhere for the long-term consequences. [10]

As has also been shown, even a small delay in the departure of the Peruvian armada for Panama, let alone its postponement or cancellation, could upset a delicate balance of related factors governing the timing and finance of imperial trade, the availability of goods for sale in Peru, and even the ability of Spain to fulfil its obligations in Europe. Delays were attributable not simply to direct action by interlopers – blockades or attacks on shipping, but merely through the reluctance of the merchant community to hazard its bullion and merchandise at times of real or presumed danger, or as a result of viceroys insisting upon having proof of the absence of intruders (or at least no evidence to the contrary), before daring to dispatch crown bullion. Ultimately the operations of the Atlantic fleets sailing to Portobello were prejudiced.

For example, if due to the tardy arrival of silver from Peru, the galleons' departure from the Isthmus was late in the season, the whole Atlantic fleet was exposed to winter conditions, the danger of shipwreck and, if these were overcome, unloading difficulties in Spain. Worse still, the fleet might be obliged to winter in the Caribbean, thus increasing the costs of the whole operation while at the same time depriving the crown of a year's shipment of silver. Early in the century, when the crown still struggled vainly to maintain the annual rhythm of sailings, it advised that Peruvian silver should be in Panama by mid-April. Since the journey from Potosí to the Isthmus took three to four months, this implied that the silver needed to leave the mining areas in January. Such timing was if not impossible at least highly detrimental to levels of bullion shipments, for it did not allow merchants returning from the previous year's voyage to Panama time to conduct their business and obtain fresh supplies of silver, most of which was produced in the period January to March when there was ample water to drive the grinding mills. Early departures from Callao, therefore, implied much reduced cargoes of silver and also increased the exposure of merchants, crews and ships to the unhealthy air and waters of the Gulf of Panama. Late departures from Peru ran the increasing risk of coinciding with the best months for foreign intrusion. If one adds to these factors, the need to take into account the appropriate season for crossing the Isthmus at a time when rivers were not in flood, then one can begin to understand the normal concern of Peruvian viceroys for this major aspect of their administration, and the sense of alarm when intruders put so much in peril.[11]

As regards the general effect of the presence of hostile vessels on the more localised trade of the South Sea ports, this too involved issues which required the attention of successive viceroys. Like his counterpart the Duke of La Palata, viceroy Mancera discovered that an enemy squadron could also endanger the levels of silver production at Potosí, by preventing the regular shipments to Arica of the mercury upon which the refining process depended. He was, therefore, obliged to use a more costly overland route. Similarly, supplies of Peruvian mercury to the mines of New Spain could be interrupted.[12] Stocks of food and their efficient distribution, especially in the area of Lima, were also disturbed. For instance, the *cabildo* in 1614 and 1615 was forced to address the question of a shortage of bread and other basic foodstuffs, including animal feeds. Less obviously, it also discussed the need to improve lighting in the Plaza de Armas and elsewhere to facilitate the work of sentinels on guard.[13] Inevitably, the danger of interruptions to the normal provision of food led to hoarding and the necessity of introducing legislation for its control. Furthermore, the principal means by which the transport of foodstuffs was achieved from the coastal valleys to major areas of settlement, that is by sea, suffered not only as a result of the blockading of harbours and the destruction of vessels at sea or in port, but later in the century due to the damage done to shipbuilding centres and the prevention of the acquisition of the vital materials for the construction of replacement craft.

However, while it is impossible to quantify accurately the relative importance of each of these effects, we are now able to estimate, with some degree of certainty, the cost to the crown of those defensive precautions for which authorisation was given in the seventeenth century.[14] From the data available, it is clear that on three occasions the cost of defending the Viceroyalty of Peru against foreign intrusion reached such levels that a greater proportion of the revenue to the Lima treasury was consumed in this manner than it was possible to ship to Spain. Suddenly in 1624, when l'Hermite interrupted normal silver operations, defence costs climbed to their highest point for the entire century, at over 1½ million pesos or almost 38 per cent of crown revenue. Such was the case in 1658, not a year of foreign intrusion but a time when viceroy Alba was rebuilding his South Sea squadron and beginning to supply Valdivia on a more regular basis as a precaution against future intervention. Defence consumed nearly 29 per cent of revenue in that year.

The above are two isolated occurrences in single years when defence costs outstripped remittances to Spain. But following a period in which silver shipments and defence costs almost coincided in the early 1670s, as a result of problems on the Isthmus of Panama and the fears provoked by Narborough at Valdivia, defence expenditure finally rushed ahead of remittances to Spain on a more permanent basis from 1679 to 1690, in response to the arrival of the buccaneers.

In general, it is apparent that with the exception of the first Dutch intruders at the turn of the century, each incursion led not to a single rise in costs, but rather to a period of increase over a short span of years, as first counter-measures, and then reappraisals resulting in a strengthening of defences, were reflected in the statistics. This was the case from 1616 to 1620, 1626 to 1630 and during the 1640s. At each of these plateaux, defence consumed about 20 per cent of the revenue to the treasury in Lima. Overall, during the first fifty years of the century, silver bullion transported to Spain accounted for about 41 per cent of revenue, and defence costs some 14 per cent. However, the increased burden of defence is most markedly obvious in the years from 1650 to 1690, when defence costs on an average reach 21 per cent and remittances to Spain drop to about 25 per cent of revenue. What is utilised for defence is not now much less than the amount imported into Spain from Peru.

More startling, however, is the fact that these overall figures conceal a rapidly gathering momentum in defence costs from the 1670s, and especially in the decade from 1681–90. In this latter period there is a dramatic slump in the proportion of revenue to the Lima treasury transported to Spain, a mere 7 per cent or 1 818 477 pesos, whereas 33 per cent or 8 350 071 pesos was consumed in defence, and that at a time when private finance played a greater role.[15]

And so, although the number of individual acts of intervention into the South Sea was not large during the seventeenth century, the repercussions in terms of a financial commitment to defence and retaliation ultimately constituted a substantial drain on crown revenue. Quite simply, Peruvian silver bought the defence of the South Sea coasts, indirectly stimulating manufactures and commerce and inevitably reducing shipments of silver to Spain; where it was supposed to go under Spanish colonial trading policy. Over the century as a whole, defence was second only to remittances to Spain as a component of treasury expenditure in Peru.[16]

Bearing in mind the remoteness of the crown at all times, and periodically the need in Peru to act swiftly in response to sudden danger, there is obviously a degree of local independence in judgements taken in the viceroyalty concerning the utilisation of financial resources available. The statistics we have quoted are also clear evidence that the crown failed in its efforts to persuade treasury officials in Lima to keep defence costs down to protect levels of remittances to Spain. This slackening of ties that bound metropolis to colony might also be perceived in the unwillingness of the crown to support military and maritime projects to the extent felt appropriate in Peru, again because of the presumed reduction this would entail for shipments of silver. Likewise, divergent perspectives are apparent in the crown and viceroy's concern to maintain a regular rhythm of trade through the Isthmus of Panama, at times when merchants were unconvinced that it was safe to transport their silver and merchandise northwards. Although one must recognise too that the commercial community in Peru, as in Seville and Cadiz, in general favoured a less than annual pattern of trade in order to push up prices through a shortage of goods.

Without a doubt, however, it is also true that these same merchants were repeatedly, and with greater frequency as the century progressed, obliged to act on their own initiative or as a result of coercion by crown and viceroy, in defence of both crown and their own private interests. This was certainly the case in the latter years of the century when the crown was no longer prepared, nor able, to finance a South Sea squadron. But in reality, throughout the whole century, by means of forced or voluntary loans, gifts and services such as the raising of companies of armed men, the *Consulado* had actively contributed to defence. Hence, just as an ever greater share of royal revenue remained in Peru to finance measures against foreign intrusion, so too greater amounts of private capital were directed to these same ends.[17] This recourse to local resolve and finance was, of course, additionally demonstrated in those coastal communities such as Trujillo and Arica which shouldered the responsibility for their own protection, at times in face of viceroys who judged they were not worthy of it and who demanded that they hand over their arms for the strengthening of the capital and the crown fleet.

Therefore, although sporadic, foreign intervention into the South Sea provoked responses that were regular and lasting. The notion of a challenge to Spanish power may have been shortlived, and weakly founded from the start, but the rumour and reality of intrusion generated a need for a defensive response – the arming and training of militias, the construction and upkeep of fortifications, the manufacture of weapons, the maintenance of a maritime squadron and the dispatch of aid to Panama and Valdivia. The financial load of all of these was one which had become markedly onerous by the latter decades of the century, at a time when the incursions were resulting in damage at sites along the entire length of the coast, and also drawing attention to the weaknesses of existing commercial routes and administrative links across the Isthmus of Panama to Spain.

As did the Spanish crown in colonial times, in the name of financial constraint, later politicians of the Republic of Peru were to neglect the lessons of the need for an effective maritime force to maintain the communications and coastal defences of the region. Finally, one is encouraged to speculate on the continuing relevance of the requirement for resourcefulness on the part of the local population of Peru, when assessing the complex formulation of an identity and of common interests in the South Sea later in the eighteenth century, separate if not yet totally opposed to those of Spain.

# Sources

## Sources in general

The preceding account of foreign intervention into the South Sea is constructed principally from two distinct groups of sources: the official journals and the personal reports of those who participated, which for the first time, in each and every case, are considered alongside the Spanish perspective of events as recorded in seventeenth-century manuscripts now in the archives of Spain, England and Peru.

The former are in part derived from the versions contained in the renowned compilations of writers such as Purchas, de Bry, de Renneville, de Lussan, Exquemelin, Callander, Harris, the Churchills and particularly Burney. To these must be added twentieth-century studies, which in the main offer the same perspectives of the official journalist or fellow participants, based on the above compilations or in some cases directly on original manuscripts. The most noteworthy are Gerhard, Spate and Kemp and Lloyd. For lists of these and associated works see Chapter 1, note 9, and Chapter 6, notes 1 and 7 for the buccaneer phase. Of the accounts in Spanish, Chilean historians at times add original material on events in that region (e.g. Ch. 1, notes 18 and 21), while overall though not always reliable coverage is offered by Fernández Duro and Lohmann Villena (Ch. 1, note 9). Particularly valuable for the Dutch expeditions are the journals and reports included in two important series of travel literature, the Werken uitgegeven door de Linschoten vereeniging, and the Hakluyt Society publications which have translations into English (Ch. 2, note 2 and Ch. 3, note 2). In some cases contemporary published versions of individual journals constitute valuable primary sources (e.g. van Noort, Ch. 1, note 23, l'Hermite, Ch. 3, note 5, Brouwer, Ch. 4, note 10 and Narborough, Ch. 5, note 5), and some scholars have chosen to concentrate on the particular features of a single venture (Javet, Ch. 1, note 9, Rodríguez Crespo, Ch. 2, note 19, Medina, Ch. 4, note 10, and Dyer, Ch. 5, note 5 and Ch. 8, note 7). The manuscript journals of those who participated in the English ventures, together with associated maps, are of course to be found in the British Library, Department of Manuscripts (Ch. 5, note 5, Ch. 6, note 7, Ch. 7, note 3 and Ch. 8, notes 7 and 8).

The Spanish and Peruvian perspectives of foreign intervention, in contrast to most of the above, are almost exclusively drawn from manuscript sources, with the exception of the *memorias* or reports drawn up by viceroys at the conclusion of their term of office (e.g. Ch. 2, note 33, Ch. 4, note 27, Ch. 5, note 17 and Ch. 6, note 16). The unpublished material consists of the official correspondence of viceroys, crown decrees and instructions, the letters of officials, the clergy and private individuals in Peru, the discussions of bodies such as the *Consejo de Indias* and the *Junta de Guerra*, the results of official enquiries into the events and consequences of specific intrusions held in Peru, the eyewitness reports of those who saw for themselves, sometimes as defenders, sometimes as captives of the intruders, and finally, conversely, the declarations of members of the various expeditions who fell into Spanish hands or delivered themselves into Spanish hands, and were interrogated in Peru. On occasions, notably during the phase of buccaneer intervention, we must rely almost exclusively on Spanish manuscript sources to unravel a complex web of movements across the South Sea (Ch. 6, notes 13 and 35, Ch. 7, notes 21 and 35, and Ch. 8, note 2).

As we would expect, the Spanish documents generally provide more accurate information about local responses in Peru and record the official reaction of the crown, its councils and officials. They are our major source of documentation with regard to all measures of an offensive and defensive nature, a topic studied in respect of land-based fortifications mainly at Lima and Callao by Lohmann Villena (Ch. 1, note 37), and more widely in my own research. From them we can also evaluate the short and long-term effects of this whole period of foreign intrusion. Furthermore, they offer comments upon the intruding ships and their crews after the long voyage, discuss the effectiveness of the threat in commercial and military terms, and by reporting the declarations of those who had once formed part of the various ventures, present at times unofficial views of an entire voyage, with comments on shipboard life, its hardships, grievances and discipline.

Finally, wherever appropriate, literary reminiscences of foreign intervention have been recorded in the notes, some by contemporary or near contemporary authors of the events, most inevitably by Ricardo Palma, who can weave an intriguing tale with a snippet of truth and a lot of imagination (Ch. 2, note 21, Ch. 3, note 26, Ch. 4, notes 23 and 32, Ch. 5, note 27, Ch. 6, note 32 and Ch. 7, note 25).

## List of Manuscript sources

*Archivo General de Indias* (AGI), Seville
Audienca de Charcas: 270
Audienca de Lima: 33, 34, 36, 37, 38, 39, 40, 41, 42, 43, 45, 47, 48, 50, 51, 52, 53, 58, 60, 65, 68, 72, 73, 77, 78, 81, 86, 88, 89, 90, 91, 98, 135, 146, 149, 155, 225, 275, 301, 304, 329, 335, 570, 571, 572, 573, 574, 575, 576, 609, 610
Audienca de México: 24, 46
Audienca de Panamá: 17, 95, 96
Contratación: 167
Indiferente General: 1863, 1868, 1869, 1879, 2574, 2665
Patronato Real: 229–16, 268–2–2, 268–2–3, 268–2–4
*Archivo General del Ministerio de Relaciones Exteriores* (AGMRE), Lima
    1–1, 1–7, 1–8
*Archivo Histórico Nacional* (AHN), Madrid
Cartas de Indias: 296, 306, 392, 403
Inquisición: 1030
*Archivo Nacional* (AN), Lima
Consulado: 1–1a, 2, 3, 4, 6a, 7

*Biblioteca Colombina* (B. Colom.), Seville
64-7-114
*British Library* (BL), London
Additional: 5414, 12429, 13964, 13974, 13975, 13977, 13992, 17581, 19571,
　　21539, 28140, 28446, 28457
Egerton: 2541
Harley: 4034, 4225, 5101
Sloane: 44, 45, 46A, 46B, 47, 48, 49, 54, 86, 239, 667, 672, 819, 1050, 2724,
　　2752A, 2752B, 3236, 3295, 3820, 3833
*Biblioteca Nacional* (BN), Lima
B. 283, B. 411, F. 160
*Biblioteca Nacional* (BN), Madrid
2341, 2348, 2355, 3043, 3044, 18719[28], 18719[29], 18719[46], 20066[61]
*Museo Naval* (MN), Madrid
Navarrete: XX, XXVI
*Public Record Office* (PRO), London
Calendar of State Papers (CSP), West Indies, 1671-80: 1150, 1188, 1199,
　　1420
1681-5: 173, 431, 632, 805, 971
High Court of Admiralty (HCA): 1-11, 1-28, 1-51
State Papers (SP), Spain: 65, 67
*Real Academia de la Historia* (RAH), Madrid
Colección Muñoz: 1-184

# Notes

## INTRODUCTION

1. See diary entry for 27 August 1520, quoted in Stechow, W., *Dürer and America* (Washington, 1971).

2. For this plunder specifically, Drake in general and those Englishmen who tried to follow him to Peru, see Hakluyt, R., *The Principal Navigations, Voiages, Traffiques and Discoveries of the English Nation* (3 vols., London, 1598–1600), Morison, S. E., *The European Discovery of America. The Southern Voyages (1492–1616)* (New York, 1974), Spate, O. H. K., *The Spanish Lake* (Minneapolis, 1979), and Andrews, K. R., *Trade, Plunder and Settlement. Maritime Enterprise and the Genesis of the British Empire (1480–1630)* (Cambridge, 1984). No one really knows the exact total, but as Andrews states, p. 159, 'a good deal of exaggerated nonsense has been written about it'. This too, in a way, is proof of the lure of the wealth of Peru. On the background to Drake, there are valuable contributions in Thrower, N. J. W. (ed.), *Sir Francis Drake and the Famous Voyage (1577–1580)* (Berkeley, 1984). For English aims in the South Sea more generally, consult Ruggles, R. I., 'Geographical exploration by the British', in Friis, H. R. (ed.), *The Pacific Basin: a History of its Geographical Exploration* (American Geographical Society, Special Publications, no. 38, New York, 1967), pp. 221–55. A wider discussion of sources on early voyages can be found in Goodman, E. J., *The Exploration of South America: an Annotated Bibliography* (New York, 1983). The peso used throughout this text is generally that of eight *reales* (piece of eight). Estimates of its value in the seventeenth century vary considerably, but a generally accepted figure would seem to be four or five shillings.

3. Useful discussions of early interpretations of the New World may be found in, Morales Padrón, F., *Historia del descubrimiento y conquista de América* (Madrid, 1973), Gerbi, A., *La natura delle Indie nove. (Da Cristoforo Colombo a Gonzalo Fernández de Oviedo* (Milan, 1975) and Cro, S., *Realidad y utopiia en el descubrimiento y conquista de la América Hispana (1492–1682)* (Troy, Michigan, 1983).

4. For an introduction to this theme, see Zavala, I. M., 'Cien años de *soledad*: crónica de Indias', in Giacoman, H. F. (ed.), *Homenaje a García Márquez* (New York, 1972), pp. 197–212.

5. Phrases from Samuel Johnson's poem, 'London'.

6. Quoted in Quinn, D. B. (ed.), *The Last Voyage of Thomas Cavendish (1591–1592)* (Chicago, 1975), p. 17.

7. Barlow, R., ed. Taylor, E. G. R. *A Brief Summe of Geography* (Hakluyt Society, 2nd series, no. 69, London, 1932), pp. xxi, xxix–xxxix and liv.

8. Taylor, E. G. R. (ed.), *The Original Writings and Correspondence of the*

*Two Richard Hakluyts* (Hakluyt Society, 2nd series, nos 76 and 77, London, 1935), no. 76, p. 87.

9. Andrews, *Trade*, pp. 139–45, and Andrews, 'Drake and South America', in Thrower, *Sir Francis Drake*, p. 50. There is a biography by Rowse, A. L., *Sir Richard Grenville of the 'Revenge', an Elizabethan Hero* (London, 1937).

10. Markham, C. R. (ed.), *Narratives of the Voyage of Pedro Sarmiento de Gamboa to the Straits of Magellan* (Hakluyt Society, 1st series, no. 91, London, 1895).

11. Taylor, *Original Writings*, pp. 140–2 and 163–4.

12. As a summary of the gathering by the English of information about the New World, see Quinn, D. B. (ed.), *The Hakluyt Handbook* (Hakluyt Society, 2nd series, nos 144 and 145, London, 1974), no. 144, chs 9, 19 and 20, and Steele, C., *English Interpreters of the Iberian New World from Purchas to Stevens (1603–1726)* (Oxford, 1975).

## 1 THE ARRIVAL OF THE DUTCH. JACOB MAHU AND OLIVIER VAN NOORT (1598–1601)

1. Boxer, C. R., *The Dutch Seaborne Empire* (London, 1965) and *The Dutch in Brazil (1624–54)* (Oxford, 1957). Sluiter, E., 'Dutch maritime power and the colonial status quo, 1585–1641', *Pacific Historical Review*, XI (1942), pp. 29–41. Goslinga, C. Ch., *The Dutch in the Caribbean and on the Wild Coast (1580–1680)* (Gainesville, 1971). For the rise and fall of Amsterdam see Braudel, F., *Civilization and Capitalism: 15th–18th century*, vol. III, *The Perspective of the World* (London, 1984), pp. 175–276.

2. Quinn, *Last Voyage*, pp. 150–5.

3. van Linschoten, J. H., *Itinerario* (Amsterdam, 1596) and Wagenaer, L. J., *Teerste deel vande Spieghel der Zeervart* (Leyden, 1584–85), translated into English in 1590 as *The Mariners Mirrour*, a title now borne by Britain's most prestigious maritime review.

4. Dispatch of the viceroy, Luis de Velasco, 8 May 1600, AGI, Lima, 34.

5. Evidence of Dirck Gerritsz, captain of the *Glad Tidings*, given at Santiago de Chile, 10 February 1600, AGI, Patronato Real, 268–2–3. Biographical and family details reveal a busy and much travelled individual, educated in Lisbon from 11 years of age, twice married, who had served in Dutch ships, and the Portuguese Indies fleet from 1568, been a resident of Goa and, since 1589, traded to Lisbon, Oporto and Germany. Further details in Ijzerman, J. W., *Dirck Gerritszoon Pomp, alias Dirck Gerritsz China, de eerste Nederlander die China en Japan bezocht (1544–1604)* (Werken uitgegeven door de Linschoten vereeniging, no. 9, The Hague, 1915).

6. Hakluyt, *Principal Navigations*, edition used is 'Everyman's Library', London, 1910, vol. VIII, p. 283. Other references in the travels of Drake, p. 59, and Cavendish, p. 217, and in the discourse of Lopes Vaz, pp. 193–4.

7. 'Copia de la instruccion que dio en el Haya el Conde de Nassau al gral Holandes Olivier de Noort', AGI, Patronato Real, 268–2–2.

8. Sluiter, E., *New Light from Spanish Archives on the Voyage of Olivier van Noort* (The Hague, 1937), pp. 40–1, which reproduces the original from AGI, Mexico, 24.

9. A basic account of the Mahu venture, at least as far as the Straits of Magellan, is provided by the journal of Bernard Jansz, surgeon with Sebald de Weert on the *Faith*. There was a Latin translation in 1602 by de Bry, followed by several other translations. Sources used are: de Bry, Theodor, *Historia Americae siue Noui Orbis* (Frankfurt, 1634), part 9. René Augustin Constantin de Renneville, *Recueil des voyages qui ont servi à l'établissement et aux progrès de la Compagnie des Indes Orientales* (10 vols, Rouen, 1725), vol. II. Purchas, S., *Purchas His Pilgrimes* (London, 1625), edition used is 20 vols, Glasgow, 1905–7, vol. II, which contains two letters from the English pilot Adams who gives the name of a second promoter as Hans Vanderueke (Van der Veken?). A more recent account is Javet, Y., 'Los primeros holandeses en el Estrecho de Magallanes', *Boletín de la Academia Chilena de la Historia*, X, no. 26 (1943), pp. 43–64. Other standard collections of voyages have been used throughout this study: Callander, J., *Terra Australis Cognita* (3 vols, Edinburgh, 1766–68), being a translation with additions of de Brosses, C., *Histoire des navigations aux terres australes* (2 vols, Paris, 1756). Churchill, A. and J., *A Collection of Voyages and Travels* (6 vols, London, 1704). Harris, J., *Navigantium atque Itinerantium Bibliotheca* (2 vols, London, 1744–48), and especially Burney, J., *A Chronological History of the Discoveries in the South Sea or Pacific Ocean* (5 vols, London, 1803–17). For more recent summaries of the voyages see: Riesenberg, F., *Cape Horn. The Story of the Cape Horn Region* (New York, 1940). Rydell, R. A., *Cape Horn to the Pacific: the Rise and Decline of an Ocean Highway* (Berkeley, 1952). Gerhard, P., *Pirates on the West Coast of New Spain (1577–1742)* (Glendale, 1960). Randier, J., *Men and Ships around Cape Horn* (London, 1968). Hough, R., *The Blind Horn's Hate* (London, 1971), and Spate, O. H. K., *Monopolists and Freebooters* (London and Canberra, 1983). Lohmann Villena, G., *Historia marítima del Perú*, vol. IV, *Siglos XVII y XVIII* (Lima, 1973), at times has factual errors due to untrustworthy sources, for example ascribing aspects of the Mahu expedition to that of van Noort. More reliable at times, though containing errors also, is Fernández Duro, C., *Armada española* (9 vols, Madrid, 1895–1903). In Dutch see Wieder, F. C., *De Reis van Mahu en De Cordes door de Straat van Magalhâes* (Werken, nos 21, 22 and 24, The Hague, 1923–25). The *Charity* is recorded in some sources as the *Love*. The *Glad Tidings* is also known as the *Flying Deer*, apparently because this motif was painted on her stern. I have not seen Sluiter, E., 'The voyage of Jacques Mahu and Simon de Cordes into the Pacific Ocean (1598–1600)', nor 'The Dutch on the Pacific coast of America (1598–1621)', (MA and PhD theses, University of California, Berkeley, 1933 and 1937).

10. AGI, Patronato Real, 268–2–3. Gerritsz refers to two English pilots

(one called Mechart?) in the *Hope*, who had been with Cavendish, and another together with a Portuguese in the *Charity*. Javet, 'Primeros holandeses', p. 46, mentions two in the *Hope*, one of whom had been with Drake and the other with Cavendish, and a further two in the *Charity*. Purchas, *Pilgrimes*, vol. II, pp. 330 and 342, has the letters of the pilot Adams, with reference also to his brother Thomas and Timothy Shotten, and mentions Thomas Spring lost at Annobón, p. 208. Spate, *Monopolists*, p. 4, has six English pilots.

11. Purchas, *Pilgrimes*, vol. II, p. 328.

12. Pigafetta, A., *Primer viaje alrededor del mundo* (Crónicas de América, no. 12, Madrid, 1985), pp. 63–4 and 66–9.

13. Hakluyt, *Principal Navigations*, vol. VIII, pp. 178, 212 and 215.

14. AGI, Patronato Real, 268–2–3, supported by observations during Drake's circumnavigation, Hakluyt, *Principal Navigations*, VIII, pp. 93–5. See also Wallis, H., 'The Patagonian giants', in Gallagher, R. E. (ed.), *Byron's Journal of his Circumnavigation (1764–66)* (Hakluyt Society, 2nd series, no. 122, Cambridge, 1964), pp. 185–96.

15. AGI, Patronato Real, 268–2–3.

16. Some reports suggest that van Beuningen survived to reach Japan, for example, de Brosses, *Histoire de navigations*, vol. II.

17. See for example: Allardyce, W. L., *The Story of the Falkland Isles* (Falkland Islands, 1909), Goebel, J., *The Struggle for the Falkland Isles* (New Haven, 1927), and Cawkell, M. B. R. *et al.*, *The Falkland Isles* (London, 1960).

18. Chilean historians relate these events in some detail. Barros Arana, D., *Historia general de Chile* (16 vols, Santiago, 1884–1902), vol. III, ch. 17. He believes that Baltasar Moucheron was one of the backers. Encina, F. A., *Historia de Chile desde la pre-historia hasta 1891* (20 vols, Santiago, 1940–52), vol. II. Rosales, D. de, *Historia general de el Reyno de Chile, Flandes Indiano* (3 vols, Valparaíso, 1877–78), vol. I, bk 1, ch. 9.

19. Dispatch of Luis de Velasco, 18 May 1602 and 'Certificación de que se envían los tres flamencos presos', 19 May 1602, AGI, Lima, 34. Lohmann Villena, *Historia marítima*, p. 384, suggests that the Dutch prisoners were released quickly but English ones held in Peru, some of the latter being sent to the *Casa de Contratación* in 1607.

20. Dispatch of Luis de Velasco, 8 May 1600, AGI, Lima, 34.

21. Gay, C., *Historia física y política de Chile* (24 vols, Paris, 1844–54), *Documentos*, vol. II, contains 'Informe de Francisco del Campo sobre los acontecimientos de la provincia de Valdivia y de Chile', Osorno, 16 March 1601. This refers to the intruders as 'English'. Rosales, *Historia de Chile*, vol. I, bk 5, ch. 13.

22. Gay, *Historia física*, vol. II, p. 135.

23. The journal of van Noort was published in Dutch at Rotterdam in 1602, and thereafter translated into Latin, French, German and English. Sources used here are: *Description du penible voyage faict entour de l'Univers ou Globe terrestre* (Amsterdam, 1602). De Bry, *Historia Americae*, part 9. De Renneville, *Recueil des voyages*, vol. III.

Purchas, *Pilgrimes*, vol. II. More recently in Dutch see Ijzerman, J. W., *De Reis om de wereld door Olivier van Noort (1598–1601)* (Werken, nos 27 and 28, The Hague, 1926), Mollema, J. C., *De Reis om de wereld van Olivier van Noort (1598–1601)* (Amsterdam, 1937), and Nijhoff, W., *Bibliographie van de Beschrijvinghe van die voyagie om den geheelen werelt cloot door Olivier van Noort* (The Hague, 1926). I have not seen Broek, J. O. M., *A Letter from O. van Noort, Circumnavigator, pertaining to the First Dutch Voyage around the World (1598–1601)* (Minneapolis, 1957). Spanish responses can be found in the dispatch of Velasco, 8 May 1600, AGI, Lima, 34, and 'Copia de un apuntamiento sobre el suceso del cossario olandes que fue a Filipinas el año passado de 1600', AGI, Patronato Real, 268–2–4.

24. Later, while sailing between Puerto Deseado and Cape Vírgenes, Pieter Esaisz de Lint assumed command of the *Hope* on the death of Huydecoper, and the vessel was renamed *Concord*.

25. The story of this gold is difficult to believe, though clearly it conforms to Dutch expectations of the area. The gold in question is usually reported to be 500 bars (or pots) and 52 chests of 100 lbs, totalling some 10 200 lbs. Supposedly, it originated from mines on Santa María worked by 2000 Indians and three or four Spanish overseers. Although southern central Chile (e.g. Valdivia) was a source of some gold in the first half of the seventeenth century, there is no evidence of such an operation on this island, nor even of such a large Indian population. If the gold had been collected elsewhere, it seems strange that it was entrusted to this ship and not to the larger and more powerful one that had accompanied her.

26. Purchas, *Pilgrimes*, vol. II, p. 197.

27. Sluiter, *New Light*, records the experience of the *Hendrick Frederick*.

28. On the perils and fears of the Straits of Magellan, and Spanish exaggeration of these, see Wallis, H., 'English enterprise in the region of the Strait of Magellan', pp. 195–220 of Parker J. (ed.), *Merchants and Scholars. Essays in the History of Exploration and Trade* (Minneapolis, 1965), pp. 198–210.

29. AGI, Patronato Real, 268–2–3, dispatch of Luis de Velasco, 8 May 1600, AGI, Lima, 34, and Sluiter, *New Light*, p. 40.

30. Boxer, *Dutch Seaborne Empire*, pp. 65–70.

31. Purchas, *Pilgrimes*, vol. II, p. 196. On Dutch travel literature in general for this period see, Commelin, I. (ed.), *Begin ende Voortgangh van de Vereenighde Nederlandtsche Geoctroyeerde Oost-Indische Compagnie* (2 vols, Amsterdam, 1645) and Tiele, P. A., *Mémoire Bibliographique sur les journaux des navigateurs néerlandais* (Amsterdam, 1867).

32. Outghersz, Jan, *Nieuwe Volmaeckte Beschryvinghe der vervaerlijker Strate Magelhani* (Amsterdam, [1600]). For Dutch geographical discoveries in the area in general, see Broek, J. O. M., 'Geographical exploration by the Dutch', in Friis, *Pacific Basin*, pp. 151–69.

33. Dispatch of Luis de Velasco, 14 September 1597, AGI, Lima, 33. This letter, and others of Velasco, is published in Levillier, R., *Gobernantes del Perú* (14 vols, Madrid, 1921–26), XIV, pp. 64–5. For a

general account of defence measures near to the capital and its port in the seventeenth century, see Lohmann Villena, G., *Las defensas militares de Lima y Callao* (Seville, 1964) and Bradley, P.T., 'The defence of Peru (1600–48)', *Ibero-Amerikanisches Archive* vol. 2, no. 2 (1976), pp. 79–111. As regards the isolation of Peru, Chaunu claims that its position on the Pacific coast of America made it three or four times more distant from Spain than any point in the West Indies or Mexico, Chaunu, H. and P., *Séville et l'Atlantique (1504–1650)* (8 vols, Paris, 1955–60), VIII₇, pp. 1061–2. The two voyages we have just discussed tend to reinforce this suggestion.

34. Dispatch of Luis de Velasco, 8 May 1600, AGI, Lima, 34.
35. For these maritime operations see Bradley, P.T., 'Maritime defence of the Viceroyalty of Peru (1600–1700)', *The Americas*, vol. 36, no. 2 (1979), pp. 156–7, and Bradley, 'Defence of Peru', pp. 81–2. Full details of ships, crews and armaments are in 'Relacion de la gente de guerra y mar, artilleros, artilleria de cada navio de los de la Rl. Armada', AGI, Lima, 34, reproduced in Bradley, 'The attack and defence of Peru in the seventeenth century' (PhD thesis, University of Leeds, 1969), p. 461.
36. Dispatch of Luis de Velasco, 10 May 1601, AGI, Lima, 34 and 'Copia de un apuntamiento', AGI, Patronato Real, 268-2-4.
37. 'Instrucción de lo que D. Graviel de Castilla . . . a de hazer en seguimiento de los enemigos corsarios', 7 July 1600, BN (Madrid), 3043, fol. 416.
38. Dispatch of Luis de Velasco, 5 May 1600, AGI, Lima, 34.
39. Crown order of 7 October 1602, AGI, Lima, 570, book 16, fols. 70–1, and Bradley, 'Attack and defence', pp. 464–5.
40. Letter of Ozores de Ulloa, 2 May 1601, AGI, Lima, 135.
41. Letter of Vázquez de Loaysa, 25 April 1601, AGI, Lima, 135.
42. Dispatches of Luis de Velasco, 7 December 1600, 2 May 1601, 1 May and 10 October 1603, AGI, Lima, 34. Vázquez preferred two forts on the island of San Lorenzo facing Callao, and a further one in the port itself, whereas Ozores limited his proposal to two forts along the Callao shoreline.

## 2 THE DEFEAT OF THE PERUVIAN FLEET BY JORIS VAN SPEILBERGEN (1614–17)

1. Boxer, *Dutch in Brazil*, pp. 2–5, and *Seaborne Empire*, pp. 23–4. Goslinga, *Dutch in the Caribbean*, pp. 35–7 and 65–88.
2. De Villiers, J. A. J. (ed. and trans.), *The East and West Indian Mirror* (Hakluyt Society, 2nd series, no. 18, London, 1906), p. 11, which contains a translation of the original narrative, *Nieuwe Oost ende West Indische Navigatien* (Leiden, 1619). For the question of mistaken attribution of authorship to Jan Corneliszoon May, see pp. xvi–xxx. Other translations into Latin, English and French can be found in de Bry, *Historia Americae*, part 11, Purchas, *Pilgrimes*, vol. II and de

Renneville, *Recueil des voyages*, vol. III. More recent Dutch studies include van Lindt van Erk, M. W. and de Winter, A. (eds), *De Reis van Joris van Spilbergen door Straat Magelhães naar Oost-Indië en terug rond Zuid-Afrika in 1614–1617* (Amsterdam, 1952), and Warnsinck, J. C. M., *De Reis om de wereld van Joris van Spilbergen (1614–17)* (Werken, 47, The Hague, 1943).

3.  Lohmann Villena, *Defensas militares*, p. 37, believes the desertions were deliberate, suggesting that the three intended to operate as spies. For proceedings against the deserters and the evidence of Lima, see AGI, Contratación, 167, no. 7, with details of the enquiry in Seville in 1618 and a crown instruction to release the prisoners a year later. AHN, Inquisición, 1030, fols. 71–77v. Dispatch of viceroy Esquilache, 6 April 1617 and findings of the Inquisition in Lima, 25 February 1617, AGI, Lima, 37. The declarations of Lima and Heinrich form the basis of BN (Madrid), 2348, fol. 233, 'Relación del viaje que el año de 1615 hizo por el estrecho a la mar del sur el holandes Jorge Esperuet'. There is a copy in BL, Additional, 17621, fol. 136, and the original is published in Fernández de Navarrete, M., *Colección de documentos inéditos para la historia de España* (112 vols, Madrid, 1842–95).

4.  BN (Madrid), 2348, 'Relación', and AGI, Contratación, 167, no. 7.

5.  *The Mirror*, pp. 27–8, which suggests Lima was sailing from Lisbon to Rio de Janeiro, whereas in his evidence in Seville on 3 March 1618 he gives Angola as his destination.

6.  Ibid., p. 45.

7.  BN (Madrid), 2348, 'Relación'.

8.  *The Mirror*, p. 53.

9.  'Instrución secreta al Gral Don R$_1^o$ de Mendoça', 6 December 1614 and 'Instruçión que a de guardar el Genl don Rodrigo de Mendoça', AGI, Lima, 36. The latter contains 57 points to be observed with reference to salutes and signals, the hoisting of standards, checks on weapons, sailing positions, punishments for swearing and gambling, and for cursing and blaspheming against the name of God and the Virgin Mary (4 years in the galleys). Dispatch of viceroy Montesclaros, 24 September 1615, AGI, Lima, 36.

10. For example, 'Relacion verdadera de persona desapazionada . . . del succeso y perdida de la armada real', BL, Additional, 13975, fols. 323–30. This 'dispassionate' commentator is generally critical of the viceroy.

11. Barros Arana, *Historia de Chile*, vol. IV, pp. 109–10, dated 12 February 1616. Rosales, *Historia de Chile*, vol. II, p. 610. Dagnino, V., *El corregimiento de Arica (1535–1784)* (Arica, 1909), p. 116.

12. The Chilean historian Barros Arana corrects the journal at this point, suggesting that when it refers to Quintero at latitude 32° 15' it was in fact Papudo. Similarly above for Valparaíso, he suggests Concón.

13. Dagnino, *Arica*, pp. 120–1.

14. Reported in an *acuerdo* of 31 October 1615, AGI, Lima, 37.

15. Dagnino, *Arica*, pp. 129–31.

16. The journal refers to a 'good sum in copper coin', *The Mirror*, p. 68, but Spanish sources agree that this was 7000 pesos in silver.

17.  For crown warnings see instruction of 28 February 1614, AGI, Lima, 571, bk 17, fols. 172v–73, and for the letters of the Duke of Lerma, AGI, Indiferente General, 1868. Each is more fully studied in Bradley, 'Attack and defence', pp. 233–7.

18.  Crown dispatch of 30 August 1614, AGI, Lima, 571, bk 17, fols. 179–80.

19.  Principal sources for warnings of Dutch intervention and the subsequent preparations for defence are: 'Relacion de las naos de enemigos que se vieron en la costa del Brasil 1614', with a letter of Montesclaros, 15 November 1614, AGI, Patronato Real, 229–16; letter of Constantino de Menales, governor of Rio de Janeiro, 10 January 1615, and a letter of Montesclaros of 2 March 1615, AGI, Lima, 275, fol. 762; reports from Martín Pacheco, governor of the fort of Arauco, and from the governor of Chile, 29 and 30 May 1615, AGI, Lima, 37; letters of viceroy Montesclaros of 2 May, 22 June and 24 September 1615, and 'R$^{on}$ dela perdida denra Armada', AGI, Lima, 36; 'Relación de la Armada', and *acuerdos generales* of 13 November 1614 and 22 October 1615, AGI, Lima, 37; letter of *licenciado* Cristóbal Cacho de Santillana, 19 May 1616, AGI, Lima, 146; 'Relacion verdadera', BL, Additional 13975, fols. 323–30; 'Relación de las operaciones de la armada del Peru contra unos nabios corsarios holandeses en el año 1614', BN (Madrid), 3044, fol. 509. There is a sound and full version in Rodríguez Crespo, P., *El peligro holandés de las costas peruanas* (Lima, 1964), and a summary in Bradley, 'The defence of Peru', pp. 83–5.

20.  BL, 'Relación verdadera', fol. 325 and 'Relación de la armada', AGI, Lima, 37.

21.  Such is the story told by Ricardo Palma in his *tradición* 'El tamborcito del pirata', which includes another famous figure of Peruvian life, Doña Catalina de Erauso, the *monja alférez*, claiming that she jumped from the sinking ship, was taken prisoner and later released at Paita. There is a reference to van Speilbergen also in Palma's *Anales del Cuzco* for the year 1615, and to the fear and alarm caused in Lima in the *tradición* 'Los duendes del Cuzco'. For other literary reminiscences of the events at Cañete see Peralta Barnuevo, P. J. de, *Lima fundada o conquista del Perú* (Lima, 1732), and Oviedo Herrera, L. A., Conde de la Granja, *Vida de Sta. Rosa* (Madrid, 1711). The former includes other Dutch expeditions to Peru and some later ones. Morales, E., *Historia de la aventura. Exploradores y piratas en la América del Sur* (Buenos Aires, 1942), is still useful on these themes.

22.  Lohmann Villena, *Historia marítima*, p. 397, believes that the *Santa Ana* sank as a result of a mistaken attack against her in the darkness by the *Jesús María*. He also lists members of famous Peruvian families who participated in the fleet, pp. 386 and 390.

23.  BL, 'Relacion verdadera', fol. 326v.

24.  On their return to Callao, the captains of these four vessels were imprisoned by viceroy Montesclaros who mockingly dismissed their claims that the wind had been unfavourable to them. They were subsequently released by his successor, the Prince of Esquilache.

Dispatch of Montesclaros, 24 September 1615, 'R$^{on}$ dela perdida denra Arm$^{da'}$, AGI, Lima, 36, 'Testimonio de los autos . . . contra D. Diego de Saravia y demás capitanes', AGI, Lima, 37. For the sake of national pride some accounts in Spanish manage to interpret this battle as a defeat for the Dutch fleet, e.g., Alcedo y Herrera, D. de, *Aviso histórico, político, geográphico* (Madrid, 1714), pp. 130–1 and Odriozola, M. de, *Documentos históricos del Perú* (10 vols, Lima, 1863–77), vol. II, p. 8.

25.   Lewin, B. (ed.), *Descripción del Virreinato del Perú, crónica inédita de comienzos del siglo XVII* (Rosario, 1958), p. 67. On the possible author and motives of this document see Lohmann Villena, G., 'Una incógnita despejada', *Revista de Indias*, vol. 119–22 (1970), pp. 315–87. According to the census of 1614, Lima at this time had a population of 25,434 (9,616 Spaniards, 2,518 religious, 10,386 negroes, 1,978 Indians, 744 mulattos and 192 mestizos), Montesinos F. de, *Anales del Perú* (2 vols., Madrid, 1906), II, year 1614. About a decade and a half later, Callao is reported to have a Spanish population of 700 souls by Vázquez de Espinosa, A., in Clark, C. U. (ed.) *Compendio y descripción de las Indias Occidentales*, (Washington, 1948), 421.

26.   Letter of Alvarez de Paz, 25 July 1618, AGI, Lima, 38.

27.   Aponte Figueroa, J. de, *Memorial que trata de la reformación del Reino del Pirú*, vol. LI of Navarrete, *Colección*, p. 545 and 'R$^{on}$ dela perdida denra Arm$^{da}$, AGI, Lima, 36. The other two guns were pedreros.

28.   Most probably this was Lobos de Tierra (as opposed to Lobos de Afuera). *The Mirror*, p. 82, note 2, discusses whether they actually caught the fish *lobo* (loach), or *lobos de mar* (seals), concluding that it was the former.

29.   *The Mirror*, p. 84. Lohmann Villena, *Historia marítima*, p. 398, records another local tradition by asserting that the gallant defence of Paita was organised by the *corregidora* rather than by her husband. He does not mention the later successful Dutch landing.

30.   Phelan, J. L., *The Kingdom of Quito in the Seventeenth Century* (Madison, 1967), p. 99.

31.   *The Mirror*, pp. 66, 65 and 55.

32.   *Ibid.*, pp. 86–99 and 100–1. Bibliographical details of each are discussed at pp. lvi–lvii, from which it transpires that the second document may have been produced originally by a pilot on the Mahu expedition who was imprisoned at Valparaíso.

33.   'Informe tocante a [las] Indias de Castilla, deduzido de los papeles del Marques de Montesclaros', BL, Additional, 28446, fols 1–70, at fol. 67, dated 12 December 1615. *Colección de las memorias o relaciones que escribieron los virreyes del Perú* (2 vols, Madrid, 1921, 1930), I, Beltrán y Rózpide, R. (ed.), p. 200. Bradley, 'Attack and defence', pp. 240–1.

34.   BL, 'Relacion verdadera', fol. 328.

35.   Letter of Alvarez de Paz, 25 July 1618, AGI, Lima, 38. He is critical also in another of 1 August 1618, AGI, Lima, 37.

36.   Various letters in AGI, Lima, 37, with a contribution from the archbishop of Lima, 8 March 1617, AGI, Lima, 301, urging new

measures and fearing intrusions every year now that the Straits are conquered.

37. 'Informe de servicios de Lozano de las Cuevas', AGI, Lima, 225. He was in charge of the construction of the fort.

38. Each has attracted interest as 'virrey poeta' (viceroy poet), for example: Cabrillana, N., 'Un noble de la decadencia: el virrey Marqués de Montesclaros', *Revista de Indias*, vol. 115–18 (1969), pp. 107–50, Miró Quesada Sosa, A., *El primer virrey-poeta en América*. *Don Juan de Mendoza y Luna, Marqués de Montesclaros* (Madrid, 1962). González Palencia, A., *Noticias biográficas del virrey poeta Príncipe de Esquilache* (Seville, 1949). Wyskota, J. de, *El virrey poeta: seis años de administración de Don Francisco Borja y Aragón* (Mexico, 1970).

39. Bradley, 'Defence of Peru', pp. 85–9 and 'Maritime defence', pp. 160–1. Lohmann Villena, *Defensas militares*, pp. 39–43, discusses the construction of forts in detail.

## 3 JACQUES L'HERMITE, THE NASSAU FLEET AND THE BLOCKADE OF CALLAO (1623–6)

1. Boxer, *Dutch in Brazil*, pp. 6–17 and *Seaborne Empire*, pp. 24–6. Goslinga, *Dutch in the Caribbean*, pp. 74–106 and 140–4.

2. *The Mirror*, pp. 165–232, contains a translation of the original narrative *Australische Navigatien* of 1618 of Jacob Lemaire. See also Engelbrecht, W. A. and van Herwerden, P. J. (eds), *De ontdekkingsreis van Jacob le Maire en Willem Cornelisz. Schouten in de jaren 1615–1617* (Werken, nos 48 and 49, The Hague, 1945).

3. The voyage is included in *Early Spanish Voyages to the Strait of Magellan*, Markham, C. R. (ed.) (Hakluyt Society, 2nd series, no. 28, London, 1911).

4. 'Relaçion del viage y subcessos de la armada olandesa', BL, Additional, 13974, fols 14–35, at fol. 21.

5. There are several translations of the original journal by Adolph Decker, *Journael van de Nassausche Vloot* (Amsterdam, 1626), e.g. de Bry, *Historia Americae*, part 13, de Renneville, *Recueil des voyages*, vol. IX, Harris, *Navigantium*, vol. I and Callander, *Terra Australis*, vol. II. A more recent Dutch version is Cannenburg, W. V. (ed.), *De Reis om de Wereld van de Nassausche Vloot* (1623–26) (Werken, no. 65, The Hague, 1964). Spanish documentation is extensive, the most important being the following: dispatches of viceroy Guadalcázar, 6 June and 9 September 1624, and 24 May 1625, which contain the testimony of the two Greek deserters and the prisoner Carstens, AGI, Lima, 40. Dispatch of the viceroy, 18 July 1624, AGI, Indiferente General, 2665. Dispatches of the President of Panama, 30 June, 2 and 28 August 1624, AGI, Panamá, 17. There are detailed manuscript accounts of the blockade: 'Relacion de lo sucedido en el Piru con la entrada de la armada de doce nabios de Olanda', and report of the *Junta de Guerra* of 25 December 1624, AGI, Indiferente

General, 2665. 'Relaçion del viage', BL, Additional, 13974, fols 14–35, and another on the same topic with the declaration of Carstens, fols 36–7. Published accounts are: *Casos notables sucedidos en las costas de la ciudad de Lima en las Indias* (Seville and Madrid, 1625), AHN, Cartas de Indias, 306, BN (Madrid), 2355, fol. 219 and BL. *Insigne victoria que el Señor Marqués de Guadalcázar ... ha alcançado en los puertos de Lima, y Callao* (Seville, 1625), AHN, Cartas de Indias, 296. The former is translated as *A True Relation of the Fleet which went under the Admirall Jaquis Le Hermite through the Straights of Magellane* (London, 1625). Declarations by those who served in the fleet can also been seen in MN, Navarrete, XXVI, no. 49, fols 319–37. There is valuable information also in the correspondence of several individuals: the accounts of the *fiscal* Luis Enríquez, 9 September 1625 and 21 February 1626, AGI, Lima, 98. Father A. Fuertes de Herrera, 1 July 1624, published in Vargas Ugarte, R., *Biblioteca peruana* (12 vols, Lima, 1935–57), vol. III, pp. 233–53. Friar A. de Lisón, 18 May 1624, AGI, Lima, 329. 'Memorial y servicios del Maestre de Campo D. Diego de Roxas y Borja', AGI, Lima, 159. The preceding are sources for Bradley, 'The lessons of the Dutch blockade of Callao (1624)', *Revista de Historia de América*, 83 (1971), pp. 53–68.

6.  De Renneville, *Recueil des voyages*, vol. IX, p. 53.
7.  *The Mirror*, pp. 190–1.
8.  Harris, *Navigantium*, vol. I, p. 68.
9.  There is a good account of scurvy and its cure in Phillips, C. R., *Six Galleons for the King of Spain* (Baltimore, 1986), pp. 173–5.
10. Harris, *Navigantium*, vol. I, p. 69.
11. Dispatches from the crown to Guadalcázar, 24 November 1622, 2 and 7 November 1623, AGI, Lima, 571, bk 19, fols 103v–04, 123v–24 and 125–25v. Dispatches of Guadalcázar, 20 May 1623, AGI, Lima, 39, 10 September and 10 December 1623, AGI, Lima, 40.
12. Letter of Benito Pérez to viceroy Guadalcázar, 6 May 1624, AGI, Lima, 40.
13. Melo, R., 'Los piratas y el Callao antiguo', *Revista Americana*, I, no. 11 (15 March 1892), pp. 168–9, Fernández Duro, *Armada española*, vol. IV, p. 34. Montesinos, *Anales*, II, year 1624.
14. In addition to the Spanish documents in note 5, see also with regard to defence: 'Acuerdo g$^l$ que se tripule la arm$^{da}$ con gente y art$^{a'}$', 24 April 1622. 'Acuerdo general de hacienda sobre que se hagan arcabuçes y mosquetes leva de soldados y gastos'. 'Copia de las Juntas de Guerra que el Virrey del Piru tubo enel puerto del Callao', AGI, Lima, 40. Report on the blockade in MN, Navarrete. XXVI, no. 50, Salinas y Cordova, B. de, *Memorial de las historias del Nuevo Mundo Piru* (Lima, 1630), ch. III. For an account of the development of militia and permanent defence forces in the vicinity of the capital, see Bradley, P. T., 'The defenders of Lima and Callao in the seventeenth century', *Revista de Historia de América*, 97 (1984), pp. 87–113.
15. Letter of Lisón, 18 May 1625, AGI, Lima, 329.
16. Letter of Salas, 8 April 1624, AGI, Lima, 155.

17. Services of Rojas and Chirinos in AGI, Lima, 159.

18. González Suárez, F., *Historia general de la República del Ecuador* (7 vols, Quito, 1890–1903), vol. IV, p. 97. The author was archbishop of Quito.

19. *Casos notables*, BN (Madrid), 2355, fol. 219v.

20. 'Relaçion del viage', BL, Additional 13974, fol. 29v.

21. His declaration is to be found in *Insigne victoria*, AHN, Cartas de Indias, 296.

22. Ibid.

23. Bradley, 'Defence of Peru', pp. 90–1 and 'Lessons', pp. 62–3.

24. BL, Additional, 13974, fols 56–9, anonymous document, and fols 60–3, 'Carta q escribi al Señor D. Fran^co de Alfaro sobre acometer por mar a los olandeses'.

25. Some Spanish accounts state that the return was made via the Straits of Magellan and the coast of Brazil, and therefore must be based on the evidence of those who deserted before the decision to sail for Chile was revoked. Dispatch of the viceroy, 20 January 1625, AGI, Lima, 40. Vargas Ugarte, R., *Historia general del Perú* (6 vols, Lima, 1966), vol. III, p. 208. Fernández Duro, *Armada española*, vol. IV, ch. XVIII.

26. *Récit véritable du grand combat arrivé sur mer aux Indes Occidentales*, in vol. 1 of Fournier, E., *Variétés historiques et littéraires* (10 vols, Paris, 1855–63). As with van Speilbergen, mention of these events in literature in Spanish often presents the opposite picture of Spanish brave and victorious and Dutchmen cruel and godless. See again, Peralta, *Lima fundada*, the *comedia* of Lope de Vega, *Amar, servir y esperar*, Quevedo's sonnet 'Al mal gobierno de Felipe IV' and his *La hora de todos y la Fortuna con seso*, 28 and 36. The latter relates how the Dutch demonstrated to Chilean Indians the use of a *cubo óptico* (telescope). Carvajal y Robles, R. de, *Poema del asalto y conquista de Antequera* (Lima, 1627), examined in the present context by Lohmann Villena, G., *Boletín de la Biblioteca Nacional*, XVI, no. 27 (1963), pp. 3–37. Palma fabricates a tale of young love rendered tragic by l'Hermite's kidnapping of a young wife, in an early *tradición*, 'Lida' or 'Un corsario en el Callao'. See Compton, M. D., *Ricardo Palma* (Boston, 1982), pp. 38–40.

27. Harris, *Navigantium*, vol. I, p. 73.

28. Burney, *History of the Discoveries*, vol. III, p. 32.

29. 'Relaçion del viage', BL, Additional, 13974, reports various losses at different stages of the blockade.

30. Lohmann Villena, *Historia marítima*, p. 412, gives the statistics for the groups sailing north and south from the blockade. Phelan, *Quito*, pp. 105–6, records damage in Guayaquil. Also on Guayaquil at this time see: Estrada Ycaza, J., *El puerto de Guayaquil*, vol. II, *Crónica portuaria* (Guayaquil, 1973). Conniff, M., 'Guayaquil through independence', *The Americas*, 33, no. 3 (1977), pp. 385–410. Clayton, L. A., *The Guayaquil Shipyards in the 17th Century: History of a Colonial Industry* (New Orleans, 1972).

31. Dispatch of Guadalcázar, 15 December 1622, AGI, Lima, 39, report-

ing for example the reduction of the Callao garrison by the *audiencia* from 500 to 300 men.

32. For local council discussions see Bromley, J., *Libros de cabildos de Lima* (Lima, 1962), vol. XIX, pp. 578–83 and vol. XX, pp. 107–8.
33. Dispatch of Guadalcázar, 6 June 1624, AGI, Lima, 40.
34. Decree of 25 January 1626, AGI, Lima, 571, bk 19, fol. 160 and a dispatch of Guadalcázar, 8 March 1627, containing a report on the state of defence by Nicolás de Retana, AGI, Lima, 41. Fuller details of the new measures are to be found in Lohmann Villena, *Defensas militares*, pp. 59–67 and Bradley, 'Attack and defence', pp. 269–74.
35. Bradley, 'Maritime defence', pp. 161–3 and 'Defence of Peru', pp. 95–6.
36. Bradley, P. T., 'Some considerations on defence at sea in the Viceroyalty of Peru during the seventeenth century', *Revista de Historia de América*, 79 (1975), pp. 77–97, at p. 83, based on a dispatch of Guadalcázar, 24 May 1625, AGI, Lima, 40 and a decree of 25 February 1626, AGI, Lima, 571, bk 19, fols 169–71.
37. Bradley, 'Considerations', pp. 83–7, using documents from AGI, Indiferente General, 2511, and Lohmann Villena, *Defensas militares*, pp. 75–9.
38. For a discussion of defence questions from the post-van Speilbergen to the post-l'Hermite period, see Bradley, 'Considerations', pp. 82 and 86–7 and 'Attack and defence', pp. 402–8, 412–14 and 485–8. As an alternative to providing protection for the silver armada, Simón Estacio da Silveira offered to open up a land and river route from Peru to the Caribbean in a report of 15 June 1626, AGI, Lima, 159. The bishop of Rio de Janeiro, Lourenço de Mendoza, advocated that Potosí silver be taken overland via Cuzco to Lima in his *Memorial a su magestad . . . en razon de la seguridad de la plata, y armada del Piru, y de los galeones de Tierra-firme* (n.p., 1635). The situation in 1627 is contained in the report of Retana, AGI, Lima, 41.
39. Crown request to Guadalcázar, 27 July 1627, AGI, Lima, 572, bk 20, fol. 45. Dispatches of viceroy Chinchón, 15 May 1629, AGI, Lima, 42, and 5 April 1630, AGI, Lima, 43. Múzquiz de Miguel, J. L., *El Conde de Chinchón, virrey del Perú* (Madrid, 1945), pp. 193–6. It is this viceroy's wife who is reputed to have divulged the curative powers against fevers of what came to be called chinchona (or cinchona) bark – quinine, portrayed on the arms of the Republic of Peru.
40. Dispatch of Guadalcázar, 6 June 1624, AGI, Lima, 40.
41. Bromley, *Libros de cabildos*, vol. XIX, p. 908. Chinchón later shared the same worries, dispatch of 11 October 1636, AGI, Lima, 48.
42. Konetzke, R., *Colección de documentos para la historia de la formación social en Hispanoamérica (1493–1810)* (3 vols, Madrid, 1953, 1958, 1962), II, no. 218. Decree of 16 December 1631, from AGI, Lima, 572, bk 20, fol. 253.
43. Lohmann Villena, 'Una incógnita despejada', pp. 317–19, *Defensas militares*, p. 50 and *Historia marítima*, pp. 489–90. Letter of Fuertes de Herrera in Vargas Ugarte, *Biblioteca peruana*, III, pp. 244–5 and 251. Medina, J. T., *Historia del Tribunal del Santo Oficio de la Inquisición de Lima* (2 vols, Santiago, 1887), vol. II, pp. 69–70.

44.    Although the 1630s saw no new Dutch fleets in the South Sea, a ⌐continuing interest in the area is indicated by the arrest of another alleged spy in September 1630. In his possession were found details of ports, their defenders and defences, together with notes for letters he intended to write. See Suardo, J. A., *Diario de Lima (1629– 39)* (2 vols, Lima, 1936), vol. I, pp. 97–8.

## 4    THE EXPEDITION OF HENDRIK BROUWER. A PROJECT FOR COLONIAL SETTLEMENT (1642–4)

1.    Boxer, *Dutch in Brazil*, pp. 14–17 and 21–158. Goslinga, *Dutch in the Caribbean*, pp. 148–58, 168–202 and 284–301.
2.    Boxer, *Dutch in Brazil*, p. 147.
3.    Very useful on the Brouwer period is Guarda Geywitz, F., *Historia de Valdivia (1552–1953)* (Santiago, 1952). I have not seen Montt Pinto, I., *Breve historia de Valdivia* (Buenos Aires, 1971).
4.    In support of Valdivia's defence: dispatch of viceroy Montesclaros, 15 November 1614, AGI, Lima, 36. Dispatches of viceroy Esquilache, 10 April and 27 March 1619, AGI, Lima, 37 and 38. Letters of Dr Carrasco del Saz, *oidor* of Panama, 30 June 1619, AGI, Panamá, 17, and of the archbishop of Lima, 16 April 1619, AGI, Lima, 301.
5.    Bradley, 'Attack and defence', pp. 414–18. Dispatches of Chinchón, 14 April 1636 and 18 March 1638, AGI, Lima, 47 and 48. Criticism of Quirós is to be found in 'Relacion . . . del Peru, que haze el Marques de Mancera', 8 October 1648, BL, Additional, 13992, fols 368–85, at fol. 381v.
6.    Decree of 16 April 1639, AGI, Lima, 609. Dispatches of Mancera, 29 May 1640 and 8 June 1641, AGI, Lima, 50. Bradley 'Attack and defence', pp. 420–2.
7.    Quoted in Guarda Geywitz, *Valdivia*, section 1.
8.    Declaration of the prisoner, named by the Spanish Antonio Juan, before the governor of Chile at Concepción on 23 November 1643, AGI, Lima, 52. He claimed to be of Catholic parents and a native of Brabant, and had worked for three years in a sugar mill in Pernambuco before enlisting as a sailor on this expedition. The names of two other Dutchmen in Spanish hands are recorded as Pedro de la Palma and Josipo Lamenes.
9.    He was born in 1581 and is described by Antonio Juan as 'very old and disabled'.
10.    Principal source for this venture is the journal of 1646 based on the diaries of some of its members, translated into German in 1649, and later included in several English collections. *Journael ende historis verhael van de Reyse gedaen by Oosten de Straet le Maire* (Amsterdam, 1646). Churchill, *A Collection of Voyages* vol. I. Callander, *Terra Australis*, vol. II. See also Burney, *History of the Discoveries*, vol. III, ch. V. Via Churchill are the following: Medina, J. T., 'Relación del

viaje de Hendrick Brouwer a Valdivia en 1643', *Revista Chilena de Historia y Geografía*, XLVIII, no. 52 (1923), and 'Documentos para la historia de la náutica en Chile', *Anuario Hidrográfico* (2 vols, Santiago, 1889 and 1892), vol. II. I have not managed to see Telting, A., *De Nederlanders im Chile, 1643* (Amsterdam, 1893). For a brief bibliography of the episode see Rodrigues, J. H., *Historiografia e bibliografia do domínio holandês no Brasil* (Rio de Janeiro, 1949), ch. V, section J. Main original Spanish sources are: 'Noticia de olandeses', 24 May 1645, AGI, Lima, 52, and 'Relacion . . . que el S<sup>r</sup> Marques de Baydes . . . embio al S<sup>r</sup> Marques de Mancera', 21 August 1643, AGI, Lima, 51. The latter estimates the three larger Dutch ships to be of 400 tons each.

11. Callander, *Terra Australis*, vol. II, p. 382.
12. Her mast broke. She subsequently reached Recife in December 1643.
13. Possibly so called as a result of the common confusion in the viceroyalty between the Dutch and the English. Otherwise referred to as Brouwershaven, situated in the NW of Chiloé island.
14. 'Relacion', of Baydes, AGI, Lima, 51. Accounts in Spanish of the events in Chile are often incorrect. The most trustworthy is Barros Arana, *Historia de Chile*, vol. IV, ch. XI. Typical of the distorted versions are Odriozola, *Documentos históricos*, vol. II, p. 10, and Alcedo y Herrera, *Aviso histórico*, section 19, which date the episode in 1633, relating how the Dutch were driven out of Valdivia by its (non-existent) Spanish garrison and allied Indians.
15. AGI, Lima, 52.
16. In Herckmans we have another poet, author of *Der Zeevaert-lof* (Amsterdam, 1634).
17. At this time the Dutch received from the Indians an exaggerated warning about the preparation of a Spanish fleet to dislodge them. This can hardly have been a comfort. To what extent it was deliberately exaggerated to induce them to leave is open to speculation. The Spanish account of the departure reveals that the informants on which it was based believed that it was Herckmans who wanted to leave, and not his men, 'because the captains and soldiers were well-disposed to the land, the climate, the fruit and gold collected there', 'Noticia de olandeses', AGI, Lima, 52. If it were true this would shed a different light on the motives of the deserters.
18. Letter dated 14 October 1643, AGI, Lima, 52.
19. 'Noticia de olandeses', AGI, Lima, 52.
20. Ibid.
21. Southey, R., *History of Brazil* (3 vols, London, 1810–19), vol. II, p. 24.
22. Boxer, *Dutch in Brazil*, p. 147.
23. Guarda Geywitz, *Valdivia*, part III, offers a full account of the process of fortification and reoccupation. There is a contemporary account, Aguirre, M. de, *Población de Valdivia, motivos y medios para aquella fundación* (Lima, 1647). See also 'Instrución que a de guardar el Maestre de Campo Alfonso de Villanueva Soberal', and instructions to Toledo, 30 December 1644, AGI, Lima, 52. Barros Arana, *Historia de Chile*, vol. IV, chs IX and XI. 'Relacion . . . del Peru', BL,

Additional, 13992. Bradley, 'Attack and defence', pp. 422–7. In his *tradición*, 'Una vida por una honra', Palma relates how the expedition won the nickname, 'the fleet of the seven Fridays'.

24.  Copy of a letter from Capt. García Tamayo y Mendoza, chief scribe of the Royal Treasury and secretary to the *Junta de Guerra*, BL, Additional, 13977, fols 333–40. Guarda Geywitz, *Valdivia*, part III, section 4, lists supplies and provisions carried, from musket balls and powder to chickpeas and lentils, hats and soap, apparently from a *Relación del feliz viaje que hizo la Armada Real a Valdivia*, also by Capt. Tamayo. He mentions another account of the expedition, Albis, J. de, *Relación sobre la Armada que envió a Chile el Marqués de Mancera* (1645). For Mancera's new galleons see Bradley, 'Maritime defence', pp. 165–8 and 'Defence of Peru', pp. 107–9, based on documents in AGI, Lima, 50 and 51.

25.  On these and later fortifications see Díaz Meza, A., 'Las fortificaciones de Valdivia y Corral', *Revista Chilena de Historia y Geografía*, IV, no. 8 (1912), pp. 163–77. Dispatches of Mancera, 5 July 1646, 8 August 1647 and 'Testimonio de los fuertes y defensas', 8 July 1647, AGI, Lima, 53.

26.  Bradley, 'The cost of defending a viceroyalty: crown revenue and the defence of Peru in the seventeenth century', *Ibero-Amerikanisches Archiv*, 10, no. 3 (1984), pp. 267–89, at p. 277. In fact, in the latter half of the century, aid to Valdivia consistently ran at an annual level of 120 000 pesos.

27.  Polo, J. T. (ed.), *Memorias de los virreyes del Perú* (Lima, 1899), p. 59.

28.  Listed in the letter of Tamayo y Mendoza, BL, Additional, 13977, fols 334v–336.

29.  Dispatch of Mancera, 11 June 1642, AGI, Lima, 51 and 'Memorial de los méritos y servicios de Manzera', AGI, Lima, 610.

30.  Dispatches of Mancera, 4 June 1643 and 16 January 1644, AGI, Lima, 51, 18 June 1644, AGI, Lima, 52, and 18 June 1645, AGI, Lima, 45, announcing completion of the work in August 1644. The Portuguese, Manuel Rodríguez, had lived in Peru for 30 years and was married to a Spanish woman. He had already contributed financially to the building of a church in Arica, but obviously now felt a further gesture was necessary to divert any suspicion from himself as a result of the recent separation of the two crowns. Viceroy Mancera was enthusiastic in the enactment of legislation against Portuguese in the viceroyalty.

31.  For a detailed account of Chinchón's pioneering work in the inland sector and the wall built by Mancera, see Lohmann Villena, *Defensas militares*, pp. 80–9 and 91–124. See also Bradley, 'Defence of Peru', pp. 96–9 and 103–6.

32.  Letter of Tamayo, BL, Additional, 13977, fols 339–339v. Major incidents of the Brouwer venture are recorded in a poem by Núñez Castaño, D., *Breve compendium hostium hoereticorum olandesium* (Lima, 1645).

# 5 NARBOROUGH AND THE MYSTERIOUS DON CARLOS (1669–71)

1. For English overseas enterprise in the New World consult Andrews, *Trade*, and *The Spanish Caribbean. Trade and Plunder (1530–1630)* (New Haven, 1978). Quinn, D. B. and Ryan, A. N., *England's Sea Empire (1550–1642)* (London, 1983). Bridenbaugh, C. and R., *No Peace beyond the Line: the English in the Caribbean (1624–90)* (New York, 1972).

2. Alcedo, *Aviso histórico*, p. 16, repeated in Melo, 'Piratas', p. 168. The captain's name is given as William Ezeten (?).

3. BL, Egerton, 2541, fols 57 and 59. The proposal was discussed in the home of Lord Conway, in the presence of Lord Bish of St David's and the Earl of Totnes. The latter turned it down in favour of projects in the West Indies.

4. Viceroy Alba de Liste wrote of rumours of English ships heading for the New World on 14 May 1656 and 20 August 1658, AGI, Lima, 58 and 60. In August 1662, the crown sent a report to viceroy Santisteban about eight English vessels planning to take Valdivia, sail to the Pearl Islands to await the silver galleons, and then proceed to Guatemala, AGI, Lima, 574, bk 26, fols 8v–9v. Though the *Junta de Guerra* was sceptical about the project on 11 June 1663, the viceroy reported receipt of a second warning issued in September 1663, AGI, Lima, 65.

5. *An Account of Several Late Voyages and Discoveries to the South and North towards the Streights of Magellan* (London, 1694, reprinted Amsterdam, 1969), p. 10. This is the official journal of Narborough. He was an associate of Sir Christopher Myngs, had served in the West Indies prior to this expedition, and subsequently in 1674 was to command a squadron in the Mediterranean. There are other versions of the journal in Dyer, F. E., *The Life of Admiral Sir John Narborough* (London, 1931), and Coreal, F., *Voyages de François Coreal aux Indes Occidentales (1666–97)* (2 vols, Paris, 1722), vol. II. There are accounts of the expedition by two of Narborough's companions: 'Journal of the voyage of the *Sweepstakes* to Magellan's Straits', by Nathaniel Peckett, BL, Sloane, 819, and 'Journal of J. Wood of a voyage from England to Patagonia', BL, Sloane, 3833, fols 3–26. The latter is mainly a collection of sailing directions. Even in recent studies, it is still possible to find Wood's account treated as a completely separate expedition, for example see Oyarzún Iñarra, J., *Expediciones españolas al Estrecho de Magallanes y Tierra de Fuego* (Madrid, 1976), p. 216, and Martinic, M., *Historia del Estrecho de Magallanes* (Santiago de Chile, 1977), p. 77. More reliable and informative is Williams, G., 'The inexhaustible fountain of gold: English projects and ventures in the South Sea (1670–1750)', in Flint, J. E. and Williams, G., (eds), *Perspectives of Empire* (London, 1973), pp. 27–54. For a listing of the locations of manuscripts associated with this and later English voyages, an invaluable, though not infallible, source is Walne, P., *A Guide to Manuscript*

*Sources for the History of Latin America and the Caribbean in the British Isles* (Oxford, 1973).

6.  *An Account*, p. 91.
7.  Ibid., pp. 42–58. On giants, superstitions and fears associated with the Straits, as well as the Narborough voyage in general, see Wallis, 'English enterprise', pp. 198–204 and 210–22, and 'The Patagonian giants', p. 185.
8.  *An Account*, p. 110.
9.  Ibid., p. 58.
10. Ibid., p. 64.
11. This is the name as recorded by Narborough and other English writers. Spanish documents contain the fuller version, Carlos Henríquez Clerque, though it is sometimes suggested that the last name is merely a reflection of his duties, i.e. clerk.
12. Dispatch of the viceroy, the Count of Lemos, 28 March 1671, AGI, Lima, 72. Even if each party were aware of the discussions which were to lead to the Treaty of Madrid, 18 July 1670 (not publicly proclaimed in Peru until a year later), the viceroy was unlikely to respond favourably to any protestations of peaceful intentions in view of the recent exploits of Henry Morgan on the Isthmus of Panama.
13. *An Account*, p. 96.
14. Ibid., p. 92.
15. Ibid., pp. 109 and 87.
16. Guarda Geywitz, *Valdivia*, part III, ch. II. A dispatch of viceroy Lemos, 28 March 1671, mentions an actual complement of 586 men, and another of viceroy Castellar, 5 September 1677, refers to a total of 728, AGI, Lima, 72 and 77.
17. Polo, *Memorias*, pp. 72–4, and Altolaguirre y Duvale, A. de (ed.), *Colección de memorias*, vol. II, pp. 297–9, from the report of the viceroy, the Count of Salvatierra.
18. *An Account*, pp. 89–90.
19. In statements made to his Spanish captors, Highway declared himself to be a mulatto, 34 years of age, born in North Africa, baptised in San Lúcar de Barrameda and in the service of English gentlemen since he was 14 years old. His present master was don Carlos. Armiger is described as being 47 years of age and a lieutenant, Fortescue 28 years old, a soldier, cosmographer and mathematician on the expedition, from the Downs, and Coe, 28 years of age, from Wapping and a trumpeter. 'Autos continuados en este Gouierno superior y tribun[1] de la Guerra de los fechos en Chile y Baldivia', 16 May 1672, AGI, Lima, 73.
20. The following discussion of don Carlos is largely drawn from Bradley, P. T., 'Narborough's Don Carlos', *The Mariner's Mirror*, 72, no. 4 (1986), pp. 465–75.
21. Ibid., p. 467.
22. 'Avisos generales en raçon de las proposiciones que se hizieron a Carlos 2° Rey de la gran Bretaña', BN (Lima), F. 160.
23. 'Testimonio de los autos fechos sobre aberiguar los designios del

enemigo inglés que dio vista ... sobre el puerto de Valdivia por Diciembre del año 1670', AGI, Lima, 73.

24. Dispatch of viceroy Lemos, 28 March 1671, AGI, Lima, 72.

25. Letter of Thomas Armiger, 28 April 1671, AGI, Lima, 73. The garbled reference to the 'King of the Indians' calls to mind the revolt of the *calchaquíes* under the leadership of Pedro de Bohórquez. See Piossek Prebisch, T., *La rebelión de Pedro Bohórquez, el Inca del Tucumán (1656–59)* (Buenos Aires, 1976), and Miller, R. R., 'The false Inca of Tucumán, D. Pedro de Bohorques', *The Americas*, 32 (1975), pp. 196–210.

26. Alcedo y Herrera, D., *Piraterías y agresiones de los ingleses* (Madrid, 1893), ch. 26, and Barros Arana, *Historia de Chile*, vol. V, p. 159, favour December. Basadre, J., *El Conde de Lemos y su tiempo* (Lima, 1948), p. 179, and Mendiburu, M. de, *Diccionario histórico-biográfico del Perú* (11 vols, Lima, 1931–5), vol. IV, p. 188, support 8 May, as do other usually reliable witnesses in Vargas Ugarte, R. (ed.), *Crónica de la época colonial de José de Mugaburu y Francisco de Mugaburu* (Lima, 1935). Edition used here is the English translation, *Chronicle of Colonial Lima* (Norman, 1975), pp. 267–8.

27. A comment by the archbishop viceroy, Liñán y Cisneros, 27 August 1678, AGI, Lima, 78. 'Memoria del virrey', 8 December 1681, BN (Lima), B. 411, ch. 99. Barros Arana, *Historia de Chile*, vol. V, p. 153, notes 31 and 32. A later English visitor to these parts, however, believes that Armiger stayed on in Valdivia and helped the Spanish to improve their fortifications. See Simson, Richard, 'Voyage through the Straits of Magellan, to the South Sea, 1689', BL, Sloane, 86. Burney, *History of the Discoveries*, IV, part II, ch. I, follows him in this. There is a literary reference to the death of 'Clerk' in Palma's *tradición*, 'Cortar el revesino', which records the name of the priest he claimed to be as José de Lizárraga.

28. Basadre, *Conde de Lemos*, pp. 182–8, Barros Arana, *Historia de Chile*, vol. V, p. 129, note 13, Lohmann Villena, *Historia marítima*, vol. IV, pp. 113–16, and dispatch of the *audiencia* of Lima, 17 April 1673, AGI, Lima, 73. From these sources it seems that Peñalosa was born in Lima, or Santa Cruz de la Sierra (Bolivia), in 1620 or 1621. Up to the time of his arrival in London late in 1669 or early in 1670, his life was as colourful as that of don Carlos. Following a quarrel with the brother of the Count of Salvatierra, viceroy in 1652, he headed for Mexico, fought against the Apaches, won a fortune in silver, fell into the hands of the Inquisition and figured in an *auto*, being reduced to poverty once again. In London, his aim was apparently to sell information about Spanish possessions in the New World. He travelled to France in 1673 with a similar objective. For further details of his background, and activities with reference to North America, see Fernández Duro, C., *D. Diego de Peñalosa y su descubrimiento del Reino de Quivira* (Madrid, 1882), and Shea, J. D. G., *The Expedition of Don Diego Dionisio de Peñalosa by Father Nicholas de Freytas, O. S. F.* (Albuquerque, 1964). Pardo, it is alleged, was exiled from Peru for secret dealings with the leader of an Indian revolt, again calling to mind the Bohórquez incident. (See note 25 above.)

29. For Gage's influence on Cromwell and the figure of Cáceres, see Fraser, A., *Cromwell our Chief of Men* (London, 1973), chs 19 and 20.

30. A number of Jews, including characters as intriguing as don Carlos, accompanied the new queen from Portugal to England, see Roth, C., *A History of the Jews in England* (3rd edn, Oxford, 1964), p. 176. A further origin of Jewish immigrants into Europe was Brazil, from where they had been expelled in 1654 following Portuguese reoccupation of Pernambuco. Most sailed directly to Amsterdam, but one or two groups sought refuge on some friendly island in the Caribbean, such as Martinique, and some eventually fell into Spanish hands in Jamaica shortly before the English seizure of the island. See Wiznitzer, A., 'The exodus from Brazil and arrival in New Amsterdam of the Jewish Pilgrim Fathers', in Cohen, M. A. (ed.), *The Jewish Experience in Latin America* (2 vols, New York, 1971), vol. II, pp. 313–30, and Wolf, L., 'American elements in the re-settlement', *Transactions of the Jewish Historical Society* (London, 1899), vol. III, pp. 80–1.

31. Wood, John, 'Description of Magellan Straits', BL, Sloane, 46A, fols 139–68 and 46B, fols 144–88, and 'A Mapp of the Streights of Magelan, drawn by Captn. John Narborough', BL, Additional, 5414, art. 29. A version of the map was published in 1673.

32. For the atmosphere and preparations, see Mugaburu, *Chronicle*, for the relevant years, also Bradley, 'Attack and defence', pp. 322–5. BL, Additional, 21539, nos 1–7 of the Meltfort Papers, contains copies of the letters of the Count of Lemos warning of the presence of intruders, as well as the testimony of those who made the original sightings. See also *Relación de los socorros del Conde de Lemos* (Seville, 1672), AHN, Cartas de Indias, 392, and viceroy's dispatch of 28 March 1671.

33. See Lohmann Villena, *Defensas militares*, pp. 125–32, for a discussion of the decline.

34. *Colección de memorias*, vol. II, p. 182, and dispatch of the viceroy, the Count of Alba de Liste, 17 July 1656, AGI, Lima, 58, reporting the state of the wall as he found it. A fuller discussion of the maintenance problems encountered by several viceroys can be found in Bradley, 'Attack and defence', pp. 309–15.

35. For example, the regular garrison of Callao was reduced from 500 to less than 400 men, and the numbers of artillerymen serving on land also cut, dispatch of the viceroy, the Count of Santisteban, 20 November 1665, with further details in Bradley 'Attack and defence', pp. 315–20, and 'Defenders', pp. 107–8. Like the wall of Callao, Mancera's large galleons also left a legacy of costly maintenance, provoking protests from the crown, e.g. 28 August 1648, AGI, Lima, 573, bk 23, fols 120–1. See also Bradley, 'Maritime defence', p. 172, and 'Attack and defence', pp. 515–17 and 520–1.

36. Little is known about these trading ventures beyond details in Seixas y Lovera, F., *Descripcion geographica y derrotero de la region austral Magallanica* (Madrid, 1690), título XIX, pp. 27–9, and *Theatro naval hydrographico* (Madrid, 1688), ch. XI. See also Gerhard, *Pirates*,

pp. 142–3, who refers to the activities of these ships in Mexico, as contained in documents of AGI, Mexico, 46, and Robles, A. de, *Diario de sucesos notables (1665–1703)* (3 vols, Mexico, 1946), vol. I, p. 122.

37.    According to Seixas, *Descripcion*, 27 and 29, de la Roche was prevented from returning via the Strait of Lemaire due to strong winds and currents, eventually making headway into the Atlantic further to the east, beyond the route used by Brouwer in 1643, and from where he glimpsed land to the south covered in snow. This discovery was printed secretly in London, he adds, in 1678. Despite the claim that de la Roche was English, the name and the return to La Rochelle on 29 September 1674 clearly indicate a French connection.

38.    Mugaburu, *Chronicle*, 223 and 226. Letters of the governor of Chile, declarations of the Indians Luis Liquema and Cristóbal Talquipillán and of others involved in the incident, AGI, Lima, 73.

39.    Although the most they achieved, apart from a rare Spanish visit to the Straits of Magellan, was the landing of dogs at the Juan Fernández Isles in an only partially successful attempt to kill off the wild goats, Vea and Iriarte were proposed as being worthy of reward for their efforts, the first the Order of Santiago and the latter the *corregimiento* of the city of Cuenca (Quito). Their expedition cost over 84 000 pesos, but this expenditure was more than covered by a *donativo* (subscription) organised in parts of the viceroyalty. Dispatches of viceroy Castellar, 20 April and 22 June 1678, AGI, Lima, 77. Both journals may be consulted in the MN, Colección Navarrete, vol. XX, fols 576–679. That of Vea is available in the Library of Congress (Washington), SA MSS, Ac. 9, and RAH, Colección Muñoz, I–184, fols 191–235. There are printed versions of the latter in Díez Gallardo y Andrade, B., *Documentos para la historia de la náutica en Chile. Del Anuario Hidrográfico. Viaje de B. Gallardo. Viaje de Antonio de Vea* (Santiago de Chile, 1886), and *Relación diaria del viaje que se ha hecho a las costas de el Estrecho de Magallanes*, in Cabreiro Blanco, L. (ed.), *Colección de diarios y relaciones* (5 vols, Madrid, 1943–47), vol. I, pp. 49–97.

# 6   SHARP AND COMPANY. THE FIRST OF THE BUCCANEERS
## (1679–82)

1.    For the history of the buccaneers in English see: Burney, J., *History of the Buccaneers of America* (London, 1891), a reprint of vol. IV of *History of the Discoveries*. Haring, C. H., *The Buccaneers in the West Indies in the Seventeenth Century* (London, 1910, reprinted Hamden, 1966). Means, P. A., *The Spanish Main: Focus of Envy (1492–1700)* (New York, 1935). Newton, A. P., *The European Nations in the West Indies (1493–1688)* (London, 1933). With regard to daily life and habits, especially of French buccaneers, the following are useful:

Charlevoix, P. F. X. de, *Histoire de l'Isle Espagnole ou de S. Domingue* (2 vols, Paris, 1730, 1731). Exquemelin, A. O., *De Americaensche Zee-Rovers* (Amsterdam, 1678). Tertre, J. B. du, *Histoire générale des Antilles habitées par les François* (4 vols, Paris, 1667–71). Other accounts may be found in: Besson, M., *Les 'Frères de la Coste'* (Paris, 1928). Corgnac, E. de, *Les flibustiers au XVIIe siècle* (Limoges, 1883). Deschamps, H., *Pirates et flibustiers* (Paris, 1952). Butel, P., *Les Caraibes au temps des flibustiers (XVIe–XVIIe siècles)* (Paris, 1982). The term 'buccaneer', then, evolves from the French *boucanier*. *Boucan* also apparently described the meat produced, in French *viande boucanée*. The actual grill or gridiron was called *barbecu* (Spanish *barbacoa*) by the Indians. The term *flibustier*, preferred by the French, was commonly considered to be a derivation from 'flyboat', an Anglicised reference to the Dutch *fluyt*. Generally nowadays it is considered to be the French pronunciation of the English 'freebooter', itself a derivation of the Dutch *vribuiter*. The Dutch, for their part, preferred the term *zee-rovers*. While the term *flibustier* might originally have more accurately described those who lived from preying on Spanish shipping, rather than those who hunted and produced cured meat, the two occupations became so closely linked that, in English at least, 'buccaneer' came to describe both.

2.   For recent accounts of Morgan's exploits, see Pope, D., *The Buccaneer King. The Biography of Sir Henry Morgan (1635–88)* (New York, 1978) and Earle, P., *The Sack of Panama. Sir Henry Morgan's Adventures on the Spanish Main* (New York, 1982).

3.   Dispatch of viceroy Lemos, 28 March 1671, AGI, Lima, 72, discussed with other documents in Lohmann Villena, *El Conde de Lemos, virrey del Perú* (Madrid, 1946), pp. 336–7.

4.   Dispatch of viceroy Lemos, 31 July 1671, AGI, Lima, 72.

5.   Dispatch of viceroy Lemos, 13 May 1672, AGI, Lima, 72, and response of 2 June 1673, AGI, Lima, 574, bk 28, fols 17–17v. The viceroy had in fact first warned of the danger to Portobello and the need to recover Jamaica on 10 March 1669, AGI, Lima, 68.

6.   Burney, *Buccaneers*, pp. 87 and 91. Dampier, W., *A New Voyage round the World* (3rd edn, London, 1698), pp. 181–3, outlines contacts with Indians and is a journal of part of Sharp's voyage in the South Sea. The manuscript is in BL, Sloane, 3236, fols 1–13 and 29–233.

7.   The principal manuscript accounts of the voyage are: 'Sharp's journal of a voyage to the South Seas 1680–82', BL, Sloane, 46A, fols 1–138 and 46B, fols 1–143. Subsequent references are to the latter. 'Coxon's journal', BL, Sloane, 2752, A and B, although part B relates events after his return and therefore cannot be wholly by Coxon. 'Cox's journal of travels into the South Seas 1680–81', BL, Sloane, 49. 'Basil Ringrose's journal of Sharp's voyage to the South Seas 1680–81', BL, Sloane, 3820, with a copy in Sloane 48. Important printed sources are: Exquemelin, A. O., *The Buccaneers of America* ed. Stallybrass, W. S. (London, 1923), based on the second edition of the 1684 English translation of *De Americaensche Zeerovers*, and the first edition of Ringrose's journal of 1685. Ayres, P., *The Voyages and*

Adventures of Captain Bartholomew Sharp and others in the South
Sea (London, 1684). Hack, W., *A Collection of Original Voyages*
(London, 1699). Wycherly, G., *Buccaneers of the Pacific* (Indianapolis,
1928). Kemp, P. and Lloyd, C., *Brethren of the Coast: British and
French Buccaneers in the South Seas* (London, 1960), covers this and
later groups from the buccaneers' point of view. Lloyd, 'Bartholomew Sharp, buccaneer', *The Mariner's Mirror*, 42 (1956), pp. 291–
301, is useful for sources and Sharp's later career.

8.  'Relación de lo sucedido en Portovelo y Panamá en el año 1680', BN
    (Madrid), 20066[61]. See also the broadly similar 'Relacion de el
    saqueo que Piratas ingleses y franzeses hicieron en la ciudad de
    Portovelo', 19 September 1680, and other documents on the same
    incident, AGI, Panamá, 95, and 'Relacion de las noticias q se han
    tenido de los insultos que Piratas Ingleses y Franceses han execu-
    tado en la ciudad de Portovelo', 24 September 1680, PRO, SP, Spain,
    65, fol. 121.
9.  Wafer, L., *A New Voyage and Description of the Isthmus of America*
    (Hakluyt Society, 2nd series, no. 73, Oxford, 1934). The manuscript
    is in BL, Sloane, 3236, fols 14–28v.
10. For example see references to them in PRO, CSP, W. Indies, 1677–
    80, nos 1150, 1188 and 1199.
11. Ayres, *Voyages and Adventures*, pp. 1–2.
12. 'Sharp's journal', fol. 7.
13. There is a brief account of this engagement by the captain of a
    Spanish bark, later released with other prisoners on the coast of
    Chile, dated Coquimbo, 17 December 1680, B. Colom., 64–7–114.
    Official reports of this incident and later action off the Peruvian
    coast can be found in 'Testimonio de acuerdos y juntas', 28 June
    1680, AGI, Lima, 81. The *Trinidad*, captained then as now by
    Francisco Peralta, had managed to evade Morgan when carrying
    valuable items away from Panama at the time of his attack, see
    Pope, *Buccaneer King*, pp. 243–4 and 246.
14. 'Sharp's journal', fol. 13.
15. 'Coxon's journal', fol. 45, refers to Sharp in this way.
16. Ayres, *Voyages and Adventures*, p. 24. Argandoña was the *corregidor*
    of Guayaquil. During their progress along the northern coast of the
    viceroyalty, Spanish sources record a landing at Barbacoas and
    Tumaco by a party of eight buccaneers. They were met by Spaniards
    led by Juan de Godoy y Prado and lost seven killed, including their
    leader Edward Dolman, who it is said had been to Lima previously.
    See 'Memoria del virrey Liñán y Cisneros', BN (Lima), B. 411,
    published in Fuentes, M. A., *Memorias de los virreyes* (6 vols, Lima,
    1859), vol. I.
17. Mugaburu, *Chronicle*, pp. 250–51, and González Suárez, *Historia del
    Ecuador*, vol. IV, p. 323, which takes a poor view of Argandoña's
    'cowardly' surrender.
18. 'Memoria del virrey Liñán y Cisneros', BN (Lima), B. 411, and
    Fuentes, *Memorias*, I, pp. 338–9.
19. Exquemelin, *Buccaneers*, p. 360.

20.    There had been until recently a total of 55 prisoners, Exquemelin, *Buccaneers*, p. 360.
21.    'Sharp's journal', fol. 44.
22.    Ibid., fol. 51.
23.    Dispatch of Liñán y Cisneros, 10 September 1681, AGI, Lima, 81.
24.    B. Colom., 64–7–114, dated 13 December 1680.
25.    'Cox's journal', fol. 24.
26.    Ibid., fol. 27.
27.    'Sharp's journal', fol. 58.
28.    These and subsequent maritime operations are listed in 'Memoria del virrey Liñán y Cisneros', BN (Lima), B. 411, and Diego de Vallejo Aragón, *Relación de la armada que despachó del Puerto del Callao . . . D. Melchor de Cisneros* (Lima, n.d.).
29.    'Cox's journal', fol. 30.
30.    Dagnino, *Arica*, ch. IV.
31.    Burney, *Buccaneers*, p. 132.
32.    B. Colom., 64–7–114, report of 16 February 1681. See also Palma's, 'La emplazada' and 'Cortar el revesino'.
33.    B. Colom., 64–7–114.
34.    'Memoria del virrey Liñán y Cisneros', BN (Lima), B. 411.
35.    'Sharp's journal', fol. 94. There are the following first-hand Spanish accounts of the *Rosario* incident: a declaration by Francisco García of San Sebastián, made at Cartagena on 24 April 1682, AGI, Panamá, 96, and the 'Deposition of Simón Calderón of Santiago Chilli, mariner', 18 May 1682, at Sharp's trial in London, PRO, HCA, 1–51, no. 181.
36.    Ayres, *Voyages and Adventures*, p. 88.
37.    By W(illiam) D(ick) in the second edition of the 1684 English translation of Exquemelin. See Lloyd, 'Sharp', p. 291.
38.    PRO, CSP, W. Indies, 1677–80, no. 1420, and BL, Sloane, 2724, fol. 3.
39.    'Sharp's journal', fol. 125. Although it was not realised at the time and not generally recognised until the voyages of Captain Cook, Sharp's penetration southwards, possibly as far as 60°S, proved incorrect theories about a Terra Australis Incognita.
40.    Letter of Sir Henry Morgan to Sir Leoline Jenkins, 8 March 1682, PRO, CSP, W. Indies, 1681–85, no. 431.
41.    Ibid., no. 713, letter of Charles II to Sir Thomas Lynch, 29 September 1682, and no. 632, letter of Jenkins to Lynch on the same topic.
42.    The proceedings of the trial are to be found in PRO, HCA, 1–11, 1–28 and 1–51. The protests of the Spanish ambassador, and the report of the trial by the *Junta de Guerra de Indias* are located in PRO, SP, Spain, 67, fols 146 and 147, and letters of the *Junta*, 20 and 22 August 1682, AGI, Panamá, 96 and Lima, 88. For the later career of Sharp, see Lloyd, 'Sharp', pp. 294–301.
43.    On the role of William Hack and his production of copies of the charts, we have Lynam, E. W. O'F., 'Hack and the South Sea buccaneers', in *The Mapmaker's Art* (London, 1953). 'Sharp's South Sea Waggoner' is to be found at BL, Sloane, 44, dated 1684. There is

another Jewish connection with the South Sea here, in that the translation of the text of the maps was undertaken by a Jewish friend of Hack, Phillip Dassigny, Kemp and Lloyd, *Brethren of the Coast*, 59. See also another manuscript by Hack of ports from Acapulco to California, dated 1687, in BL, Sloane, 45, fols 1–35, and charts of the entire South Sea coast in BL, Harley, 4034. There is a book of original Spanish charts at BL, Sloane, 239, and sailing instructions for the same coast by a Captain Bartolomé Villegas at BL, Sloane, 47, and Harley, 4225.

44. The well documented distributions of pesos in coin amount to a little over 1000 pesos per man, for an individual who stayed with Sharp to the end. This takes no account of silver plate, jewels, other items of value and unrecorded seizure of plunder.

45. Dispatch of viceroy Castellar, 29 August 1682, with declaration of Francisco García, 24 April 1682, and dispatch of *Junta de Guerra de Indias*, 20 August 1682, AGI, Panamá, 96.

46. Bradley, 'Defenders', pp. 97–9 and 109.

47. Bradley, 'The loss of the flagship of the Armada del Mar del Sur (1654) and related aspects of viceregal administration', *The Americas*, 45 (1989), pp. 383–403. See also 'Maritime defence', pp. 168–9 and 172.

48. 'Relacion del . . . Conde de Castellar', 4 August 1681, AGI, Lima, 610, section 128, and Fuentes, *Memorias*, I, pp. 235–6.

49. Artíñano y de Galdácano, G. de, *Historia del comercio con las Indias durante el dominio de los Austrias* (Barcelona, 1917), p. 225.

50. Costings dated 24 August 1681, AGI, Lima, 81.

## 7   ENGLISH AND FRENCH BUCCANEERS: THE SECOND WAVE (1684–9)

1. See Ch. 6, note 1, for general sources on the history of buccaneers.

2. For details of Dampier, Wafer and companions up to the time of their return to the South Sea, see Dampier, *New Voyage*, chs II, III and IV, and Wafer, *New Voyage*, pp. 4–29.

3. 'Journal of a voyage round the world (1683–86)', BL, Sloane, 54 and 1050, fol. 2.

4. Ibid., fol. 4v.

5. Kemp and Lloyd, *Brethren of the Coast*, p. 87, and chs VI–XI for an account of subsequent episodes from English and French sources. See also Spate, *Monopolists*, pp. 145–55. Cowley, who had been handling negotiations with the local chieftain along with the doctor, recalls that they were each offered a woman 'to sleepe by us as long as we stayed there', but claims to have refused 'by reason I did not like her hide', BL, Sloane, 54, fol. 4v.

6. Burney, *Buccaneers*, p. 162. W. Hack dubbed this land Pepys' Island. See Allardyce, *Falkland Isles*, p. 5, and Cawkell, *Falkland Isles*, p. 10. For an alternative view of its identity, see Chambers, B. M., 'Where

was Pepys' Island? A problem in historical geography', *The Mariner's Mirror*, 19 (1933), pp. 446–54.

7.    Although there are points of comparison with Crusoe, the Indian William was more likely the prototype of Defoe's Man Friday. For this aspect of the islands and their history in general, see Woodward, R. L., *Robinson Crusoe's Island – A History of the Juan Fernández Islands* (Chapel Hill, 1969).

8.    Cowley's journal, BL, Sloane, 54, fols 6v–7.

9.    Dampier, *New Voyage*, p. 99. There is a useful Spanish summary of events until the early months of 1686, 'Resumen que se a formado por la secretaria del Peru de las operaz[nes] que los piratas han hecho en el mar del sur', 25 October 1686, AGI, Panamá, 96.

10.   See 'Charts and description of the Galapagos Isles and of Pepys' Island: 1687', BL, Sloane, 45, fols 37–69. There are names such as King Charles I, Duke of Norfolk, John Narborough and those of several buccaneers, including Cowley himself.

11.   Cowley's journal, BL, Sloane, 54, fol. 10.

12.   'An examination of Richard Arnold', 4 August, PRO, CSP, W. Indies, 1685–88, no. 805 (also found at BL, Additional, 12429, fols 154–9), an account by one who was a member of the Harris party, claims to have taken booty of 24 ozs per man at Sta María, and a further £1000 in gold dust from a prize. 'Resumen que se a formado', AGI, Panamá, 96, records only the gold at Sta María, as 30 000 *castellanos*.

13.   Quoted in Kemp and Lloyd, *Brethren of the Coast*, p. 110.

14.   Dampier, *New Voyage*, p. 146.

15.   For events at Guayaquil, see González Suárez, *Historia del Ecuador*, IV, pp. 329–31.

16.   Dampier, *New Voyage*, p. 159. Preoccupied at this point with ways of getting rich, Dampier also alludes to the existence of another rich wreck in the vicinity of Guayaquil.

17.   Ibid., p. 192.

18.   Ibid. Arnold adds a nationalistic slant to Swan's decision, suggesting that he 'utterly refused to wear french Colours or fight under any other Colours than ye King of Englands', PRO, CSP, W. Indies, 1685–8, no. 805.

19.   First published in Paris in 1689, the edition used here is Raveneau de Lussan, *Journal du voyage fait à la mer du sud*, vol. III of Exquemelin, A. O., *Histoire des aventuriers flibustiers* (Trevoux, 1775). Rose, of course, had spent a short time with Sharp on the north side of the Isthmus in 1680.

20.   The activities of the buccaneers in the Gulf of Panama and the gradual accumulation of a force of 10 ships and approximately 1000 men, is documented in a dispatch of the President of Panama, 5 May 1685, and in the report of Juan de Molina, who spent 22 months as a prisoner, contained in a letter of viceroy Palata, 7 June 1686, part of 'Resumen de . . . las cartas q ha escrito el Señor virrey', AGI, Panamá, 96.

21.   For the viceroy's view of this latest incursion, and for his reaction to

it, see *Noticias del Sur* (Lima, 1685), AHN, Cartas de Indias, 403, sections 22–37, and 'Piratas en el Mar del Sur y despacho de la Armada del Año 1685', fols 291–332 of 'Relacion de el Estado de el Peru ... que haze el Duque de la Palata', BL, Additional, 19571, fols 24–420. The latter is published in Fuentes, *Memorias*, vol. II, pp. 289–332.

22. Ibid., and Bradley, 'Considerations', p. 91.
23. 'Piratas en el Mar del Sur', BL, Additional, 19571, fols 305 and 293.
24. *Noticias del Sur*, Section 41.
25. Ibid., Sections 38–40 and 42–56, and Llamosas, L. de las, *Manifiesto apologético* (Madrid, 1692), BL, Additional, 19571, fols 1–23, at fols 11–14. The author of this document is perhaps better known as a dramatist. See Lohmann Villena, *El arte dramático en Lima durante el virreinato* (Madrid, 1945). Vea has left his own account of the forces in opposition in the Gulf of Panama, together with a detailed description of the sea battle, dated 11 March 1686, AGI, Panamá, 96. The same bundle of manuscripts contains an exchange of letters, from 15 March to 21 October 1684, regarding the most appropriate use of Peruvian maritime forces, between Vea who supported the idea of an armed squadron specifically to search out intruders, and the viceroy who was increasingly concerned with the need to transport silver to Panama. Mugaburu, *Chronicle*, 290–3 claims that unpaid volunteers raised the total complement of the expedition to 1700 men. Palma, in 'El traquido de la capitana', considers the appointment of three commanders to be a 'very great blunder'.
26. 'Piratas en el Mar del Sur', BL, Additional, 19571, fol. 295.
27. Dampier, *New Voyage*, p. 209.
28. De Lussan, *Journal*, p. 71.
29. Estimates of losses range from 200 to 400 deaths. Vea believed 360 were burnt, letter of 11 March 1686, AGI, Panamá, 96. The figure quoted here is taken from Crahan, M., 'The administration of Don Melchor de Navarra y Rocafull, Duque de la Palata', *The Americas*, 27, no. 4 (1971), pp. 389–412, at p. 402.
30. Dampier, *New Voyage*, p. 209. The causes of the dispute and subsequent division of forces are also documented by the Spanish prisoner, Juan de Molina, 'Resumen de ... las cartas', 7 June 1686, AGI, Panamá, 96.
31. De Lussan, *Journal*, pp. 73–4.
32. Radell, D. R. and Parsons, J. J., 'Realejo: a forgotten colonial port and shipbuilding center in Nicaragua', *Hispanic American Historical Review*, 51, no. 2 (1971), pp. 295–313, records this and later raids in the area.
33. Following the departure of Dampier, the remaining English sources for the events of 1686 are Arnold (though only until April) and Wafer, *New Voyage*, pp. 115–16, who skips rapidly over the first eight months of the year. Later accounts in English, e.g. Burney, Kemp and Lloyd, and Spate reflect this lack of detailed information. The gaps can be filled in from 'Relazon de los Suzesos de la America en el mar del Sur y Costas del Piru', BL, Additional, 13964, fols 314–50,

which is especially concerned with the exploits of Davis in the *Bachelor's Delight* during 1686 and the first half of 1687. De Lussan remains the main source for French activities.

34. Wafer, *New Voyage*, p. 116, claims this was so, but Arnold believes Harris was still with Davis and Knight in April. This may be so, and Harris may not have departed until the later division of forces in August 1686.

35. 'Relazon', BL, Additional, 13964, fol. 320, and 'Resumen de . . . las cartas', 7 and 8 April and 7 June 1686, AGI, Panamá, 96. The poor defence at Saña is surprising when one considers that it was in the hands of the *Sargento General de Batalla*, Luis Venegas Osorio, sent from Spain with the title of Inspector of the Fortifications of Tierra Firme and the South Sea Coasts, and who was soon to be called to Lima to advise on the construction of a wall. Viceroy Palata was moved to comment that one could only understand how Venegas had managed to forget all that he had learnt from years of military service as a 'blow from the hand of God'. But he was doubtful that the losses claimed by the people of Saña could be so great, suggesting that 100 000 pesos was a more sensible estimate.

36. Dispatch of viceroy Palata, 22 March 1687, AGI, Lima, 86.

37. The seizure of the *Asunción* and subsequent experiences are recorded by a crew member who became a prisoner of the buccaneers, 'Declaración de Joseph Benítez, Indio del $R^{no}$ de Chile', AGI, Lima, 86.

38. Cuéllar's letter, 24 June 1686, AGI, Lima, 335.

39. Odriozola, *Documentos históricos*, vol. II, p. 17.

40. 'Relazon', BL, Additional, 13964, fol. 325v. Palata's excuse was that in a small port like Pisco, where there were several alternative landing points, the guns could not prevent the buccaneers from coming ashore. Moreover, once in the town, they could only be driven out by cannonfire at risk of damage to buildings.

41. Ibid., fol. 328v.

42. Ibid., fol. 329v.

43. Wafer, *New Voyage*, p. 116. His account becomes more detailed again at this point.

44. Ibid., p. 140, in fact part of Wafer's *Secret Report*, published as Appendix I.

45. Ibid., pp. 121–2.

46. Mugaburu, *Chronicle*, pp. 303–4, and 'Relazon', BL, Additional, 13964, fols 324–5 and 336.

47. Activities off the coast of New Spain are reported by the President of Panama, 'Relación de las operaciones de los piratas que infestan el mar del sur', AGI, Panamá, 96. De Lussan joined Townley at this point.

48. De Lussan, *Journal*, pp. 172–5. The reference to the English as Catholics is an allusion to the accession of the Catholic James II in 1685.

49. Ibid., p. 175.

50. Useful for the Guayaquil attack, especially where it relies on sources

in Spanish, is Bernal Ruiz, M. del P., *La toma del puerto de Guayaquil en 1687* (Seville, 1979). See also González Suárez, *Historia del Ecuador*, IV, 332. De Lussan rejoined his French comrades at this point.

51. Most Spanish accounts mention a buccaneer force of 500–600 men, rather than the more likely 300 which de Lussan records.
52. De Lussan, *Journal*, p. 236.
53. Ibid., p. 245.
54. Ibid., pp. 243–4. Kemp and Lloyd mistakenly suggest that Davis met his former companions off the coast of Mexico.
55. Bradley, 'Considerations', pp. 93–5. See also Clayton, L. A., 'Local initiative and finance in defense of the Viceroyalty of Peru', *Hispanic American Historical Review*, 54, no. 1 (1974), pp. 284–304.
56. Crown instructions of 29 September and 6 November 1689, AGI, Lima, 576, bk 32, fols 39–41, 54v–57v and 58–9.
57. Burney, *Buccaneers*, pp. 233–4 and de Lussan, *Journal*, p. 258.
58. Wafer, *New Voyage*, p. 125 and footnote 1, pp. 125–6. See also Spate, *Monopolists*, p. 372, note 44.
59. Wafer, *New Voyage*, pp. xliv–xlv.
60. Kemp and Lloyd, *Brethren of the Coast*, pp. 131–2.
61. It was, of course, viceroy Palata who ordered the execution of Carlos Henríquez Clerque, and also of 19 others who had fallen into Spanish hands during the recent attacks, 'Relación de . . . Palata', BL, Additional, 19571, fols 339v–342v and Fuentes, *Memorias*, vol. II, pp. 340–4.
62. González Suárez, *Historia del Ecuador*, vol. IV, p. 346.
63. Crown order of 7 December 1682 and response of Palata, 26 December 1684, AGI, Lima, 88. 'Relación de . . . Palata', BL, Additional, 19571, fols 343–44v and Fuentes, *Memorias*, vol. II, pp. 344–6. Like his predecessor, Palata recognised that only the former viceroy Castellar's *San Juan Evangelista* was fit for a commercial and quasi-military role.
64. Crahan, 'Administration of Palata', p. 398. For repercussions of the buccaneers in general, and on the Isthmus of Panama in particular, see Céspedes del Castillo, G., 'La defensa militar del Istmo de Panamá', *Anuario de Estudios Americanos*, 9 (1952), pp. 235–75.
65. Letter of the Marquis of Los Velez, 9 November 1686, AGI, Panamá, 96.
66. Letter of the President of Panama, 5 May 1685, AGI, Panamá, 96.
67. Letter of the Marquis of Los Velez, 9 November 1686, AGI, Panamá, 96.
68. Bernal, *Toma de Guayaquil*, pp. 91–6.
69. 'Relazon', BL, Additional, 13964, fols 347–9.
70. Letter of Molesworth to the Earl of Sunderland, 4 August 1686, PRO, CSP, W. Indies, 1685–8, no. 805.
71. PRO, SP, Spain, no. 67, 15 March 1685.
72. PRO, CSP, W. Indies, 1685–8, no. 971, 5 November 1686.
73. Dispatch of the *Consejo de Indias*, 7 December 1685, AGI, Panamá, 96.
74. 'Parecer que se dio sobre si era conbeniente o no el fortificar la voca de el Rio de la ensenada de el Dariel', BN (Madrid), 18719[46].

75.  'Voto del Sr. Conde de Castellar', 13 April 1683, AGI, Panamá, 96.
76.  'La Junta particular sobre la defensa de América', 29 September 1685, AGI, Panamá, 96.
77.  'Relación de . . . Palata', BL, Additional, 19571, fols 322–32. Fuentes, *Memorias*, vol. II, pp. 319–29.
78.  'Junta particular', 29 September 1685, AGI, Panamá, 96.
79.  Dispatch of the *Junta de Guerra*, 1 August 1687, AGI, Panamá, 96 and Indiferente General, 1879.
80.  Bradley, 'Defenders,' pp. 100–3, 'Relación de . . . Palata', BL, Additional, 19571, fols 271 and 287v–88, Fuentes, *Memorias*, vol. II, pp. 266–9 and 285–8.
81.  Bradley, 'Maritime defence', pp. 173–4.
82.  Bradley, 'Defenders', p. 110.
83.  'Relación de . . . Palata', BL, Additional, 19571, fol. 273, and Fuentes *Memorias*, vol. II, pp. 268–9.
84.  Bradley, 'Attack and defence', pp. 452–5.
85.  Feijoo de Sosa, M., *Relación descriptiva de la ciudad y provincia de Truxillo del Perú* (Madrid, 1763), p. 8. For an illustrated view of aspects of life in the city, see López Serrano, M. (ed.), *Trujillo del Perú* (Madrid, 1976).
86.  For a full account of the wall, see Lohmann Villena, *Defensas militares*, pp. 151–217, and also Bradley, 'Attack and defence', pp. 348–84 and 608.

# 8  THE END OF AN ERA AND THE ONSET OF A NEW PHASE. THE LAST BUCCANEERS, JOHN STRONG PRIVATEER AND THE ARRIVAL OF THE FRENCH (1686–1701)

1.  The journal is published by Ducéré, E. (ed.), *Journal de bord d'un flibustier (1686–93)* (Bayonne, 1894). It is used by Dahlgren, E. W., *Les Relations commerciales et maritimes entre la France et les côtes de l'Océan Pacifique (commencement du XVIII$^e$ siècle)*, vol. 1, *Le Commerce de la Mer du Sud jusqu'à la Paix d'Utrecht* (Paris, 1909). Only this volume was published, being a detailed account of early French ventures.
2.  Dispatches of viceroy Monclova and accompanying reports, 15 March 1690, AGI, Charcas, 270, 14 November 1690, 31 December 1691 and 7 April 1692, AGI, Lima, 88, published in Moreyra y Paz-Soldán, M. and Céspedes del Castillo, G., *Virreinato peruano. Documentos para su historia* (3 vols, Lima, 1954–55), vol. I, nos. 6B, 30, 57 and 67.
3.  There was a division of forces on 8 June 1690, evident from the discovery of a message from a Captain Michel, informing the rest of his intention to head for New Spain, AGI, Lima, 89 and Moreyra, *Virreinato*, vol. I, no. 88, attached document B.
4.  Dispatch of Monclova and accompanying report, 13 October 1693, AGI, Lima, 89, and Moreyra, *Virreinato*, vol. I, no. 105.

5. Dispatch of Monclova and accompanying report, 15 August 1695, AGI, Lima, 89, and Moreyra, *Virreinato*, vol. II, no. 155.

6. Froger, F., *A Relation of a Voyage made in the Years 1695, 1696, 1697 to the Coasts of Africa, Streights of Magellan, Brasil, Cayenna, and the Antilles* (London, 1698), p. 8. This is a translation of the French original of the same year, and an account of the de Gennes expedition to be discussed later.

7. Strong, John, 'Journal of his voyage to Magellans Straits and the South Sea, 1689', BL, Sloane, 3295, 1v, and BL, Harley, 5101. See also Dyer, F., 'Captain John Strong. Privateer and treasure hunter', *The Mariner's Mirror*, XIII (1927), pp. 145–59.

8. Simson, Richard, 'Voyage through the Straits of Magellan to the South Sea, 1689', BL, Sloane, 86, 667 and 672.

9. Ibid., fol. 4v.

10. Simson in fact refers to this successful mission. Phipps (1651–95) was the governor of Massachusetts and obtained a commission from the English crown to search for the treasure ship. See Cotton Mather, *Magnalia Christi Americana* (London, 1702), and Dyer, 'John Strong', pp. 146–7.

11. Dispatch of Monclova, 14 November 1690, AGI, Lima, 88, and Moreyra, *Virreinato*, vol. I, no. 30.

12. Dispatch of Monclova, 26 January 1691, AGI, Lima, 88, and Moreyra, *Virreinato*, vol. I, no. 40.

13. Simson's journal, BL, Sloane, 86, fols 39v–40.

14. Ibid., fol. 28.

15. Strong's journal, BL, Sloane, 3295, fols 67 and 65, for references to the Río Tumbes and the wreck. Simson gives the names of the French privateer as Lodovicus de la Roche, fol. 34v.

16. See Bradley, 'The loss of the flagship', pp. 383–8. Various papers on the reasons for the accident and the subsequent salvage operations can be found in AGI, Indiferente General, 2574, and AN (Lima), Consulado, 1–1a, 2, 3, 4, 6a and 7.

17. To be precise, Simson records that the first two Englishmen contacted on 12 October were joined on the following day by two others 'with their boyes'. His suggestion that 'the history of their life and adventures would be worth the while', clearly was not unheeded. BM, Sloane, 86, fols 39–39v.

18. Strong's journal, BL, Sloane, 3295, fol. 83v. Spanish reports refer only to 10 men.

19. See Dyer, 'John Strong', pp. 155–9, for a fuller discussion of the prizes.

20. Simson's journal, BL, Sloane, 86, fol. 1.

21. Dispatch of Monclova, 14 November 1690, AGI, Lima, 88, and Moreyra, *Virreinato*, vol. I, no. 30.

22. Ibid.

23. Report of the *Junta de Guerra*, 7 September 1692, AGI, Lima, 89, repeated in *cédulas* to the governor and Audiencia of Chile, and President of the Audiencia of Panama, 25 November 1692, AGI, Lima, 570, bk 32, fols 227v–235.

24. Dispatches of Monclova, 22 March 1691 and 20 July 1695, AGI, Lima, 88 and 89 and Moreyra, *Virreinato*, vol. I, no. 47 and vol. II, no. 144.

25. Dispatch of Monclova, 15 March 1690, AGI, Charcas, 270, and Moreyra, *Virreinato*, vol. I, no. 6B.

26. Dispatch of Monclova, 14 November 1690, AGI, Lima, 88, and Moreyra, *Virreinato*, vol. I, no. 30.

27. Dispatch of Monclova, 15 August 1695, AGI, Lima, 89 and Moreyra, *Virreinato*, vol. II, no. 155.

28. Bradley, 'Maritime defence', pp. 170–1, and Dispatch of Monclova, 3 September 1696, AGI, Lima, 90, Moreyra, *Virreinato*, vol. II, no. 190. The *San Lorenzo* was sold for 10 000 pesos, soon to be followed by the *Guadalupe* in 1696 for 15 200 pesos.

29. Undated instruction of the crown to viceroy Monclova, with a dispatch of the *Consejo de Indias*, 9 August 1684, AGI, Indiferente General, 1879. For Peñalosa among the French from 1673 to 1686, see Basadre, *Conde de Lemos*, pp. 189–97. One should not forget in this context the poorly documented de la Roche expedition of 1674 which was reported to have ended its voyage at La Rochelle in the following year.

30. The journal of the expedition is Froger, *Relation of a Voyage*. Valuable also is Dahlgren, *Voyages français à destination de la Mer du Sud avant Bougainville (1695–1749)* (Paris, 1907), reprinted from *Nouvelles Archives des Missions Scientifiques*, 14 (1907), pp. 423–568. See also Fernández Duro, *Armada española*, V, ch. XIX, Campos Harriet, F., *Veleros franceses en el Mar del Sur* (Santiago de Chile, 1964), ch. 1, Kemp and Lloyd, *Brethren of the Coast*, ch. 12, and Spate, *Monopolists*, pp. 154 and 180–2.

31. Froger, *Relation of a Voyage*, p. 80.

32. Dispatch of the *Junta de Guerra*, 8 August 1684, AGI, Indiferente General, 1863.

33. Dispatch of Monclova, 3 September 1696, AGI, Lima, 90, Moreyra, *Virreinato*, vol. II, no. 190, and dispatch of the *Junta de Guerra*, 27 April 1695, AGI, Indiferente General, 1880.

34. Dispatch of Monclova, 8 November 1697, AGI, Lima, 91, and Moreyra, *Virreinato*, vol. II, no. 206.

## EPILOGUE

1. Barbour, J. S., *A History of William Paterson and the Darien Company* (Edinburgh, 1907). Hart, F. R., *The Disaster of Darien* (Boston, 1929) and *Spanish Documents Relating to the Scots' Settlement in Darien* (Boston, 1931). Insh, G. P., *The Company of Scotland Trading to Africa and the Indies* (London, 1932) and *The Darien Scheme* (London, 1943). Prebble, J., *The Darien Disaster* (London, 1968). There are shorter accounts in Howarth, D., *The Golden Isthmus* (London, 1967), pp. 102–44, and Spate, *Monopolists*, pp. 169–80.

2. Main sources on the French are again Dahlgren, *Relations commerciales*, and *Voyages français*. The latter, p. 24, shows that 168 French vessels sailed for the South Sea between 1698 and 1726. See also the following studies: Campos Harriet, *Veleros franceses*, Villalobos, S., 'Contrabando francés en el Pacífico (1700–24)', *Revista de Historia de América*, 51 (1961), pp. 48–88, and *Comercio y contrabando en el Río de la Plata y Chile (1700–1811)* (Buenos Aires, 1965), Vignols, L., 'Le "Commerce interlope" français à la Mer du Sud au début du XVIIIe siècle', *Revue d'Histoire Economique et Sociale*, 13 (1925), pp. 240–99, and the accounts in Spate, *Monopolists*, pp. 189–94, Dunmore, J., *French Explorers in the Pacific* (2 vols, Oxford, 1965 and 1969), vol. I, *The Eighteenth Century*, and Moreyra y Paz-Soldán, M., *El Tribunal del Consulado de Lima* (2 vols, Lima, 1956 and 1959), vol. I, pp. xxxvi–lxxii.

3. Triennial sailings from Callao to Panama continued from 1666 to 1681. In part due to foreign intervention, further departures until the Treaty of Utrecht were reduced to those of 1685, 1690, 1696 and 1707. See Rodríguez Vicente, M. E., 'Los caudales remitidos desde el Perú a España', *Anuario de Estudios Americanos*, 21 (1964), pp. 1–24, Moreyra y Paz-Soldán, M., *El tráfico marítimo en la época colonial* (Lima, 1944), and Walker, G. J., *Spanish Politics and Imperial Trade (1700–89)* (Bloomington, 1979), pp. 22–3, which makes the point about commercial necessity.

4. Spate, *Monopolists*, p. 187.

5. Rogers, W., *A Cruising Voyage round the World* (London, 1712).

6. *Description of a Buccaneer's Atlas by W. Hacke* (London, 1914), p. 12, one of *A Collection of Monographs and Miniatures Offered for Sale by B. Quaritch* (London, 1904–14).

7. Allen, R., *An Essay on the Nature and Methods of Carrying on a Trade to the South Sea* (London, 1712), from BL, Additional, 28140, fol. 29. See Alsop, J. D., 'A Darien epilogue: Robert Allen in Spanish America (1698–1707)', *The Americas*, 43, no. 2 (1986), pp. 197–201.

8. 'Proposall for takeing Baldivia in ye So Seas by Thos Bowrey', and 'Proposal for settlement in ye way to ye So Seas', BL, Additional, 28140, fols 31–31v. The same collection of manuscripts contains a letter from Bowrey to a Director of the South Sea Company on commercial prospects in the South Sea, fol. 32, and an account by Edward Cooke of places visited in the area by the Woodes Rogers venture, fols 29–30.

9. Carswell, J., *The South Sea Bubble* (London, 1960), Sperling, J. G., *The South Sea Company* (Boston, 1962), and McLachlan, J. O., *Trade and Peace with Old Spain (1667–1750)* (Cambridge, 1940).

10. For example, see Hamilton, E. J., *American Treasure and the Price Revolution in Spain (1501–1650)* (Cambridge, Mass., 1934), p. 19.

11. Such upsets are dealt with by Rodríguez Vicente, M. E., *El Tribunal del Consulado de Lima en la primera mitad del siglo XVII* (Madrid, 1960), pp. 215–21, and Domínguez Ortiz, A., *Política y hacienda de Felipe IV* (Madrid, 1960), p. 282.

12. For example, see dispatches of Mancera, 21 July 1644 and 17 July 1646, AGI, Lima, 52 and 53, and Crahan, 'Palata', p. 398.

13. Bromley, *Libros de cabildos*, vol. XVII, pp. 702 and 816–17.

14. See Bradley, 'The cost of defending a viceroyalty', pp. 267–89, from which these conclusions are taken. Some of the data on which this study is based appears in TePaske, J. J. and Klein, H. S., *The Royal Treasuries of the Spanish Empire in America* (3 vols, Durham, N. C., 1982), vol. I, *Peru*.

15. The inclusion of the cost of military aid to Chile would add over 250 000 pesos annually to defence costs, a further 8 per cent of annual revenue over the century as a whole. So, for the period 1650–90, defence against intruders and the Chilean war consumed more annually than it was possible to remit to Spain, and in the 1680s almost 41 per cent of income.

16. Defence expenditure may be studied in the broader context of viceregal financial operations in Andrien, K. J., *Crisis and Decline. The Viceroyalty of Peru in the Seventeenth Century* (Albuquerque, 1985).

17. In a *cédula* to viceroy Alba, dated 25 February 1655, AGMRE, bk 1–1, fols 375–76, the crown refers to contributions from the merchants of Peru over the last 40 years of over 277 000 pesos. Caracuel Moyano, R., 'Los mercaderes del Perú y la financiación de los gastos de la monarquía (1650–1700)', *XXXVI Congreso Internacional de Americanistas. Actas y Memorias* (Seville, 1966), pp. 335–43, at p. 339 suggests a figure of 650 to 700 000 pesos for the second half of the century. However, a further *cédula* to viceroy Monclova, dated 3 October 1690, mentions services and gifts over the last decade alone worth over 900 000 pesos, AGMRE, bk 1–8, fols 95–6. Contributions in respect of the armada amounted at least to 300 000 pesos, *cédula* of 24 June 1697, AGI, Lima, 576, bk 33, fols 197–201v, and AGMRE, bk 1–7, fol. 515.

# Index